LEXICAL
AND SEMANTIC
ASPECTS
OF PROVERBS

FRANTIŠEK **ČERMÁK**

UNIVERZITA KARLOVA
NAKLADATELSTVÍ KAROLINUM 2019

Reviewers:
PhDr. Hana Bouzková
Mgr. Bohdana Divišová

ISBN 978-80-246-4358-8
ISBN 978-80-246-4369-4 (pdf)

CONTENTS

Introduction: Linguistic Aspects of Proverbs in System and Text

This collection of papers on proverbs in English, Czech and other languages is mostly a second edition of those already published elsewhere. However, most did originate as the author's contribution to his fairly regular participation in *Interdiciplinary Colloquium on Proverbs. Colóquio Interdisciplinar sobre Proverbios*, held yearly in Tavira, Portugal. This colloquium, the only one of its kind, has become a lively platform for exchanging views on proverbs, whether linguistic, literary, historic or other, both in English and Portuguese. Due to the limited means and range of publication (through by the care of Runo Soares and Outi Lauhakangas, there appears a separate locally printed volume every year), proceedings of the Colloquia are mostly unknown and it is difficult to find them in shops.

Thanks to the efforts of Wolfgang Mieder, the major background figure on the field of proverbs, author of many books and editor of the unique yearly Proverbium, some of my contributions have been published as *Proverbs, Their Lexical and Semantic Features* in 2014. However, the present edition is much more comprehensive since other studies published elsewhere have been added, and some are new. The contributions found here have been read previously by Runo Soares, Outi Lauhakangas, and Wolfgang Mieder, editors who are familiar with them, and they can be considered as reviewed.

The volume is rather broad, linguistic in nature, offering a number of aspects and languages studied, though mostly on lexical, semantic and pragmatic aspects, and corpus findings leading to proveb minima.

Apart from smaller publishers (such as Europhras), all of them are given with each respective paper, the main sources of the papers here are **Actas ICP** and **Čermák Proverbs** (see below):

ACTAS ICP, Proceedings, International Association of Paremiology,
eds. Rui Sores, Outi Lauhakangas, Interdisciplinary Colloquium on Proverbs. Colóquio Interdisciplinar sobre Proverbios, eds. Rui JB Soares, Outi Lauhakangas, Tavira (= **Actas**).

František Čermák PROVERBS: THEIR LEXICAL AND SEMANTIC FEATURES
'Proverbium' in cooperation with the Institute of the Czech National Corpus
The University of Vermont Burlington, Vermont 2014
Supplement Series of Proverbium
Yearbook of International Proverb Scholarship Volume 36 (= **Čermák Proverbs 2014**).

PROVERBIUM, Yearbook of International Proverb Scholarship, ed. W. Mieder

The traditional field of Proverbs which is being enriched by the colloquia and subsequent proceedings seems to be drawing attention and it is hoped that the present edition might contribute to satisfy the attention.
My thanks go to the reviewers who have enabled this publication.

Reviewed by Rui Soares, Wolfgang Mieder, Outi Lauhakangas.

A
Aspects of Proverbs: Lexical, Semantic and Pragmatic

The most general and obvious aspect and feature of proverbs is their lexical basis. The nature of their lexical setup is examined here, in part A, mostly in their relation to meaning, a feature often neglected.

1. LEXICAL FOUNDATIONS OF PROVERBS: BASED ON DATA FROM ENGLISH, GERMAN, FRENCH AND CZECH

In **Actas ICP 1, 2011**, 197–207, **Čermák Proverbs 2014**, 91–110.

ABSTRACT

Proverbs in four languages are concentrating around the central key-word 'dog' and 7 other, mostly animal names (bird, cat, gold, hand, horse, stone, water) are examined as to the lexical components that they are made of with the ultimate goal to trace the relations between both levels, that of the lexicon and the sentence. Data used are those from Wictionary, the Czech data, somewhat larger coming from a large and comprehensive Czech Dictionary. On the basis of these, some basic statistics and correlations are calculated and offered arriving at the four vocabularies that the proverbs in the languages inspected are made of. The relevant proverbs are then compared and searched as to correspondences that, surprisingly, are few.

1. INTRODUCTION

Linguistically, everything about proverbs is proverbially vague, including their meaning, use, variant forms, and many other aspects if they are viewed in general. These include, on the one hand such derived notions as their metaphorical character while, on the other hand, there is hardly any consensus as to what exactly proverbs are and how to distinguish them from other types of phraseology. A part of the problem is due to proverbs sitting proverbially on too many fences, one pertaining to ethnography, one to literary science, one to linguistics, specifically to phraseology, with further background relationships to history, law, etc. Yet, the core of proverbs has never raised any major objection as to its substance. The complicated network of links, ties and adherences is interdisciplinary and does not, accordingly, have any distinctly satisfactory and clear-cut face that would satisfy everyone. It does have, in fact, many faces depending on the point of view taken, as the father of modern linguistics Ferdinand de Saussure has repeatedly stressed, though he has never dealt with proverbs.

Despite these many aspects, sometimes mutually contradictory, there is one indisputable fact, behind all of this, recognized as the very basis of proverbs as well as of anything related to meaning in languages, namely words as building blocks of every single proverb, on which any other interpretation and analysis of any aspect must be based.

2. From the Lexis to the Proverb: Are the Two Semantically Linked?

Generally, it is acknowledged that some proverbs are viewed almost literally, such as:
(1) *Knowledge is power*,
while others are not and their interpretation depends on the context much more. Such is the case of, for example, (2) *Barking dogs seldom bite*
which can be read in many ways. Here, for example, either a literal or functional approach may be applied:

(a) Dogs who bark instead of bite usually use barking as a defence instead of biting.
Or, a logical one:
(b) What is meant by barking dogs seldom bite? If a dog is using its mouth for barking, how can it bite at the same moment?
Or, an acoustical and psychological one:
(c) Forget about the bite because their bark is just as annoying. So what can be done to stop their nuisance barking?
Or, finally, a metaphorical and causal one, referring to people:
(d) People who say they are going to do something bad to us usually sound like a dog barking that does nothing to us.

Although the last reading usually prevails, it is, without a specific context, still very far from saying what kind of person provided with what authority and under what circumstances is meant, etc.

Obviously, some very simple general questions may and should be asked:
A Is there a Causal Relationship between the Vocabulary Used and the Proverb? If there is,
B What Are the Major Building Blocks of Proverbs?
C Is There a Metaphorical Process Involved?

The first two simple examples above provide a basic answer to the last (C) question. Without going into the intricacies of metaphors, it is the **concrete nouns** and, perhaps, verbs (such as *dogs*, *bite*), as opposed to the abstract ones (*knowledge*, *power*) that are involved in metaphoric formation. That, as we have seen in the interpretations of (2), can give rise to various readings and meanings. A repeated use of some frequent proverbs may also give rise to fixed meanings and/or related associations. In Tavira 2010 we have shown that there are at least 10 tentative and broad types of meaning related to proverbs based on the *dog* constituent (Čermák – Lindroos 2010), such as:

man threatening is not dangereous • *Pes, kterej/který štěká, nekouše. (A barking dog never bites).*

Here, the barking dog is consensually associated with danger, being, however, only a part of the overall meaning of the proverb used about the man: in fact, the whole proverb contradicts this general association and expectation. Hence, the semantic link of the component *dog* to the proverb viewed as a whole is, at best, only partial and indirect. In view of the 9 remaining meaning types using the component *dog*, it is obvious that meaning attributes are different in other cases (see Čermák – Lindroos 2010) and there is nothing stable about the semantic role of *dog* in various proverbs.

3. Proverb Data and Their Comparison

In order to get at a more consistent picture of this semantic part vs the whole relationship, one would need to examine more data that would be representative. As we know, paremiological minima, which are far from being wide-spread (Čermák 2003, Mieder 2004, etc.) are widely different and represent a mostly subjective collection (with the exception of those for Czech and English based on large corpora). The only option left for a kind of comparative proverb data seems, then, to be what Web-based Wiktionary (Wikiquote) offers. Despite obvious problems and discrepancies in size and approach applied, the proverb lists offered by Wiktionary (spring 2011) have been used for English (755 proverbs), German (214), and French (308), as there is nothing else even remotely useful. Since the Czech Wikipedia collection was too small (82), data for this language have been selected from a recent comprehensive and very large dictionary of the Czech phraseology (Čermák et al. 2009, offering 876 proverbs). Hence, data for English and Czech are similar in size, while data for German and French are about 3–4 times smaller. It is hoped that the list has been compiled with the best of intentions aiming at a representative picture, although one does have some doubts about this, cf., for example, an odd inclusion, such as:

The difference between a man and a cat or a dog is that only a man can write the names of the cat and the dog.
Please don't retouch my wrinkles. It took me so long to earn them.

4. Lexical Stock of Proverbs

Breaking down these probably basic English, German, French, and Czech lists separately in word forms, some statistics (despite unequal sizes of the collection compared) and word lists could be obtained. First the overall statistics:

English: **755** proverbs, Word : Proverb ratio = 2.15 words per 1 proverb (Wiki)
1,624 words altogether, 386 types, Word: Type ratio = 4.21
German: **214** proverbs, Word : Proverb ratio = 3.06 words per 1 proverb(Wiki)
655 words altogether, 92 types, Word: Type ratio = 7.12
French: **308** proverbs, Word : Proverb ratio = 2.55 words per 1 proverb (Wiki)
785 words altogether, 638 types!, Word: Type ratio = 1.23 words per 1 proverb
Czech: **876** proverbs, Word: Proverb ratio = 2.82 words per 1 proverb (SČFI)
2,470 words altogether, 458 types, Word: Type ratio = 5.41

It is the proportions that are of interest here. Note, at least, the highest word-type ratio for German meaning that German proverbs rely heavily on a repetition of words which is in sharp contrast to French, where the ratio is the lowest of all (while the number of types is the highest of all languages). This picture would be different, should all the variants, plentiful in Czech due to its high inflection, be included.
Since the figures are rather high but most of the words belong to low frequency levels, it has been decided, on the basis of four frequency dictionaries based on the four proverbs collections, to cut-off the data at frequency 3 (inclusive).

This has led to reduced data having a similar and, hopefully, comparable qualities. Thus,
English data (frequencies 345-3) were reduced to 23.77% (386 words),
German data (frequencies 46-3) were reduced to 14.02% (92),
French data (frequencies 34-3) were reduced to 18.73% (147),
Czech data (frequencies 190-3) were reduced to 18.54% (458).

While figures for hapaxes and near-hapaxes (frequency 1 and 2) are prone to chance and there is nothing systematic there, it might be of some interest to give, on the other hand, (predictable) figures for the most frequent words found here, namely:

English: *the, a, is, to, you*
German: *ist, der, nicht, die, das*
French: *la, le, qui, pas, les*
Czech: *se, je, kdo, na, a*

It is obvious that the proverb meaning is carried and built by nouns that name entities, people, places, etc., and, to some extent, by verbs that tell what relations, actions, states, etc., are named. All the grammar words are, basically, negligible in that they do not express content notions; a separate study of relations related to these, would be a different study. Going thus into content and meaning, at least in a moderate way, the following frequency lists have been compiled (actual frequencies preceding):

English: 40 man, 34 it's, 34 are, 30 will, 28 life, 26 make, 26 have, 22 makes, 21 do, 20 can, 20 can't, 19 get, 18 know, 14 you're, 13 want, 12 world, 12 things, 12 lie, 12 give, 12 love, 12 take, 12 time, 11 doing, 11 day, 11 let, 11 put, 11 thing, 11 go, 11 gets, 11 has, 10 need, 10 heart, 10 horse, 10 cry, 10 mouth, 9 may, 9 truth, 9 try, 9 say, 9 success.

German: 46 ist, 23 man, 13 kommt, 13 was, 10 es, 9 hat, 7 muss, 6 ende , 6 macht, 5 sagen, 5 brot, 5 will, 5 morgen, 4 arbeit, 4 teufel, 4 sind, 4 machen, 4 wird, 4 taten, 4 kartoffeln, 3 haben, 3 wahrheit, 3 hunde, 3 leute, 3 hand, 3 gott, 3 gold, 3 vater, 3 lass, 3 sein, 3 not, 3 ehrt, 3 gedanke, 3 gehen, 3 lernt.

French: 34 est, 28 faut, 24 fait, 20 c'est, 17 n'est, 15 vaut, 13 peut, 12 sont, 11 veut, 9 n'a, 7 faire, 7 l'argent, 6 fais, 5 chose, 5 font, 5 jour, 5 dieu, 4 dort, 4 avoir, 4 mange, 4 dire, 4 monde, 4 chat, 4 loup, 4 nuit, 4 chien, 4 femme, 4 beurre, 4 vérité, 4 amis, 4 ennemis, 3 porte, 3 l'homme, 3 passe, 3 place, 3 fin, 3 chasse, 3 âne, 3 vole, 3 ont, 3 chiens, 3 vent, 3 vient, 3 vin, 3 aime, 3 mort, 3 mettre, 3 rit, 3 trouve, 3 vivre, 3 jeunesse, 3 perdu, 3 temps, 3 poison, 3 vache.

Czech: 110 je, 56 není, 46 má, 22 chce, 19 štěstí, 15 člověk, 13 voda, 13 bude, 13 rozum, 13 nemá, 13 peníze, 12 být, 12 konec, 12 musí, 11 smrt, 11 pravdu, 10 pán, 10 poznáš, 10 pánbůh, 10 bejt, 10 člověka, 10 strom, 10 láska, 9 bývá, 9 jest, 9 čas, 9 máš, 9 jsou, 9 nebylo, 9 bůh, 9 dává, 9 slovo, 9 chválí, 9 děti, 9 chodí, 9 život, 8 víno, 8 chyby, 8 práce, 8 srdce.

In the following, the view about the primary semantic (and motivational) role of nouns and, even more so, a much more important role played here by **Concrete** nouns as opposed to Abstracts (see examples (1) and (2) above) will be supported. It is primarily Concrete nouns, such as *gold* or *horse*, that have been selected for comparison and an inspection of their semantic contribution to proverbs. The reason for this is their obvious capacity to form metaphorical meanings in the sense we have seen above in (2), namely **dog → (angry) man**.

Proportions of Nouns and Concrete Nouns (the classification may be arbitrary): English: 66/37, German: 17/8, French: 27/11, Czech: 89/37.

However, before going into this, let us, briefly, have a look at the verb and the type of meaning it contributes to the proverb meaning. Using German as the smallest set (without frequencies), namely:

ist, kommt, was, hat, muss, macht, sagen, will, sind, machen, wird, haben, lass, sein, ehrt, gehen, lernt it is evident that verbs expressing, broadly, static, relational meanings are represented, such as *sein, haben, lassen, ehren, müssen*, while dynamic verbs are represented only by verbs of motion and general activity, such as *kommen, gehen* and *machen*. Even further on, in lower frequencies, very specific verbs are scarce. Thus, the burden of conveying the bulk of meaning rests with nouns.

Coming back to (concrete) nouns, it was surprising to find out that there are very few nouns that are common to all four languages inspected so that this could become a basis for proverb identification in the Wiki lists (and the Czech dictionary data). On the basis of its highest frequency, it was **dog** again, that proved to be quite basic. The rest, inspected in the following (5) consisted of only 7 (concrete) nouns, namely:

bird, cat, gold, hand, horse, stone, water,

nouns that are mutually exclusive and rather different.

Surprisingly, the basic stock of proverbs examined lacked words such as *bread, hat, coat, house, sand, foot, apple* in French (*pain, chapeau, manteau, maison, sable, pied, pomme*) or *tree, tooth/teeth, pig* in German (*Baum, Zähne, Schwein*), *knife* or *bread* in Czech (*nůž, chleba*), or *wine* and *gold* in English. However, all, if not most of them are to be found in lower frequency words.

5. SOME FREQUENT PROVERBS EXAMINED IN 4 LANGUAGES

Most proverbs, also in this kind of core selected from Wikiquote, are widely different in the four languages examined. Therefore, only those few based on 7 nouns that the four languages share are briefly looked into, although only the *dog*-proverbs will be given in full, the rest is to be found in the Appendix 1.

The few correspondences across languages are indicated.

DOG Proverbs

English: 16 proverbs
Barking dogs seldom bite. **Ger, Fr, Cz**
Brag is a good Dog, but Holdfast is better.
The difference between a man and a cat or a dog is that only a man can write the names of the cat and the dog.
The dog is nude though the clothing cost a penny.
Even a dog can distinguish between being stumbled over and being kicked.
Even a dog can make it to the top when there's a flood.
Even an old dog likes to be patted on the head and told, 'Good boy!'
Every dog has its day.

Give a dog a bad name and hang him.
Let sleeping dogs lie. **Ger**
Lie down with dogs, wake up with fleas. **Fr**
Meaner than a junk-yard dog.
An old dog will learn no tricks. **Cz**
Rather be a dog in peace, than to be a man in chaos.
Straighten not the dog's tail even in the bamboo hollow.
Take an old dirty, hungry, mangy, sick and wet dog and feed him and wash him and nurse him back to health, and he will never turn on you and bite you. This is how man and dog differ.

German: 4 proverbs
Bellende Hunde beißen nicht. **En**
Den Letzten beißen die Hunde.
Der Knochen kommt nicht zum Hund, sondern der Hund zum Knochen.
Schlafende Hunde soll man nicht wecken. **En**

French: 7 proverbs
Chien qui aboie ne mord pas. **En, Cz**
Les chiens aboient, la caravane passe.
Les chiens ne font pas des chats.
Qui m'aime aime mon chien.
Qui se couche avec les chiens se lève avec des puces. **En**
Qui veut noyer son chien l'accuse de rage.
Un chien regarde bien un évêque.

Czech: 14 proverbs
Mrtvej/mrtvý pes nekouše/neštěká.
Pes psa nekouše.
Pes je nejlepší přítel člověka.
Pes, kterej/který štěká, nekouše. **En, Ger, Fr**
Starýho/starého psa novejm/novým kouskům nenaučíš. **En**
Kdo chce psa bít, hůl si najde.
Mnoho psů, zajícova smrt. n. Mnoho myslivců zajícova smrt.
Život je pes.
Ranní déšť, ženský pláč a psí kulhání nemají dlouhého trvání.
Kde nesvrbí, nedrbej a psa, když chce spát, za vocas netahej.
Pánbůh /pánbu psí hlas neslyší.
Tím řeka není horší, že z ní pijí psi.
Lepší dobrá vejmluva než psí hovno.

Out of the varying number and content of these proverbs, there is only a single one that the data have in common, namely *Barking dogs seldom bite* which refers, though in a roundabout way, to the semantic feature of danger. The remaining correspondences are scarce. Oddly enough, only one other semantic feature out of the ten mentioned above and analysed for *dog* elsewhere (Čermák – Lindroos 2010, see also Appendix 2) may be found here, too, namely the one where *dog* is a victim of maltreatment, cf. *Give a dog a bad name and hang him* and, possibly, *Even a dog can distinguish between being stumbled over and being kicked*. Let us notice, yet again, a rather odd inclusion of a not so frequent proverb in English, ascribed to Lord Byron, namely:

Take an old dirty, hungry, mangy, sick and wet dog and feed him and wash him and nurse him back to health, and he will never turn on you and bite you. This is how man and dog differ.

The profusion of dog-proverbs in English contrasting with the other languages, may reflect a rather special character of *dog* in the English-speaking countries, but any speculation along theses lines is just that, speculation.

A detailed comparison of these proverbs would be interesting but there is no scope for this here.

The seven proverb components mentioned above, given in their proverb form in Appendix 1 below, also record correspondences between languages, if any, and similar modest observations about their semantic character and features may be followed here. Perhaps, the sheer disproportion of specific components in proverbs in some languages is worth noticing. Thus, it is conspicuous that *bird-*, *gold-* and *water*-proverbs are so highly represented in Czech, not giving much grounds for any reasonable explanation, while the predominance of *horse*-proverbs in English may be perhaps vaguely explained.

6. Summary

Though laborious and data-burdened, this contribution should not be viewed as anything more than an attempt and illustration of the initial line of thinking for at least two reasons. First, the data are problematic as to their content, way of composition and size, and second, the data is too small to allow for any safe generalization. Accordingly, one might wonder why there are no more objective paremiological minima, based on corpora perhaps, that would enable such comparison and, hence, offer an insight into the cultures compared, not to speak of their usefulness in school, in the dictionary-making business, etc.

In doing so, the status of proverbs, at least from the linguistic point of view, should be reviewed, and some proverbs excluded, such as the English *Not enough room to swing a cat* which is an idiom all right but may formally defy the proverb definition. Likewise, the status of such expressions (all of them being uncritically included here) such as *A camel is a horse designed by committee*, could be revised.

LITERATURE

ČERMÁK, František, HRONEK, Jiří, and MACHAČ, Jaroslav. 2009. *Slovník české frazeologie a idiomatiky. Výrazy větné*. Praha: Leda (= Dictionary of Czech Phraseology and Idiomatics. Sentence Expressions = SČFI).

ČERMÁK, František, LINDROOS, H. 2011. "Dog and Cat Proverbs: a Comparison of English, Czech, Finnish and Other Languages." In *4. Colóquio Interdisciplinar sobre Proverbios. 4th Interdisciplinary Colloquium on Proverbs. Actas ICP Proceedings, International Association of Paremiology*, edited by R. Sores and O. Lauhakangas, 131–140.

ČERMÁK, František. 2003. "Paremiological Minimum of Czech: The Corpus Evidence." In *Flut von Texten - Vielvalt der Kulturen. Ascona 2001 zur Methodologie und Kulturspezifik der Phraseologie*, edited by H. Burger, A. Häcki Bufofer, and G. Greciano, 15–31. Hohengehren: Schneider Verlag.

Čermák, František. 2007. *Frazeologie a idiomatika česká a obecná*. Praha: Karolinum. (= Czech and General Phraseology)

ČERMÁK, František. 2010. "Frequent Proverbs and Their Meaning: A Proposal of a Linguistic Description" (The Core and Paremiological Minima Described). In *3rd Interdisciplinary Colloquium on Proverbs. Actas ICP Proceedings, International Association of Paremiology*, 40–65.

ČERMÁK, František. 2010. "The Paremiological Minimum of English." In *... for thy speech bewrayeth thee. A Festschrift for Libuše Dušková*, edited by M. Malá and P. Šaldová, 57–71. Praha: Univerzita Karlova, Filozofická fakulta.

APPENDIX 1

BIRD PROVERBS

English: 4 proverbs
A bird in the hand is worth two in the bush.
Birds of a feather flock together.
The early bird catches the worm. **Cz**
Fine feathers make fine birds.

German: 1 proverb
Friss, Vogel, oder stirb!

French: 1 proverb
Petit à petit l'oiseau fait son nid.

Czech: 12 proverbs
Člověka po řeči, ptáka po peří poznáš.
Kůň k tahu, pták k letu a člověk k práci.
Každej pták svý hnízdo chválí.
Vrabec je taky pták .
Každý pták tak zpívá, jak mu zobák narost.
Pečený ptáci/holubi tam nelítaj/nelítají do huby.

Neuč rybu plavat a ptáka létat.
Ptáka poznáš po zpěvu.
Jen drápkem uvíz, a chycen je ptáček celý.
Ranní ptáče dál doskáče. **En**
Když ptáčka lapají, pěkně mu zpívají.
Pečení ptáci tam nelítají do huby?

CAT PROVERBS

English: 7 proverbs
All cats love fish but hate to get their paws wet.
A cat may look at a king.
The difference between a man and a cat or a dog is that only a man can write the names of the cat and the dog.
Not enough room to swing a cat.
Put a cat amongst the pigeons.
There's more than one way to skin a cat.
When the cat is away, the mice will play. **Fr, Cz**

German: 2 proverbs
Die Katze im Sack kaufen.
Bei Nacht sind alle Katzen grau. **Cz, Fr**

French: 5 proverbs
Chat échaudé craint l'eau froide.
Il ne faut pas réveiller le chat qui dort.
La nuit tous les chats sont gris.
Les chiens ne font pas des chats.
Quand le chat n'est pas là, les souris dansent. **En**

Czech: 4 proverbs
Potmě je každá kočka/kráva černá. **Ger, Fr**
Kočce o myších se snívá.
Když není kocour doma, mají myši pré. **En, Fr**
Nemá vždycky kocour posvícení.

GOLD PROVERBS

English: 4 proverbs
All that glisters is not gold. **Cz, Ger**
Old is Gold.

A coin of gold is delighting in a bag of silver coins.
Time is gold.

German: 3 proverbs
Es ist nicht alles Gold, was glänzt. **Cz**
Morgenstund hat Gold im Mund.
Reden ist Silber, Schweigen ist Gold. **Cz, Fr**

French: 1 proverb
La parole est d'argent, mais le silence est d'or. **Cz, Ger**

Czech: 8 proverbs
Dobrý/dobrej přítel nad zlato.
Dobrá rada nad zlato.
Sůl nad zlato.
Začal na zlatě, skončil na blátě.
Zlato brány otevírá.
Zlata se rez nechytá.
Není všechno zlato , co se třpytí. **En, Ger**
Mluviti stříbro, mlčeti zlato. **Ger, Fr**

HAND Proverbs

English: 8 proverbs
A bird in the hand is worth two in the bush.
Don't bite the hand that feeds you.
Idle hands are the devil's playthings.
A good surgeon has an eagle's eye, a lion's heart, and a lady's hand.
Let us go hand in hand, not one before another.
Many hands make light work.
Never let the right hand know what the left hand is doing.
One hand washes the other. **Cz**

German: 3 proverbs
Beiß nicht in die Hand, die dich füttert.
Besser ein Spatz in der Hand, als eine Taube auf dem Dach.
Eine Hand wäscht die andere. **Cz, En**

French: 1 proverb
Moineau à la main vaut mieux que grue qui vole.

Czech: 6 proverbs
Podej/dej/nastrč čertu prst a hned chce celou ruku.
Host do domu, hůl do ruky.
Hledáš-li pomocnou ruku , najdeš ji na konci svýho/svého vlastního ramene.
Ruka ruku myje/meje. **En**, **Ger**
Mnoho rukou, málo díla.
Studený ruce, upřímný srdce. n. Studené ruce, upřímné srdce.

HORSE Proverbs

English: 10 proverbs
Don't look a gift horse in the mouth. **Cz**, **Fr**
A camel is a horse designed by committee.
Don't shut the barn door after the horse is gone.
For want of a nail the shoe is lost, for want of a shoe the horse is lost, for want of a horse the rider is lost.
Hung like a Horse.
If wishes were horses, beggars would ride.
It's a good horse that never stumbles.
Put a beggar on horseback and he'll ride it to death.
You can lead a horse to water but you can't make it drink.
Don't put the cart before the horse.

German: 2 proverbs
Auf alten Pferden lernt man reiten.
Wenn der Reiter nichts taugt, ist das Pferd schuld.

French: 2 proverbs
À cheval donné on ne regarde pas les dents. **En**, **Cz**
L'argent ne se trouve pas sous le sabot / le pas d'un cheval.

Czech: 4 proverbs
Vůl je nebezpečný zepředu, kůň zezadu a blbec ze všech stran.
Darovanému koni na zuby nahleď! **En**
Nech to koňovi, ten má větší hlavu!
Království za koně! (Shakespeare)

STONE Proverbs

English: 5 proverbs
Failure is the stepping stone for success.

Let him who is without sin cast the first stone.
People who live in glass houses shouldn't throw stones.
A rolling stone gathers no moss. **Cz, Fr**
Sticks and stones may break my bones but words will never hurt me.

German: 1 proverb
Steter Tropfen höhlt den Stein. **Cz**

French: 1 proverb
Pierre qui roule n'amasse pas mousse. **En, Cz**

Czech: 5 proverbs
Kámen často se hýbající neobroste. **En, Fr**
Kdo do tebe kamenem, ty do něj/ného chlebem.
Kdo do tebe kamenem, ty do něj dvěma.
Těžko z kamene olej vytlačit.
Častá krůpěj /kapka i kámen prorazí/proráží. **Ger**

WATER PROVERBS

English: 6 proverbs
Seek water in the sea.
Still waters run deep. **Cz**
Blood is thicker than water. **Cz, Ger**
You can lead a horse to water but you can't make it drink.
Don't throw the baby out with the bathwater.
Like water off a duck's back.

German: 2 proverbs
Wasser unter der Brücke.
Blut ist dicker als Wasser. **En, Cz**

French: 3 proverbs
C'est la goutte d'eau qui fait déborder le vase.
Chat échaudé craint l'eau froide.
Il n'est pire eau que celle qui dort.

Czech: 13 proverbs
Tak dlouho se chodí se džbánem pro vodu, až se ucho utrhne.
Krev není voda. n. Krev je hustší než voda. **En**
Hoď rybu do vody, ať plave.
Sítem vodu nenabereš.
Co je do studánky, když v ní voda není.

Škoda je, jen co voda veme/vezme.
Škola bez kázně, mlýn bez vody.
Vodu s ohněm nesmícháš. n. Voda se s ohněm nesnáší.
Voda rozum nekalí.
Snáze jest v kalné vodě ryby loviti.
Voda teče, řeči plynou.
Co má viset, neutopí se, i kdyby voda přes šibenici ležela.
Tichá voda břehy mele/bere. **En**

APPENDIX 2

Ten onomasiological lemmas ('meanings') for DOG-proverbs
(In English and Czech only, though more languages have been examined, see Čermák – Lindroos 2010.)

1 · **man old learns with difficulty**
 • *Starýho/starého psa novejm/novým kouskům nenaučíš.* (You can't teach an old dog new tricks.)

2 · **man threatening is not dangereous**
 • *Pes, kterej/který štěká, nekouše.* (A barking dog never bites.)

3 · **man punishes under a pretext easily**
 • *Kdo chce psa bít, hůl si najde.* (It's easy to find a stick to beat a dog.)

4 · **dog is loyal**
 • *Pes je (nejlepší) přítel člověka.* (A dog is a man's best friend.)

5· **man disregards the unimportant**
 • *Psi štěkají a karavana jde/de dál.* (Dogs bark, but the caravan goes/rolls on.)

6 · **man believes in superstition**
 • *Černá kočka přes cestu znamená neštěstí/smůlu.* (It is unlucky have a black cat cross your path.)

7 · **supervising tempts wilfulness**
 • *Když kocour není doma, myši mají pré/hody/posvícení.* (When/while the cat's away, the mice will play.)

8 · **it is difficult to discriminate, they all merge**
 • *Potmě je každá kočka/kráva černá.* (All cats in the dark are grey.)

9 · **man yields to superiority**
 • *Mnoho psů, zajícova smrt.* ('Too many dogs is the hare's death', He didn't have a cat's/snowball's chance in hell.)

10 · **life is hard**
 • *Život je pes.* (It's a dog's life.)

2. Lexicon and Proverbs: Basics and Foundations (Lexical Origins of Proverbs)

In **Actas ICP 12, 2013**, 229–238, **Čermák Proverbs 2014**, 133–146.

Abstract

The obvious and yet hardly ever explored problem of how and on what basis proverbs are constructed out of words is examined here. As a basis, The Routledge Book of World's Proverbs is chosen which has been turned into a specific corpus and examined as such in an attempt to find the nature of the very basic foundation stones of proverbs in thousands of proverbs (translated into English) from over 100 languages. The first part of the contribution concentrates on aspects of the compilation of the book and origins of the proverbs included. This is followed by a discussion of the much neglected metalanguage (summarised in the Subject Index) describing, briefly and largely inadequately, the meaning of proverbs which is used as the only classificatory principle of the dictionary. Finally, some basic statistics, based on the proverb corpus are offered, specifically from the field of the Lexicon.

1. Introduction

Since linguistically it is words that are the building blocks of any text, including proverbs, it might be useful to examine these words in some detail. As this contribution is based on compact data from some 130 languages as published in *The Routledge Book of World's Proverbs* (Jon R. Stone, Routledge, London New York 2006), one of those few intimating that the whole universe of proverbs might be covered by a single book, the aim of this contribution is to follow, first, some formal characteristics of these and, second, their dictionary treatment. The total number of proverbs included in the book is, approximately, 17,000.

Under the heading **Proverb** some ten proverbs are given including a German one:

A country can be judged by the quality of its proverbs,

which may be viewed as somewhat chauvinistic by non-Germans. Two other proverbs, however, might be a good starter characterizing the collection:

A proverb is a short sentence based on long experience (Spanish),
A proverb is to speech what salt is to food (Arabian),

the first one going to the core linking experience and language, the second characterizing the use of proverbs by their comparison to eating and the relation of food and salt. Both open a rather wide horizon of what may be found here, formally and semantically, with the stress laid on the former.

Obviously, the Routledge dictionary is a rather small one and it says so. What it does not admit, however, is how the proverbs included here have been selected, it does not even suggest the size of the original proverb collections used. Hence, the **selection** must inevitably be viewed as arbitrary and subjective. Given a lack of any criteria for a selection of proverbs the choice presented in the book is just as good as any. There is no attention paid to paremiological minima and there is an almost complete absence of proverb frequencies observable.

Even though the problem of the **identity** of proverbs which is not handled at all, being left to the original sources, no doubt heterogenous, at least some attention paid to the **classification** of proverbs could be expected, but the author has hardly given it any systematic thought. The only attempt is to be found in a usually one-word head-word suggesting implicitly that the meaning of proverbs can be squeezed into a single word (more about this in 3.).

2. Origin of Given Proverbs

Should we start proverbially, then the German:

Proverbs are like butterflies: some are caught and some fly away,

neatly sums up the reality reflected in this dictionary: there are proverbs with a better record in large dictionaries as against those that are rather modest and small, which does not mean, however, that either is exhaustive and that most proverbs, especially in the latter case, have been recorded. Many have not. This has had its impact on the compiler reflecting, thus, his **bias** towards some cultures and languages in contrast to other. This explains, for example, the fact that there are almost 26 times more proverbs of Roman origin included than of Greek (both being classical languages), while, on the other hand, there are some 11 times more German proverbs than Russian ones.

To be more precise, the frequency of proverbs by country (or culture) given here is headed by Roman 3320 (probably Latin), followed by 1807 German ones, 1287 Spanish, 1018 Italian, French 976, English 927, Chinese 926, Danish 889, Dutch 615, Irish 545, and Yiddish 945, followed by 374 Japanese, 352 Portuguese, 305 unknown, 255 Korean, 237 Poor Richard, 166 Egyptian, 163 Russian, 146 Yoruban, 128 Greek, 125 Arabian, 123 African, etc. Also other countries and/or languages are occasionally mentioned, such as Afghani, Albanian, Ancient, Argentine, Armenian, Ashanti, Balinese, Madagascar, and Puerto Rico, while, on the other hand, more than one country is lumped together bearing the label West-African or Slavic.

Next to **geographical origins**, some of which are highly problematic, also the **names of persons**, **ethnic groups**, religions or cultural traditions, important books etc, such as *Jesus, Poor Richard, Big Head, little wit, Bible, Native American, Taoist, Samurai* are given as sources.

The problem of according the **place or language of origin** to a proverb is, perhaps, best illustrated by the only version of the proverb familiar from many languages, at least in Europe, quoted as coming, surprisingly, from Armenian:

You are as many a person as languages you know (Czech *Kolik umíš jazyků, tolikrát jsi člověkem*).

It is just impossible to accept that this relatively distant language has vastly influenced many other European languages, the proverb (*As many languages you know, as many times you are a human being*, being strongly accented by the first Czech president T. G. Masaryk), being used elsewhere. One can point at, for instance,

Spanish *Cuantas lenguas hablas, tantos hombres vales*, or
Bulgarian *Struvaš tolkova, kolkoto ezici govoriš*, etc.

However, going by the list of sources in the bibliography, it has to be pointed out that only the English written resources are given, hence proverb selections are due to the English compilers of the resources. This also accounts for the English translations of proverbs where no original versions are given.

3. SUBJECT-INDEX AND METALANGUAGE USED

Some idea of the semantics or content of the book may be got from its subject-index. There are 2130 entries in the Subject-Index, this number representing, thus, crude semantic 'groups' of proverbs listed alphabetically. An example of such **semantic labels** may be illustrated by a part of the letter B:

Baby, Bachelor, Bachelorhood, Back, Backbite, Bacon, Bad, Bad Luck, Bad Name, Bad News, Bagpipe, Bagpiper, Bait, Bake, Baker, Balance (Scale), Bald, Bale, Ball, Bamboo, Baptize, Barbarians, Barber, Barefoot

Apparently, nouns are in the majority as labels, rarely followed by other word classes, such as *applaud, approve, baptize, bad* or *bald, apart, far*, there being no grammar words at all. Only two aspects have been paid some attention while planning the form of the labels occasionally, namely opposite character of some and their multiword character, i.e. where it seemed to be useful to the compiler, e.g.:

Above and Below, Bad Luck, Bad Name, Bad News, Begin and End, Birds of Prey, Blind and Deaf, Boundary Marker, Cats and Dog, Cloudy Day and Night, Eat and Drink, Get Along, Give and Take, Golden Age, Golden Rule, Good and Bad, Good and Evil, Good Deed, Good Faith, Good Humor, Good Life, Good Man, Good Person, Good Name, Good News, Good Sense, Good Thing, Good Things, Good Works,Quid Pro Quo, Scylla and Charybdis, Tit for Tat, Too Much, Up and Down, War and Peace, Wax and Wane, Women and Men, Yes and No, Young and Old, Last Straw.

Some of these rather subjectively selected labels are just plain idioms (*Quid pro Quo*), an approach to be generally avoided, other reflect some kind of psychological association (*Good Life*), some are terms (*Boundary Marker*), and for some it is just difficult to see any motivation at all (*Good Thing*, while there is no *Bad Thing* listed). Yet also some of the single-word labels seem to lack motivation, cf. *nothing, nobody, something* while *somebody* is missing, etc. It is specifically appalling that proverbs may be labeled and thus explained by another proverb (*Tit for tat*), where the **metalanguage** used for explanation and identification of it is mixed up with the object language.

The **inconsistency** of labelling makes one wonder: why, should one ask, (1) next to *bachelor, bachelorhood* is given as a separate label, while *child* has no *childhood* to accompany it, or why (2) *Frenchman* and also *German* and *Russian* are given though not *Englishman*, etc., or (3) *Capitalism* but no *Communism* or *Socialism*, etc.

Some labels are based on very special **parts of idioms**, which may hardly be used to indicate that a proverb should be looked for under these, such as *Bygones*, or they are just rather uncommon, such as *Chaff, Cobbler*, etc.

These 'quasisemantic' labels should **semantically** point to proverbs, but mostly they do not. Reversing the point of view, i.e. let us start from the **form** of proverbs and parts of them and have a look at the label pointed at. Thus, to offer just a single example, it is readily seen that the 50 proverbs containing the joint component *company* are labeled very differently, even widely so; there is a correlation to be found. Out of these 50 proverbs, the label **Company** offers only 15 proverbs containing the word *company*. Let us have a look at the distribution and coverage of the notion 'company' by some examples:

Acquaintance: *A person is known by the company it keeps.* (English)
Alone: *Better to be alone than in bad company.* (German)
Bad: *He keeps his road well enough who gets rid of bad company.* (Portuguese)
Boast: *He that boasts of himself affronts his company.* (Danish)
Bread: *The bread eaten, the company departs.* (Spanish)
Character: *You can judge a man by the company he keeps.* (Danish)
You know the man by the company he keeps. (English)

Cheerful: *Cheerful company makes any meal a feast.* (Korean)
Cheerful company shortens the miles. (German)
Companion: *For a good companion, good company.*(Spanish)
Company: *You will be sad if you keep company with only yourself.* (Roman)
Tell me the company you keep, and I will tell you who you are. (Dutch)
Tell me your company and I will tell you thyself. (Irish)
Better to be alone than in bad company. (German)
Choose your company before you choose your drink. (Irish), etc.
Crowd: *A crown is not company.* (Danish)
Feast: *The Company makes the feast.* (English)
Knave: *The hatred of knaves is to be preferred to their company.* (Roman)
Late: *The later the evening, the fairer the company.* (German)
Man: *A man is known by the company he keeps.* (American)
Morals: *Bad company corrupts good morals.* (Christian)
Pleasure: *Pleasure requires company.* (Mexican)
Seven: *Seven is company, nine is a brawl.* (American)
Two: *Two's company but three's a crowd.* (American)

It is hardly worth analyzing this; the approach adopted is a mere repetition of the traditional and **unsatisfactory ordering of proverbs** in most traditional proverb collections, not really enabling, without the help of an electronic search, to find what one is looking for. The old problem is an attempt, over and over again, to express or capture complex proverb meaning by a **single word**, which has been criticized long ago and is doomed to fail. It is just impossible, even relying on a very wild stroke of imagination, to connect or associate **company** with all of the labels given above, namely *bad*, *bread*, *character*, *cheerful*, *crowd*, *feast*, *late*, *morals*, etc.

4. Statistics of Proverbs: Lexemes (Words) and Collocation

The proverb corpus is made up of 149 648 words which, due to repetition of some, amount to 9425 different word types. These have been subjected to several types of formal analysis.

4.1 Length of Proverbs

From the point of view of the user, most proverbs appear to fit and be printed in a single line in the dictionary. The **average length** of proverbs may be estimated to be somewhere between 6–9 words, but there exist interesting extremes. Obviously, the **shortest proverbs** are made up of two and three words only, such as

Improve thyself, Know thyself, Shit happens, Truth prevails (not in the dictionary);
Anger increases love, Arms carry peace, Count your blessings.

On the other hand, some proverbs may be **unusually very long** having an untypical
structure, such as:

*Keep five yards from a carriage, ten yards from a horse, and a hundred yards from an ele-
phant; but the distance one should keep from a wicked man cannot be measured* (Indian).
*Monday's child is fair of face, Tuesday's child is full of grace; Wednesday's child is full of woe,
Thursday's child has far to go; Friday's child is loving and giving, Saturday's child works hard
for its living; and a child that's born on the Sabbath day is bonnie and blithe and good and gay*
(English).
*One Russian is a drunk; two Russians a chess game; three Russians a revolution; four Russians
a string quartet* (French).

4.2 Lexical Stock in Proverbs

The **frequency list** of words (altogether 14,914) the proverbs are composed of (altogether 17.182), starts, naturally, with grammar words going down to rare frequencies (2-1 x) that make up most of proverbs. Thus words with frequencies down to 5
(*illness*) correspond to the first 3,000 words out of the total, i.e. 33.51% of all proverbs, while the lowest frequency words (3-1 x) covers 9,914 words, i.e. 66.49% of all
proverbs.

It is difficult to give any brief and, at the same time, deep-going analysis of the
word stock (149,648 words, amounting, without repetition, to 9,425 forms) used in
proverbs. In order to offer some insight and idea of a reference frame, similar numbers of words in the (**A**) frequency dictionary made up of the proverbs' word stock
(221 words) and (**B**) the Routledge frequency dictionary (255 words, Mark Davis, Dee
Gardner) have been chosen and compared; moreover, these have been limited to nouns
and verbs only, as these carry meaning mostly.

Since the number of these autosemantic words (i.e. nouns and verbs) have been
so severely limited, having been cut off at the very top, the degree of overlapping may
not seem great. Should more or even all words be included, the overlapping, i.e. words
contained both in the proverbs frequency dictionary (A) and the general frequency
dictionary (B) will grow; at the same time, one would soon get into problems, as the
frequency dictionary is rather small (5000 words) and many words to be found in proverbs have a very low general frequency (see more in 4.4).

Thus the **Proverb Frequency dictionary (A)** projected onto the general Frequency
dictionary and its 221 nouns and verbs, selected from the 500 most frequent words in
(A) gives a rough idea of both agreement and differences. Words marked in bold are
those that the list of the general frequency dictionary (B) does NOT have:

adversity, *advice*, age, *anger*, *are*, ask, *ass*, *beauty*, become, *becomes*, *bed*, *been*, *beginning*, *being*, believe, *bird*, *bite*, *born*, *bread*, break, bring, *brings*, buy, call, can, *can't*, *cannot*, care, *cat*, catch, *catches*, come, *comes*, *cow*, day, death, *devil*, die, do, *does*, *doesn't*, *dog*, *dogs*, *don't*, *done*, door, *drink*, *eat*, *eats*, end, *enemy*, *envy*, *evil*, eye, *eyes*, face, fall, father, *fear*, *fears*, find, *finds*, *fire*, *fish*, *fly*, *fool*, *fools*, forget, *fortune*, *fox*, friend, *friends*, *friendship*, *fruit*, get, *gets*, give, *given*, *gives*, go, *god*, *goes*, *gold*, grow, *grows*, *had*, hand, *hands*, *has*, *hath*, have, head, hear, heart, *heaven*, help, hold, home, *honey*, *honor*, hope, *horse*, house, *hunger*, change, child, *children*, *is*, *judge*, keep, *keeps*, *king*, know, *knowledge*, *known*, *knows*, *laughs*, law, learn, leave, let, *lie*, *lies*, life, live, *lives*, look, lose, *loses*, *lost*, love, *loves*, *made*, make, *makes*, man, *man's*, *master*, may, *men*, *men's*, mind, *misfortune*, money, mother, *mouth*, must, *nature*, need, *needs*, *ox*, *peace*, people, person, *play*, *pleasure poverty*, *praise*, *purse*, put, road, run, said, say, *says*, see, *seek*, *sees*, sell, *shall*, *sheep*, should, *silence*, son, *sorrow*, speak, *speaks*, *stone*, *sun*, take, *takes*, talk, tell, *thief*, thing, *things*, think, *thinks*, *throw*, time, *tongue*, *tree*, *trust*, *truth*, use, *virtue*, want, *wants*, war, *was*, water, way, *wealth*, *were*, wife, will, *wind*, *wine*, *wisdom*, *wish*, *wolf*, woman, *women*, *won't*, word, *words*, work, world, would, *years*, *youth*.

If one reverts the direction and tries to see the overlapping from the point of view of the general frequency dictionary, the result is, by and large, complementary. Thus the **Frequency dictionary (B)** is projected onto the general Proverb Frequency dictionary (A) and its 255 nouns and verbs, selected from the 500 most frequent words in (B). Words marked in bold are those that the list of the Proverb frequency dictionary (A) does NOT have, i.e. within the limits of the cut-off part:

add, age, **air**, **allow**, **appear**, **area**, **arm**, **art**, ask, **be**, become, **begin**, believe, **body**, **book**, **boy**, break, bring, **build**, **business**, buy, call, can, **car**, care, **carry**, **case**, **city**, **class**, **college**, come, **community**, **company**, **consider**, **continue**, **control**, **could**, **country**, **course**, **create**, **cut**, day, death, **decide**, **decision**, **develop**, **development**, die, **difference**, do, door, **drive**, **drug**, **education**, **effect**, **effort**, end, **expect**, **experience**, **explain**, eye, face, **fact**, fall, **family**, father, **feel**, **field**, find, **follow**, **food**, **foot**, **force**, friend, **game**, get, **girl**, give, go, **government**, **group**, grow, **guy**, hand, **happen**, have, head, **health**, hear, heart, help, **history**, hold, home, hope, **hour**, house, change, child, **idea**, **include**, **information**, **interest**, **issue**, **job**, keep, **kid**, **kill**, **kind**, know, law, **lead**, **leader**, learn, leave, let, **level**, life, **light**, **line**, live, look, lose, love, make, man, **market**, may, **mean**, **meet**, **member**, **might**, **million**, mind, **minute**, **moment**, money, **month**, **morning**, mother, **move**, **music**, must, **name**, **nation**, need, **night**, **number**, **offer**, **office**, **open**, **parent**, **part**, **party**, **pass**, **pay**, people, person, **place**, **plan**, play, **point**, **police**, **policy**, **power**, **president**, **price**, **problem**, **process**, **program**, **provide**, **pull**, put, **question**, **raise**, **rate**, **read**, **reach**, **reason**, **receive**, **relationship**, **remain**, **remember**, **report**, **require**, **research**, **result**, return, **right**, road, **role**, **room**, run, say, see, **seem**, sell, **send**, **sense**, **serve**, **service**, **set**, should, **show**, **school**, **side**, **sit**, son, speak, **spend**, **stand**, **start**, **state**, **stay**, **stop**, **story**, **student**, **study**, **suggest**, **system**, take, talk, **teacher**, **team**, tell, **thank**, thing, think, time, **town**, **try**, **turn**,

understand, *use*, **value**, **view**, **voice**,**wait**, **walk**, *want*, *war*, *water*, **watch**, *way*, **week**, *wife*, *will*, *win*, *woman*, *word*, *work*, *world*, *would*, **write**, **year**.

Of course such common words as *age*, *ask*, etc. listed in both lists which do not seem to be represented, are in fact represented in both, but lie beyond the arbitrary frequency indicated by the cut-off point (i.e. 221 or rather 255 nouns and verbs).

4.3 Collocations, N-grams and Proverbs

Due to the diversity of the lexicon used, most metaphors are found at the level of the proverb as a whole. Looking below it, at **n-grams** of various size, the whole scale of septagrams (made up of 7 words), hexagrams (6), pentagrams (5), down to bigrams (2) has been calculated. As expected, in this vast array of combinations there are more combinations that

(A) have no meaning (due to chance and neighbourhood, such as *servant but a*, *are often the*, *and tide wait for*), that are
(B) part or fragment of larger meaningful combinations (*the last straw that breaks the camel's*, a septagram, 3×) or
(C) are of grammatical nature only (*there are* 74×, *must be* 60×)
could be found, while only marginally some meaningful collocations could also be found, including some multiword collocations.

Most n-grams (over half of them) consisted of bigrams. Septagrams have been chosen as the extreme that, basically, coincides with many proverbs viewed as a whole. In what follows, some examples of various n-grams (referred to by the first bold figure in the parentheses) shown with their frequency (the second figure followed by ×) are given. They cannot be but random examples selected from a vast amount of data (out of 38,613 combinations).

what cannot be cured must be endured (**7**/2×, i.e. a septagram),
a woman's work is never done (**6**/4×, i.e. a hexagram),
if you want to be (**5**/5×), *by the company he keeps* (**5**/4×), *cast your pearls before swine* (**5**/3×), *all roads lead to rome* (**5**/4×), *a slip of the tongue* (**5**/4×), *it is too late to* (**5**/6×), *bird in the hand is* (**5**/6×), *it is too late to* (**5**/6×), *bird in the hand is* (**5**/6×), *it is too late to* (**5**/6×), *bird in the hand is* (**5**/6×, i.e. pentagrams),
on its own dunghill (**4**/7×), *sky in the morning* (**4**/3×), *the one who has* (**4**/10×, i.e. tetragrams),
on its own (**3**/9×), *where there are* (**3**/11×), *he is a fool* (**3**/9×), *is known by* (**3**/19×), *nothing is certain* (**3**/4×),
an old man (**3**/19×), *better to lose* (**3**/11×), *does not make* (**3**/24×), *he that would* (**3**/27×), *it is easier* (**3**/25×), *he who has* (**3**/84×), *no one knows* (**3**/8×), *in the morning* (**3**/15×), *for the sake of* (**3**/11×), *there is no* (**3**/127×, i.e. trigrams),

power corrupts (2/2×), *be silent* (2/15×), *good counsel* (2/8×), *your friend* (2/22×), *poor man* (2/35), *while rich man* (2/21×), *as well* (2/29×), *has its* (2/50×), *he that*(2/252×), *there are* (2/74×), *good deed* (2/11×), *better than* (2/158×), *good man* (2/26×, , i.e. bigrams)...

The highest frequencies can be observed with those (mostly meaningful) collocations that are lexically not interesting but have a grammatical or structural role to play (cf. *he that, there are,* etc., in the bigrams).

It is obvious that due to the unique character of proverbs most **metaphors** found here are very rare (with a frequency one usually), cf.:

it rains honey and wine (1×), *bed of roses* (1×), *saying and doing* (1×), *scratch a king* (1×), *the smoke of friendship* (1×), *at a snail's pace* (1×), *speaking law* (1×), *spare the rod* (2×).

Out of these, only some metaphors are stable, such as (*at a snail's pace, bed of roses*).

4.4 OLD AND NEW LEXEMES IN PROVERBS

Since most proverbs are rather old (though it is difficult to determine their age precisely), at least two aspects related to time are obvious.

There are words whose age makes them **rare and obsolete** in today's usage. These include, for example,
apothecary, befoul, blithe, bonnie, conservative, disuse, ducat, eaglet,grape-gatherer, luckless, muckle, out-monkey, parley, thou, thy, etc.

Obviously, problems related to their understanding may arise here.
The time scale, if approaching modern times, may still cause a low frequency representation of such words as *car, drug, include, information, issue, police, president, process, rate, research*
that are not to be found at all here, or have a marginal frequency, so far, such as *democracy* (1×), *bicycle* (1×), *million* (1×), *nation* (2×), *parliament* (1×, in a Danish proverb), *party* (1×), *policy* (1), *problem* (2×), *relationship* (3×), *whiskey* (2×).
On the other hand, some relatively new words have not found their way into proverbs yet, such as
airplane, locomotive, mobile phone, radio, submarine, television, etc.

5. CONCLUSIONS

Obviously, any subjective selection from the vast amounts of data is a problem: the Routledge edition should not be viewed as a good *pars pro toto* illustration.

Despite limitations due to formal approach only, some general aspects of the proverb corpus and its building blocks have, hopefully, become somewhat clearer.

On the other hand, limitations due to the initial design of the dictionary partly explain some ambiguousness and difficulties in analysis. This is primarily due to the old, and unacceptable trend of trying to squeeze the complex meaning of the proverb under a single word label.

Last but not least, as an evergreen almost: there is the problem of the metalanguage used here again: it is often academic, sometimes obsolete and, worst of all, even identical with the object language.

LITERATURE

ČERMÁK, František. 2012. "Lexical Foundations of Proverbs. Based on Data from English, German, French and Czech." In 5. *Colloquio Interdisciplinar sobre Proverbios – Actas, 5th Interdisciplinary Colloquium on Proverbs*, edited by R. Soares, O. Lauhakangas, 203-217. Lisbon: AIP-IAP.

DAVIES, Mark and GARDNER, Dee. 2010. *A Frequency Dictionary of Contemporary American English*. London – New York: Routledge.

STONE, Jon R., ed. 2006. *The routledge book of world's proverbs*. London – New York: Routledge.

3. Frequent Proverbs and Their Meaning: A Proposal of a Linguistic Description (The Core and Paremiological Minima Described)

In **Actas ICP 3, 2010**, 47–88, **Čermák Proverbs 2014**, 47–90.

Abstract

Starting with the nominative function of proverbs, which is to be distinguished from its mea-ning, one might ask where to start looking, should one try to get at the proverbs meaning. Next to the traditional and subjective resources of proverbs in traditional dictionaries, one might turn to a modern corpora and frequency-based proverb minima extracted from them. A number of basic lexico-semantic classes for English and Czech have been found in this way and are examined.

1. Introduction: Social Function of Proverbs and Their Nominative Power

The major functions proverbs have in human communities have been discussed for a long time many times over and examined from various aspects and a consensus seems to be that there is no substitute for them in social communication, even in our modern times and society. Proverbs are generally held to be universal for any society in its multifaceted nature and its language, too. Accordingly, the sheer mul-titude and varied social functions of proverbs have led to designs of general classifi-catory frameworks or systems, too. However, should we reverse the traditional look of viewing proverbs through their form first and start considering them from their meaning and linguistic functions, one might also ask other questions; such as, what type of propositional meaning proverbs have in the universe of human thought that traditionally recur and are repeatedly found useful by successive generations. Hence a question that one could ask:

Do proverbs as specific language stereotypes cover, from this semantic or onomasiological po-int of view, any recurrent type of thought, based on shared and inherited experience?

However, in a brief follow-up to this question, one may become wary should he/she realize that some of the valuable old proverbs, such as the Egyptian:

If you search for the laws of harmony, you will find knowledge,

do not seem to have many modern counterparts and may be lost nowadays. Does this mean that some valuable types of experience and their apposite expression in language have not been recurrent after all?

Generally, the question may seem either trivial, as the answer might be, or most probably, that one does not really know, since there is no mapping of recurring human thought projected into language available. Yet, systems devised by M. Kuusi and G. L. Permjakov seem to suggest a lot along the lines leading to a potential core of an answer, though they do not represent a real answer yet. Nonexistence of proverbs, for example, in chemistry, mathematics or physics, may suggest that proverbs appear in the traditional fields linked to practical human life and its recurrent aspects and repeated patterns shared by the whole community over a period of time. Thus, it seems that proverbs in their coverage and use belong to the social sciences (including linguistics), rather than to exact ones, as it is clear from, for example, the main categories registered by M. Kuusi.

There is a special aspect of proverbs that deserves mention and attention. Using a proverb means that the speaker invariably takes an attitude that is of necessity *evaluative*, approving or disapproving of the actions of somebody else, giving him/her advice, warning, etc., all of this against the background of common and inherited wisdom and experience, which is viewed as normative. This evaluative aspect, being basically of a pragmatic nature, which is to be distinguished from the content or basic meaning of proverbs, is so common, that it is hardly ever mentioned. Using a proverb one assumes, rather automatically, an evaluative and hence a subjective role (though shared by many), which is incompatible with the exact sciences, hence their absence from the general systems of proverbs. Although this evaluative aspect in the use of proverbs requires more attention, there is not much scope for it here.

Not being able to come up with a comprehensive answer to our question, so far, does not mean that one could not eventually be able to formulate it. Since there is now at least a modest experience with thesauri mapping the universe of words and lexemes in a more or less accepted way (such as Roget's), there is no reason to believe that this is impossible for fixed combinations of words, including proverbs. Yet, problems involved in this are far greater than in the traditional taxonomy of words in a vocabulary according to their meaning.

An obvious first step in search of the answer to the initial question is to have a look, first in a modest way, at the core of proverbs and the type and features of meaning involved here. To be able to do that, however, one will have to find a reliable core of proverbs, based on real usage, whose evidence and record may be found in corpora. Having these, one would have to devise a solid and unified metalinguistic framework for their description and see what is to be found in this core. This is, then, also the aim of this contribution.

2. Nominative Foundations of Proverbs: Taxonomy

The existence of proverbs has not gone unnoticed for long, the earliest attempts to collect them are known in Europe from the time of Greek antiquity at least (see also Mieder 2004), but a general boost in this direction was started in Europe with Erasmus at the beginning of 16th century (1500 onwards). Though containing more than proverbs only, his *Adagia* was a major impetus boosting national proverb collections in many countries. Collection of proverbs gradually inspired at least some people, mostly ethnographers at first, and made them notice some of general features of proverbs, gradually leading to modern descriptions. However, the bulk of what has been published in the field starts after World War II. Names such as A. Taylor, M. Kuusi, G. L. Permjakov and W. Mieder have become representative of the field and as the field opened more to allow, next to ethnographers, also semioticians, and linguists, a more complex picture of the proverb topic has emerged.

The early proverb collections have traditionally been organized in a simple and primitive way by enlisting a number of topics covered by proverbs, which were, however, rather haphazardly lumped together under such loose labels as those in the seminal collection of Czech proverbs by Čelakovský (1852). Under broad and ill-defined fields called, such as:

2 *Good-Bad... egoism, hypocrisy, swindle, prodigality, unjustified wealth, gratitude*, or
3 *Truth-justice-lie-language, chattering, slander, jokes, promise...*

The specific proverbs one is interested in are to be found with some difficulty and there is no guarantee that each of his 17 fields (*work, happiness, mind, world, health, household...*) is descriptive enough as to cover all specific proverbs unequivocally.

This kind of mapping the proverb universe into rather loose fields, used in many languages, has been later offered in an alternative solution in the type of system of M. Kuusi, based on his vast knowledge of many languages, using only 13 themes or fields such as *The world and human life, Social interaction,*and *Agreement and norms* (with many subdivisions). Though having many drawbacks, it remains to be seen if a different and better system can be devised in future. The perennial and major problem is how to translate the sentential character of the proverb into a combination of a few suitable words, if not sentences, namely, a suitable metalanguage.

Linguistically, proverbs are seen as specific ready-made language nominations (lexemes) that are much more complex than one-word or multiword lexemes requiring, however, more research into their nominative aspects that has not even begun. It is evident that a taxonomy should become the final goal of any classification though it might not exactly copy the one that is known from biology and elsewhere. A specific problem, for linguists too, is the status of criteria reasonably dissecting the whole universe and individual fields as such. So far, only notions and categories of the external classifications, taken over from the sciences, philosophy, and their disciplines are used which are not really applicable in linguistics and linguistic description. Ultimately, one must decide between a classification and description (in dictionaries). While the former may be of interest for specialists, the latter may be used by the broader public.

2.1 Paremiological Minimum or Something Else?

The idea of cutting down the realm of proverbs to a core, studying its features (mostly semantic here), and trying to generalize so that all proverbs can be covered calls for such a selection that would, however, be based on reliable criteria. The obvious, and in fact only, basis so far are pareminological minima started by G.L. Permjakov and available for several languages now (including Czech and German, but not English). Since they raise some doubts one should be wary and look for alternatives, if available. Basically, the situation is not much different here from that of lexicology. However, lexicology has produced, for many languages, two useful products, *frequency dictionaries* (a modern and corpus-based one has recently been published for the Czech language, too) and statistical *mappings of text coverage* by the growing numbers of lexemes enabling one to know how many items one must know to be able to understand various percentages of texts. Thus for the Czech language it holds that the most frequent 50 thousand lexemes cover 98,3% of all texts, while the first 10 lexemes correspond to almost 10% of texts (Čermák – Křen 2004).

Such useful instruments as frequency dictionaries do not exist for proverbs, so far. Should one have them, a selection of proverbs both for a proverb minimum and a solid probe of the core would, then, be based on a solid basis, as one would really know how many proverbs are needed for the selected and well-specified goal.

2.2 Problems of the Methodology of Paremiological Minima

Though based on a limited field of research along ethnographical lines, these minima are far from reliable and representative. Paremiologists often seem to discard frequency (1) as a criterion, in some cases they even disregard the synchrony-diachrony division (2) cherishing proverbs that are not much in use any longer. However, some of their problems are related to the methodology of proverb verification (3), they are suggesting that asking people only the first half of the proverb he/she will supply the second half. This, in fact, may be wrong, as it may actually be the second half of the proverb that might be more familiar and should be used in the research based on questions (such as *silver lining* for **Every cloud has a silver lining**, and not, traditionally, *Every cloud*, see Čermák 2007a).

Also, it may not be true that all proverbs are automatically divisible into two neat halves that one might use here (it would seem rather difficult to ask, as the leading question, just *Money...* hoping the respondent will correctly supply *Money talks*). It is also difficult to know the social range (4) and number of people to be asked to get a representative distribution of the knowledge of the proverb. Moreover, such research has no way of telling in what situations and contexts (5) and how proverbs are used. Finally, one of the most serious major problems of this ethnographical method is that it does not include any discovery procedure (6) and just verifies what paremiologists already know. To find new, unknown proverbs is not possible in this way.

On this insecure basis, paremiological minima are, then, biased. This, in turn, leads to another question: how many proverbs constitute a minimum? Is it 300 (Permjakov's number) or 100 (used by some other)? Apart from the mere availability of data, what real criteria in the selection should apply? The name *minimum* is a misnomer signalling that a minimum, even though one does not know what it exactly is, is the number one should not go under since it represents a standard. However, the idea of a standard is not based on any kind of solid research. In sum, it all seems to boil down to data, their number, and the criteria of their selection. An obvious solution, even if one takes into account the prerequisites just mentioned would be knowing what the needs of the target users are to make this kind of solution useful and needed. To illustrate this briefly, let me point to some Russian examples. It seems that some of Permjakov's basic proverbs included in his minimum, such as *Бумага все терпит* (Paper will endure everything) or *Перемелется – мука будет* (It is a long lane that has no turning) are not to be found in the Russian National Corpus. Inevitably, this casts some doubts on his selection and criteria behind it.

The aspect of data and usage can be vastly improved now by exploration of very large representative corpora offering such a great variety of speakers ethnographers could never dream of having (though there is a problem of the difference between written and spoken usage). Though this approach is definitely based on more solid grounds as to the quality of information obtained, the old problem persists here, too: basically, one still does not know how to discover proverbs one has not already known before. Yet, some modest improvements are to be found here; one of them being, next to the range of possible formal methods, is based on statistical association measures, such as mutual information (not systematically used, however) and identification of proverbs by some typical forms accompanying them, such as introducers (Čermák 2003).

2.3 SEMANTICS AND FUNCTION OF PROVERBS

If one compares definitions for the same single proverb provided by various dictionaries, one may often wonder whether they are describing the same thing. Thus the proverb,

Let bygones be bygones,
semantically rather simple, so to speak, is rendered as:
forget past offences or causes of conflict and be reconciled (NODE),
forget about unpleasant things that have happened in the past (Free Dictionary by Farlex),

forget past differences and be reconciled (Oxford Compact Dictionary) and
to decide to forget past disagreements; become reconciled (Dictionary.com).

Surprisingly, there is precious little these definitions have in common, in fact only three words (*forget, past, be*) are to be found in all of the definitions. This is just an illustration of how difficult and problematic it may get in trying to explain things, i.e. capture their meaning. Going by old elementary school experience, it should hold that the longer (and, supposedly, more explicit) the definition is the better. Since the numbers of words the dictionaries use here is: 10, 10, 6, 6/8 it should be the longest definition that is the best. But is it really true? On the other hand, definitions in specialized dictionaries tend to be much longer and more explicit and, accordingly, probably better. A recent Czech dictionary (Čermák et al. 2009) offers definitions for proverbs ranging from over 40 to almost 60 words used for the definition.

Obviously, a very short semantic(-ethnographic) label a proverb gets, if it is fitted into a type system of Kuusi's, offers much less and it should not be mistaken for a lexicographic definition.

In the business of describing proverb meaning, there are at least two other aspects worth considering. The first is discrimination of the *function*, set in a typical situation and context of use as well as major relevant factors, including reasons for its use from the very meaning, a bit more will be said about this point later. Suffice to say that it is hardly ever done anywhere (though the Czech dictionary observes the difference systematically). There is a vast difference between a mere statement of the *meaning* and recommendation that is implicitly involved, i.e. urging someone, cf.:

Better late than never
and its meaning *It's better to do something, even if it's late, than not do it at all,*
while its *function* might be rendered by *do it by all means!*

However, it is perhaps the other aspect that is more important, namely that of a suitable *metalanguage* used for description of both. Unlike lexicography and its traditional techniques, there is no methodological consensus found here used for proverb definitions and dictionaries are left to their own devices and idiosyncrasies.

3. RESOURCES PROBLEM

The data problem and ways how to get reliable information from them has been mentioned above. It seems that in our time people are less in favour of undertaking painstaking field research and collection than before. Hence, the only apparent solution is to found in large corpora (though not so much Internet). Of course modern corpora with their emphasis laid on typicality and representativeness are much different from individual, often regional resources that had been collected by some dedicated people earlier. However, the variety of this kind of resources raises the obvious question about the extent of their distribution among most users, since they have invariably been based on small samples only.

3.1 IDENTIFICATION OF PROVERBS

Some methodological problems related to finding and identifying proverbs in available resources have been briefly mentioned above. It is just not possible to ask people on the street a simple but naive question 'which proverbs do you know?' which amounts to asking a computer corpus 'which proverbs are there somewhere inside?'

But there are other, different problems related to:

(a) *discrimination* of proverbs from among other similar *sentence-like idioms,*
(b) *identification* of a proverb invariant from *variants* or, perhaps, deciding that there is more than one proverb found in the maze of forms and semiforms assembled.

There is no simple answer to the (a) question of identification as it clearly depends on how one views the broader framework, at least that of phraseology and idiomatics (e.g., see a description by Čermák 2007b). The worst solution is if paremiologists consider their field a closed and self-contained field without links and transitory phenomena shared by other disciplines. The field of sentence-like or propositional idioms, where proverbs belong, is vast and lacking in a solid and recognized description. Yet it seems possible to say that within this vast and manifold realm proverbs take probably no more that some 10% of this kind of sentence idiom, displaying, naturally, many obvious transitory types, that are difficult to classify. This appears to be, for example, the Czech situation, too.

Using corpora again brings more urgently forward the necessity to deal with (b) variants that are to be found everywhere. Even if one separates variants that appear stable from those that are not, i.e. filters that belong to *la langue* and to *la parole*, there are still many problems to be solved. These include, for example finding answers to questions such as (A) how to grasp variants and use them for description, (B) to decide which one is the invariant, (C) involving the problem of the extent to which the alleged proverb may be changed and still preserve its identity and (D) where it is no longer the case, namely from where one has to acknowledge the birth of a new and independent form. These are not easy questions. Some illustration may help to understand the case better. Having been examined in a large representative 100-million word corpus of Czech (Čermák 2004), 243 highly frequent Czech proverbs have been found to have variants (almost 42 percent).

4. Paremiological Minima Revised

A number of paremiological minima (PM) have been devised, all of them building on ethnographical principles using demographic methods, based on field research (see Mieder about this 2004, 127ff). The only exception has been the second minimum of Czech based on corpus data (Čermák 2003). In both cases, however, the drawbacks of both approaches have not been overcome. In order to arrive at comparable data, a paremiological minimum of Czech has been completely revised arriving at a third minimum. For English, various data available (starting with Mieder's list, 2004, 129-130) have been lumped together. The data for both languages (in fact rather long lists of them) have then been searched in the Czech National Corpus (SYN2005, i.e. CNC) and British National Corpus (i.e. BNC), both offering 100-million words in a representative selection. The first 100 proverbs with their frequencies, i.e. those with the highest frequencies, have been selected (which are to be found in the Appendix). In order to standardise the job, only one canonical form for each proverb has been selected, leaving all variants behind. For purposes of comparison, a list by Baur-Chlosta (1996) and Grzybek (1991) for German, though not based on a corpus, has been added. Even a cursory look at the English and Czech suggests that proverbs seem to be used in Czech much more often.

For the sake of a closer analysis, however, shorter lists, based on these three minima, have been mechanically selected containing only the first 20 proverbs for each language, ordered by corpus frequency. It is to be regretted that no other comparable data (with the exception of the Slovak, whose corpus, however, is still not balanced, Ďurčo 2004), that could be included in the research and comparison, are not available.

4.1 English Paremiological Minimum: A Core of the First 20 Proverbs (BNC: down to frequency 15)

Easier said than done. 62
Every cloud has a silver lining. 52
Still waters run deep. 33
Chickens come home to roost. 31
First things first. 31
Small is beautiful. 30
Forgive and forget. 27
Birds of a feather flock together. 25
There is safety in numbers. 25
Time is money. 22
Out of sight, out of mind. 21
First come, first served. 20
Every man for himself. 20
No smoke without fire. 19
Money talks. 18

Better late than never. 16
You cannot have your cake and eat it too. 16
Knowledge is power. 15
There is no such thing as a free lunch. 15
Fight fire with fire. 15

4.2 Czech Paremiological Minimum: A Core of the First 20 Proverbs (CNC: down to frequency 23)

The Czech minimum is, next to frequencies, provided by English equivalents, so that a comparison is possible.

Do třetice všeho dobrýho. 90× *Third time lucky.*
Účel světí prostředky. 69× *The end justifies the means.*
Kdo s koho. 56× *May the best man win.*
Něco za něco. 53× *One good turn deserves another.*
Oko za oko, zub za zub. 52× *An eye for an eye and a tooth for a tooth.*
Přání je otcem myšlenky. 46× *The wish is father to the thought.*
Nikdy neříkej nikdy. 40× *Never say die, Never say never.*
Jiný kraj jiný mrav. 38× *Other countries other manners.*
Jablko nepadne daleko od stromu. 32× *The apple never falls far from the tree, Like father like son.*
Všeho moc škodí. 32× *You can have too much of a good thing.*
Zdání klame. 31× *Appearances can be deceptive.*
Všechno zlý/zlé je k něčemu dobrý/dobré. 29× *Every cloud has a silver lining.*
Odvážnýmu štěstí přeje. 28× *Fortune favours the brave/bold.*
Všeho s mírou. 28× *Too much of one thing, good for nothing.*
Můj dům můj hrad. 28× *My house is my castle.*
Pod svícnem bývá tma. 27× *Still waters run deep.*
Ráno moudřejší večera. 26× *Let's sleep on it.*
Moc řečí a skutek utek. 26× *(be) all talk and no action.*
Konec dobrý, všechno dobré. 25× *All's well that ends well.*
Lepší vrabec hrsti než holub na střeše. 24× *A bird in the hand is worth two in the bush.*
Štěstí/náhoda přeje připraveným. 24× *Fortune favours only the prepared mind.*
Život je boj. 23× *Life is one long struggle.*
Rozděl a panuj. 23× *Divide and rule/conquer.*

5. Meaning and Function of Core PM in English, Czech and German

A rather simple hypothesis may be formulated stating that the most proverbs should express the most common meanings that are repeatedly used with a high frequency.

Accordingly, these common proverbs, or rather a proverb core, relate to the most typical, frequent and useful meanings and contents speakers resort to in many types of their communication. To learn more about this, at least in a preliminary way, proverbs will have to be selected to form a manageable amount, obviously from a paremiological minimum. In order to achieve some balance at least, three languages will be compared, namely Czech, English, and German, though the last offers a much different minimum than Czech and English (being smaller and not supported by corpus data). In this case, the number of proverbs to be inspected boils down to the first 20 from each language. However, to be able to make any comparison going forward, all of the sixty proverbs, or rather their meanings, will have to be in inspected within a uniform semantic framework based on a metalanguage able to cover it in its most relevant aspects. For this, two obvious frameworks, those by Matti Kussi and G. L. Permjakov seem to suggest themselves. However, for a number of reasons, another, and hopefully, a more relevant onomasiological framework will be used, based on a lexicographical approach.

To be able to ask questions of the type, why this or that proverb means just this and not something else, a brief look at the component parts (words) of these proverbs might show to what extent there is some kind of motivation behind the proverb meanings. The German minimum being different, only the English and Czech vocabulary will be inspected briefly.

To illustrate this, let us look at the English proverb:

Still waters run deep.

Comparing the lexical stock it is built from with the semantic metalaguage used (and explained later), namely **man inconspicuous surprises**,
it is obvious that none of the components is made part of the metalanguage (though there might be other that do this, at least partly).

5.1 Proverb Components and Their Meaning

To find out if there is a more general type of semantic relation between the chosen proverbs and their components, a list of the latter will be made making it possible to see any motivation.

The Alphabetical English Word List was made of 114 words representing these component parts. It is heavily based on 25 nouns that are used only once or twice; an exception are somewhat more frequent occurrences of *a* (3×), *fire* (3×), *first* (4), *is* (5×), *first* (4×) and *of* (3×). Though the most common proverbs have been selected, also some less frequent and rare words occur here, including *feather, flock, chickens*, and *roost*.

a, and, as, beautiful, better, birds, cake, cannot, cloud, come, deep, done, easier, eat, every, feather, fight, fire, first, flock, for, forget, forgive, free, has, have, himself, home, chickens, in, is, it, knowledge, late, lining, lunch, man, mind, money, never, no, numbers, of, out, power, roost, run, safety, said, served, sight, silver, small, smoke, still, such, talks, than, there, thing, things, time, to, together, too, waters, with, without, you, your.

However, the Alphabetical Czech Word List is made up of a much smaller stock of 79 words, where nouns dominate (22), too, but there is only a single word more frequent, namely the preposition *za* (3×), the rest having a frequency of 1 or 2. Also here, some less frequent and rare words occur, namely *holub* (pigeon), *hrst* (handful, fist), *svícnem* (candleholder), *třetice* (three, archaic), *vrabec* (sparrow),

a, bývá, daleko, do, dobré, dobrého, dům, holub, hrad, hrsti, jablko, je, jiný, k, kdo, klame, koho, kraj, lepší, moc, moudřejší, mrav, můj, na, něco, něčemu, nepadne, než, od, odvážnému, oko, pod, prostředky, přeje, ráno, s, stromu, střeše, světí, svícnem, škodí, štěstí, tma, třetice, účel, utek, večera, vrabec, všeho, všechno, za, zdání, zlé, zub.

It is the presence of rare words at least that makes any general type of semantic relationship difficult to find as the proverbs inspected represent very general and the most common types of meanings. For more, a much more detailed analysis would be necessary.

5.2 MEANING OF CORE PROVERBS

5.2.1 MEANING, FUNCTION AND CLASSIFICATORY FRAMEWORKS

The problem of the meaning of the core proverbs under inspection, whose selection under the name of proverb minima has been discussed above (4.), is closely linked to that of form, though it is, basically, independent of the meaning of the component parts, as it seems, just like any other type of idiom. Nevertheless, one must specify, even here, what is meant by meaning, since the term is generic and largely a broad one. If specified, the term of *meaning* should then be inspected here as to whether the proverb meaning is constructed in and dependent on some general framework using a kind of metalanguage and, at the same time, distinguished from function. While meaning, basically, is any semantic feature or a cluster of features lying behind the form, *function* may be best viewed operationally as a pragmatic feature or features, related to types of language action one performs when a proverb is used.

In spite of the remarkable contributions of many, only a couple of men have been able to offer such a general framework, or suggested the general conditions and features it is supposed to have. None of these, however, approached the field from a linguistic point of view. The two, basically familiar to paremiologists, Matti Kuusi and G. L. Permjakov, have viewed proverbs in a universal framework as ethnographers, basically, though the emphasis on Kuusi's side had been laid on a broader cultural framework, while with Permjakov it had been the sign and semiotical as well as logical aspects of proverbs he had relied on. However, at least two other figures, largely unknown in this context, should be recalled here, too, that of Otakar Zich, a Czech logician who has written a book *Folk Proverbs from the Logical Point of View* (Lidová přísloví z hlediska logického, 1956) and, above all, Charles Sanders Peirce, an American philosopher and founder of the modern science of semiotics. Though there might be some awareness of each other, it seems, mostly, that there had essentially been none and that these outstanding people had worked independently. This can, partly, be read from the dates when their major contributions were published: Peirce 1940 (Selected Writings), Zich 1956, Kuusi 1957, 1972 and Permjakov 1970 (in English 1979, though later also thanks to Grzybek, in German, Permjakov 2000). While O. Zich did not offer any systematic framework for proverbs, his main concern was with criteria and their application in logical construction of proverbs viewed as propositions and it seems by far to be the best analysis of this field that is available.

Because of his general importance for science, however, it might be useful to remind ourselves, of the semiotic system of Peirce's. His system, reconstructed from his numerous letters primarily, is a comprehensive one, including signs of all levels, starting from those related to psychological types (perception), through those related to reality (real objects), lexicon, and up to logical processes. In the final framework we know today, signs have been viewed by him as means mediating relations between objects and meanings in a triadic system of mental processes. These were made up by categories that he usually called Firstness, Secondness and Thirdness. It is the highest type, Thirdness, that is of immediate concern for linguists and, specifically, paremiologists, as it is viewed as a mode of signs revealed in their representation, continuity, order, and unity. Later, more familiar names characterized these categories as being made up of signs for quality, existence, and representation, the last one corresponding to Thirdness. Representation, including signs of the highest order, is hierarchically split into three levels, including signs for (A) **rheme** (yes-no), (B) **proposition** (sign representing its object that can be stated), and (C) **argument** (sign interpreting its object as habit or law). Since his ten-level hierarchical system of interconnected and mutually interdependent signs is rather elaborate, it may be, for practical reasons, necessary just to mention that only the last and highest two levels, that of the dicent symbol and argument are relevant here. While *dicent symbols* amount to sentences and propositions, *arguments* are solely, in Peirce's mind, made of syllogisms. Within these limits, one may, then, try to view proverbs.

In contradistinction to the systems of Kuusi and Permjakov, based on non-linguistic criteria, basically, below an attempt will be made to show how a descriptive linguistic framework and system may be designed. In fact, it has been used and proven to work in the description of proverbs and other sentential idioms (some 10,000) in the edition of the *Dictionary of Czech Phraseology and Idiomatics* (2nd ed.), namely for its last volume containing this type of idiom. It is to be noted, however, that this lexicographical approach, adapted for English and German from Czech here, is originally meant to be an onomasiological dictionary (comprising some 5,000 lemmas) that accompanies the dictionary proper and it is here where extensive definitions are given, next to this brief skeleton characteristic of the onomasiological system which stands apart. It is obvious that many lemmas, because of their brief character, relate to more than one idiom entry. Hence, this system, through its lemmas, has to be viewed as a shortened version of the full lexicographical definition (not given here).

Due to the character of idioms and proverbs included, the general idea was to construct such a system that has the form and structure of a sentence, too, being built on autosemantic word classes in a fixed word order using common and frequent words only. This type of metalanguage guarantees a uniform approach and enables both standardization of varieties of form and a possibility for a reliable search in the alphabet which starts with the alphabetical order of the first component, followed, if needed, successively by other components that are ordered alphabetically, too. This requires that the first component always has to be, because of its primary importance, a noun or pronoun and that, for example, an adjective (usually preceding it) has to be placed after the noun. To keep the lemma form as short as possible and avoid cluttering it, all articles, particles and interjections have been left entirely. Hence, a simplified general sentence-like form of the proverb definition in this onomasiological dictionary has acquired the shape of a single structure (allowing for many variants)

$$S^1_{Hum} - (A) - S^2_{Hum} - (A) - S^3_x - V - S^4_y - ADV$$

where the first two nouns (S^1_{Hum}, S^2_{Hum} representing the speaker and listener, both of them being humans)

may be left out of the onomasiological lemma here as unnecessary (though they are duly characterised in the dictionary proper in full definitions). Thus, the onomasiological lemma that we are interested in here starts with the third noun of the pattern above, followed by other arguments (up to a fourth noun, verb, and an adverb). The bottom index x stands for more possibilities in the semantic classes of the noun, such as Hum(an), An(imal), Abs(tract), Res (concrete thing), Loc(ative), etc. It seems that, in contrast to nouns, a semantic subclassification of other word classes, such as adjectives and verbs, is not really necessary, though it is possible.

In order to make this type of lexico-semantic lemma representative and indicative of the proverb's meaning, that would be useful and intuitive, other considerations have been paid attention to. These then offer, in contradiction to Permjakov or Kuusi, much more meaning as described in a simple and accessible way for the user, which he/she can also easily find in the whole system (i.e. main dictionary). It is evident that more of the proverbs's meaning can be mediated in this way than the binary, and in fact, non-linguistic approach that Permjakov offers. Lacking any criteria for classification and ordering of items here, it is yet again the old and familiar alphabet that safeguards both the ordering and search within the system.

Though useful and feasible, however, this is not meant as a description of the whole system; that would require much more. In the following, this lexico-semantic system has been used here as a basis for classification of all the proverbs included in the Czech, English, and German minima, illustrating basic types of meaning that the most frequent proverbs have, showing also differences and correspondences between the three languages. If a given onomasiological lemma has Czech and German proverbs only, these are provided with English equivalents or translations (in italics). The full survey of the system is to be found in the Appendix, only two first large groups are given here.

5.2.2 Lexico-Semantic Classification (-S³-)

I Simple

A Declarative Structures (ordered by the third component only)

HUMAN (man):
- **man better wins** • Kdo s koho. (*May the best man win.*)
- **man coming sooner gains the privilege/claim** • First come, first served.
- **man courageous is successful**, **man timid does not achieve result** • Odvážnýmu štěstí přeje. (*Fortune favours the brave/bold.*)
- **man inconspicuous surprises** • Still waters run deep.
- **man irrational wants two contrary things** • You cannot have your cake and eat it too.
- **man rational settles for a result smaller (and does not risk)** • Lepší vrabec v hrsti než holub na střeše. (*A bird in the hand is worth two in the bush.*)
- **man refusing advice refuses help too** • Wer nich hören will, muss fühlen. ('*He who doesn't want to listen will have to experience.*')
- **man threatening is not dangerous** • Hunde, die bellen, beissen nicht. (*His bark is worse than his bite., Barking dogs don't bite.*)
- **man wise terminates dispute** • Der klügere gibt nach. (*The wiser head gives in.*)
- **man forgets and does not think of people absent** • Out of sight, out of mind.
- **man is influenced by parents** • Jablko nepadne daleko od stromu. (*The apple never falls far from the tree.*)
- **man is punished for deed evil likewise** • Wer anderen eine Grube gräbt, fällt selbst hinein. ('*Who digs a pit for others falls into it himself.*')
- **man learns/knows from experience** • Es ist noch kein Meister vom Himmel gefallen. (*Practice makes perfect.*)
- **man loses easily what he gained without effort / what he does not appreciate** • Wie gewonnen, so zerronnen. (*Light come light go.*)
- **man must deserve result, do not expect something free!** • There is no such thing as a free lunch.

- **man must finish thought consistently (despite consequences)** • Wer A sagt, muss auch B sagen. (*If you say A, you have to say B as well.*)
- **man must practice/to achieve for achieving perfection** • Üben macht den Meister. (*Practice makes perfect.*)
- **man profits from discord of other two** • Wenn zwei sich streiten, freut sich der dritte. (*'When two quarrel, the third rejoices.'*)
- **people have tastes different** • Über den Geschmack lässt sich nicht streiten. (*There is no accounting or taste.*)
- **people equal associate** • Birds of a feather flock together.
- **people in group make man feel secure and confident** • There is safety in numbers.
- **I want to be alone, home is inviolable/untouchable** • Můj dům můj hrad. (*My house is my castle.*)
- **I will do it under condition** • Něco za něco. (*One good turn deserves another.*)
- **he talks much and does nothing** • Moc řečí a skutek utek. (*(Be) all talk and no action.*)
- **they cover and support themselves** • Eine Hand wäscht die andere. (*You scratch my back and I'll scratch yours.*)
- **everyone looks for interests own** • Every man for himself.

ABSTRACT:

- **advice is easier than to do it** • Easier said than done.
- **appearance is deceptive, do not believe impression external!** • Zdání klame. (*Appearances may be deceptive.*)
- **appearance effective may be deceptive, it is deceptive** • Es ist nicht alles Gold, was glänzt. (*Not all that glitters is gold.*)
- **appearance tiny/fine is pleasant** • Small is beautiful.
- **beginning is difficult** • Aller Anfang ist schwer. (*All beginnings are difficult, Every beginning is hard.*)
- **certainty is better than hope** • Lepší vrabec v hrsti než holub na střeše. (*A bird in the hand is worth two in the bush.*)
- **deed evil/hostile is punished severely** • Oko za oko, zub za zub. (*An eye for an eye and a tooth for a tooth.*)
- **deed good requires master, team is irresponsible** • Viele Köche verderben den Brei. (*(Too) Many cooks spoil the broth.*)
- **end is decisive/decides** • Konec dobrý, všechno dobré. (*All's well that ends well.*)
- **experience unfavourable brings gain too** • Všechno zlý/zlé je k něčemu dobrý/dobré. (*Every cloud has a silver lining.*)
- **failure small brings good fortune/luck, you will be lucky** • Scherben bringen glück. (*Broken crockery brings you luck.*)
- **goal justifies use of crime also** • Účel světí prostředky. (*The end justifies the means.*)
- **it is necessary to proceed systematically** • First things first.
- **it is sign of danger** • No smoke without fire.

- **knowledge is weapon, information is advantage** • Knowledge is power.
- **love goes through discords, people close irritate themselves often** • Was sich liebt das neckt sich. (*The quarrel of lovers is the renewal of love.*)
- **mistake backfires, it will backfire** • Chickens come home to roost.
- **money decides/ is decisive** • Money talks.
- **morning is inspirational / brings inspiration, postpone it!** • Ráno moudřejší večera. (*Let's sleep on it.*)
- **place of hiding best is visible** • Pod svícnem bývá tma. (*Still waters run deep.*)
- **places different have customs different, do not be surprised and accept it!** • Jiný kraj jiný mrav. (*Other countries other manners*)
- **situation bad has way out too** • Every cloudhas a silver lining.
- **thing best can be escalated/stepped up to unbearableness (and harmful effect)** • Všeho moc škodí. ('*Too much (of anything good) is harmful*'.)
- **three is lucky number** • Do třetice všeho dobrýho. (*Third time lucky.*)
- **waiting costs money, it is urgent** • Time is money.

5.2.3 A DISCUSSION AND SUMMING UP

There seem to be two major types (structures) of general meaning found above that are called *Declarative* (A, in the sense of a mere statement, remark, etc.), and *Imperative* (B, lumping together commands, recommendations, suggestions, etc.). It is evident that the nature of the Imperative type of meaning is in fact pragmatic in nature and, hence, this type of notation registers semiotic functions. It must be noted that functional aspects (i.e. where descriptive declarative structures do not obtain or are marginal only) show the extent to which both semantics and pragmatics are interconnected, both being necessary for a description of proverbs side by side. In fact, in those cases where both a description of meaning and function are possible standing on an equal basis, pragmatic structures are not recorded here again (under B), cf.:

man must deserve result and **do not expect something free**!

valid for

There is no such thing as a free lunch.

Altogether, there are some 15% of these pragmatic types of structures, used for description here.

Inspecting usage of proverbs in corpus texts, it is obvious that they are often used pragmatically and **functionally** in the sense that an appeal is made towards the listener, addressee (noun argument S^2_{Hum}), cf.

Time is money (used, next to explanation, as argument, reminder, and advice),
Out of sight, out of mind (argument, reminder or commentary),
No smoke without fire (argument, recognition, concession or commentary), etc.

In fact, such a function can be found for any of the proverbs inspected.

The approach used here is pragmatic and flexible, open to additional features and being as close to an intuitive understanding of the proverb as possible. Hence, if need be, also a more elaborate extension of the Simple structures presented so far into **II Extended Structures** is easy to add, covering, by means of an additional subclassification, other arguments than S³ followed above; in fact, for each of the remaining arguments of S³ (-A) - V - (S⁴) - (ADV), including -S³$_x$ (-A) -... Accordingly, this approach where, due to the subclasses for each argument may be made into an elaborate hierarchy and used in future taxonomies and for the design of a thesaurus of this kind. As it refuses to use a limited supply of fields and labels only and may be easily expanded, it may be difficult to reconcile it with what is dominant in the obviously more or less closed systems of Kuusi and Permjakov.

Despite the differences between the languages involved, it may be useful, however, to compare, by way of a brief illustration only, coverage of proverb meaning by the three approaches, which happens to be the main topic pursued in this contribution.

Thus, a single German (and English, and Czech) proverb has been chosen for comparison as it happens to be explicitly mentioned and covered by all three approaches, though not in the first 20.

Es ist nicht alles Gold, was glänzt

which is dubbed here as:

appearance effective may be deceptive, or **it is deceptive**.

Some of the salient aspects of this proverb are covered by three of the classificatory labels of Permjakov (the interpretation is that of P. Grzybek, p. 173) which have to be read and understood together, though there is no way of knowing without further study which salient features have been included and which have not. Thus, Permjakov's labels cover the following aspects:

FG Formative group (Formbildend group) 13KC: *revelation-nonrevelation* (Offenbarung-Nichtoffenbarung), TP I1 Thematic Pair: *content-form* (Inhalt-Form), and IIa20: *beautiful-not beautiful* (Schŏn-häßlich). Obviously, the amount of meaning expressed by Permjakov's approach and by the lexicographical one advocated here, is quite different. Thus, labeling the proverb by revelation is a very roundabout and general way of saying that something has been revealed though revelation may not be the case; likewise the opposition non/beautiful may not always fit as the proverb does not necessarily include the aspect of beauty only, but, rather that of glamour, an external effect that is not mentioned. Moreover, two major semantic features, that of appearance, outward look and deception are not covered at all.

It seems that Kuusi's system offers even less descriptive features, though it is rather the idea of thematic fields that prevails here. It is obviously the class C5 (Signals and Their Meaning/Interpretation) or C6 (Appearance: Internal Values) that might be relevant; in fact this proverb is included under C6c (subclass called *everything is not as it appears; the deceptiveness of identifying marks*) and the proverb fits here rather nicely. Yet the aspects of glamour/effect and deception are not included in the first of the two characteristics. Hence, to capture the feature of deception both characteristics have to be used in conjunction. On the other hand, there is no semantic feature mentioned or implied by Permjakov nor Kuusi that the lexicographical onomasiological definition would not include. Both Permjakov and Kuusi fail, however, in recording the pragmatic features of the proverb's use: these are not included at all. As it is implied, this can easily be added to the lexicographical declarative characteristic (**do not believe it!**).

In 5.2, an inventory of words making up the lexical stock of the proverbs inspected has been mentioned. Without going into detail, even a brief comparison of these components and metalinguistic meaning structures used for the description of proverbs reveals that there is hardly any relation between the two, let alone meaning motivation of the latter through the former.

What is, then, the semantic space covered by these top proverbs? Admittedly, the mere 20 most frequent proverbs from each of the three languages is too little for any comparison of the proverb usage, mostly due to the incompatibility of resources that the three minima have been based on. Yet it is amazing that no single type of meaning (represented by a meaning structure) occurs here in at least two languages, let alone in all three. Hence each language is completely different and no comparison is possible. Of course, this does not mean that the three languages are totally different as it might seem from such a meagre selection of items compared. On the contrary, going through larger lists of proverbs, it becomes readily evident that it is just difficult to find a single proverb in one language that the other two might not have, too, though with different frequencies and sometimes forms, too. Trying, thus, to pin down the most frequent types of meaning, the obvious conclusion must, due to a total absence of overlapping of the languages here, be that the most frequent types of meaning are to be sought, if at all, in the sum of all three languages when brought together, as above.

6. Summary and Open Questions

Despite the heterogeneous character of data and, accordingly, specific results and conclusions that it was possible to make, it does not really allow for a more sweeping generalization. That would point to features valid for a larger field of proverbs and it seems that this may be a way to go, suggesting perhaps, repetition of the same descriptive procedure on more data. Then one might hope that some more general features of the whole field will emerge.

A number of aspects, both in form and usage, had to be left out, though the most pertinent ones, those of meaning and, hopefully, function have been shown to be amenable to a lexicographic description that can easily be applied for any language.

On a higher and general level, the semantic structures included and inspected here do present, however, a rather consistent picture of the most common aspects of human behaviour and life, viewed dynamically as there are hardly any types of static meaning represented.

Thus, it is first, *man*, being both rational and irrational, who strives to achieve a goal, being able to learn on his way (from mistakes and experience). Our egocentrism prevents us to include any thought given to *things, animals*, etc., however. Nouns that make the first (= third) argument in the metalanguage used here are all invariably anthropocentric in their nature, too, being derived from man's actions. Specifically, they point to some of the most important aspects of human activity, such as *appearance, deeds, their beginning and end, goals, mistakes and means* (money, knowledge, information), etc. The pragmatic Imperative structures are related to human actions, too, pointing, by means of *advice, recommendation or warning*, etc., to the quality of these. At least one case reflects our societies' awareness that the needs and habits of our neighbours and foreigners should be respected, too (see the Appendix).

LITERATURE

BAUR R. S., CHLOSTA Ch. 1996. *Sprichwörter: ein Problem für Fremdsprachenlehrer wie -lerner?!*, Deutsch als Fremdsprache, 91–102.

ČELAKOVSKÝ František Ladislav. 1852. *Mudrosloví národa slovanského ve příslovích*. Praha: České museum.

ČERMÁK, František. 2009. České frazémy a idiomy propoziční, in *Slovník české frazeologie a idiomatiky. Výrazy větné*. Praha: Leda. (= Czech Proposional Phrasemes and Idioms)

ČERMÁK, František, KŘEN, Michal, BLATNÁ, Renata. 2004. *Frekvenční slovník češtiny*. Praha: NLN (= Frequency Dictionary of Czech).

ČERMÁK, František. 2003. "Paremiological Minimum of Czech: The Corpus Evidence." In *Flut von Texten - Vielvalt der Kulturen. Ascona 2001 zur Methodologie und Kulturspezifik der Phraseologie*, edited by H. Burger, A. Häcki Bufofer, and G. Greciano, 15–31. Hohengehren: Schneider Verlag.

ČERMÁK, František. 2004b. "Jazyková variabilita: případ přísloví." In Čeština - Universalia a specifika 5, edited by Z. Hladká and P. Karlík, 99–109. Praha: NLN. (= Language Variability: the Case of Proverbs).

ČERMÁK, František. 2004b. "Text Introducers of Proverbs and Other Idioms." In *Phraseologismen als Gegenstand sprach- und kulturwissenschaftlicher Forschung*, edited by C. Földes and J. Wirrer, 27–46. Hohengren: Schneider Verlag.

ČERMÁK, František. 2007a. *What One Can Do with Proverbs in Text*, In Čermák 2007b Frazeologie a idiomatika..., s. 536–548.

ČERMÁK, František. 2007b. *Frazeologie a idiomatika česká a obecná. Czech and General Phraseology*. Praha: Karolinum.

ĎURČO, Peter. 2004. "Paremiologické minimum slovenčiny. Výsledky a porovnania." In *Jazyky a jazykoveda. Sb. k 65. narozeninám prof. PhDr. Františka Čermáka, DrSc*, 45–62. Praha: FF UK, Ústav Českého národního korpusu. (= Paremiological Minimum of Slovak)

GRZYBEK, Peter. 1987. "Foundations of Semiotic Proverb Study." *Proverbium* 4: 39–85.

GRZYBEK, Peter. 1991. *Sinkendes Kulturgut? Eine empirische Pilotstudie zur Bekanntheit deutscher Sprichwörter Wirkendes Wort*, 240-264.

KRIKMANN, Arvo. 1974. *"Some Difficulties Arising at Semantical Classifying of Proverbs"*, *Proverbium* 23: 865-879.

KUUSI, Matti. 1957. *Regen bei Sonnenschein: Zur Weltgeschichte einer Redensart*. Helsinki: Academia Scientiarum Fennica

KUUSI, Matti. 1972. *Towards an International Type-System of Proverbs*. Helsinki: Academia Scientiarum Fennica.

LAUHAKANGAS Outi. 2001. *The Matti Kuusi International Type System of Proverbs*. Helsinki: Suomalainen Tiedeakatemia.

MIEDER, Wolfgang. 2004. *Proverbs. A Handbook*. London: Greenwood Press Westport.

PACZOLAY G. 1997. *European proverbs in 55 languages with equivalents in Arabic, Persian, Sanskrit, Chinese and Japanese*. Veszprém: Veszprémi Nyomda Rt.

PEIRCE CH. S. 1931-1958. *Collected Papers of Charles Sanders Peirce*, Vol. 1-8. Cambridge, Mass.: Harvard University Press.

PERMJAKOV, Grigorij Ľvovič. 1970. *Ot pogovorki do skazki. Zametki po obščej teorii kliše* (From Proverb to Folk-Tale. Notes on the General Theory of Cliché, Moskva 1979).

PERMJAKOV, Grigorij Ľvovič. 1971. *Paremiologičeskij Eksperiment. Materialy dlja paremiologičeskogo minimuma*. Moskva: Nauka.

PERMJAKOV, Grigorij Ľvovič. 2000. *Die Grammatik der sprichwörtlichen Weisheit*, edited by P. Grzybek. Hohengehren: Schneider Verlag.

TAYLOR, A. 1931. *The Proverb*. Cambridge, Mass.: Harvard University Press.

ZICH, Otakar. 1956. *Lidová přísloví z hlediska logického*. Praha: NČSAV.

APPENDICES

Paremiological Minimum of Czech (100, down to frequency 10 in CNC)

Do třetice všeho dobrýho. 90
Účel světí prostředky. 59
Kdo s koho. 56
Něco za něco. 53
Přání je otcem myšlenky. 46
Nikdy neříkej nikdy. 40
Jiný kraj jiný mrav. 37
Oko za oko, zub za zub. 35
Jablko nepadne daleko od stromu. 32
Všeho moc škodí. 32

Zdání klame. 31
Všechno zlý/zlé je k něčemu dobrý/dobré. 29
Odvážnýmu-připravenému štěstí přeje. 28
Můj dům můj hrad. 28
Všeho s mírou. 28
Pod svícnem bejvá tma. 27
Ráno moudřejší večera. 26

Moc řečí a skutek utek. 26
Konec dobrý, všechno dobré. 25
Lepší vrabec hrsti než holub na střeše. 24

Štěstí přeje připraveným. 24
Život je boj. 23
Rozděl a panuj. 23
Ruka ruku myje/meje. 23
Není šprochu, aby na něm nebylo pravdy trochu. 22
Bližší košile než kabát. 22
Sejde z očí, sejde z mysli. 22
Nejlepší obranou je útok. 22
Ať si každý zamete před vlastním prahem. 21
Náhoda/štěstí přeje připraveným. 21

Nic není zadarmo. 21
Světská sláva polní tráva. 21
Komu není shůry dáno, v apatyce nekoupí. 21
Nevstoupíš dvakrát do téže řeky. 21
Boží mlýny melou pomalu ale jistě. 20
Kam vítr, tam plášť. 20
Po bitvě je každý generálem. 19
S jídlem roste chuť. 19
Proti gustu žádnej dišputát. 18
Lepší pozdě než nikdy. 18

Stará láska nerezaví. 18
Peníze nejsou všechno. 18
Pravda vítězí. 18
Bez práce nejsou koláče. 18
Nemá smysl plakat nad rozlitým mlíkem. 17
Dvakrát měř, jednou řež! 18
Konec vše napraví. 17
Méně je někdy více. 17
Dobrá rada nad zlato. 17
Co na srdci, to na jazyku. 16

Co není zakázáno, je dovoleno. 16
S poctivostí nejdál dojdeš. 16
Ryba smrdí od hlavy. 16
Co se stalo, nemůže se odestát. 15
Když se kácí les, lítaj třísky. 15
Pýcha předchází pád. 15

Co je psáno, to je dáno. 14
Mluviti stříbro, mlčeti zlato. 14
Sliby chyby. 14
Sůl nad zlato. 14

Zvyk je železná košile. 14
Kde není žalobce, není (ani) soudce. 13
Všude je chléb o dvou kůrkách. 13
Na hrubý pytel hrubá záplata. 13
Napřed práce potom zábava. 13
Vrána k vráně sedá, rovný rovného si hledá. 13
Zázraky se nedějou. 12
Dobrá rada nad zlato. 12
Všude dobře, doma nejlíp. 12
Všeho do času. 12

Komu čest tomu čest. 12
Pozdě bycha honit. 12
Škola základ života. 12
Boží mlýny melou pomalu, ale jistě. 12
Kdo dřív přijde, ten dřív mele. 12
Ranní ptáče dál doskáče. 12
Život je pes. 12
Co je doma, to se počítá. 12
Krev není voda. 12
Lež má krátký nohy. 12

Pes je (nejlepší) přítel člověka. 11
Když se dva hádají/perou, má z toho třetí užitek/třetí se směje. 11
Lepší něco než nic. 11
Kdo se bojí, nesmí do lesa. 11
Poturčenec horší Turka. 11
Cesta do pekla je dlážděna dobrými úmysly. 11
Kdo jinému jámu kopá, sám do ní padá. 11
Nula do nuly pojde. 11
Rodina je základ státu. 11
Kde nic není, ani smrt nebere. 11

Starého psa novým kouskům nenaučíš. 11
Příklady táhnou. 11
Lež má krátké nohy. 11
Žádná kaše se nejí tak horká, jak se uvaří. 11
Kdo lže, ten krade. 10

Každý je svého štěstí strůjcem. 10
Práce kvapná málo platná. 10
Žádnej učenej z nebe nespad (ale blbce jako by shazovali). 10 (jen kratší ver.)
Kdo nic nedělá, ten nic nezkazí. 10
Nevděk světem vládne. 10

Paremiological Minimum of English (100, BNC, down to frequency 1)

Easier said than done. 62
Every cloud has a silver lining. 52
Still waters run deep. 33
Chickens come home to roost. 31
First things first. 31
Small is beautiful. 30
Forgive and forget. 27
Birds of a feather flock together. 25
There is safety in numbers. 25
Time is money. 22

Out of sight, out of mind. 21
First come, first served. 20
Every man for himself. 20
No smoke without fire. 19
Money talks. 18
Better late than never. 16
You cannot have your cake and eat it too. 16
Knowledge is power. 15
A picture is worth a thousand words. 15
There is no such thing as a free lunch. 15

Fight fire with fire. 15
When in Rome, do as the Romans do. 14
Let sleeping dogs lie. 14
Beggars can't be choosers. 14
All's well that ends well. 13
Forewarned is forearmed. 13
Live and let live. 13
Let bygones be bygones. 12
Look before you leap. 12
Practice makes perfect x. 12

A bird in the hand is worth two in the bush. 11
The end justifies the means. 11

Easy come, easy go. 11
Two wrongs don't make a right. 11
Like father, like son. 11
Actions speak louder than words. 10
Don't look a gift horse in the mouth. 10
An applea day keeps the doctor away. 10
First come, first served. 10
No man can serve two masters. 10

Once bitten, twice shy. 9
Wastenot, want not. 9
Two heads are better than one. 9
Bad news travels fast. 9
A stitchin time saves nine. 8
Beautyis in the eye of the beholder. 8
Too many cooks spoil the broth. 8
No news is good news. 8
Charity begins at home. 8
Absence makes the heart grow fonder. 7

No man is an island. 7
Strike while the iron is hot. 7
Make hay while the sun shines. 7
Curiosity killed the cat. 7
Blood is thicker than water. 7
Out of sight, out of mind. 6
It takes two to tango. 6
The early bird catches the worm. 5
All good things come to an end. 5
Don't count your chickens before they're hatched. 4

Where there's a will, there's a way. 4
Silence is golden. 4
Early to bedand early to rise, makes a man healthy, wealthy, and wise. 4
The grass is always greener on the other side of the fence. 4
All that glitters is not gold. 3
Dounto others as you would have them do unto you. 3
Spare the rod and spoil the child. 3
To err is human, to forgive divine. 4
Lightning never strikes in the same place twice. 4
Beauty is only skin deep. 3

He who hesitates is lost. 3
Love is blind. 3
One swallow doesn't make a summer. 3
Businessbefore pleasure. 2
If at first you don't succeed, try, try again. 2
An ounce of prevention is worth a pound of cure. 2
A rolling stone gathers no moss. 2
You can't teach an old dognew tricks. 2
Don't put all your eggs in one basket. 2
A fooland his money are soon parted. 2

Many hands make light work. 2
Don't change horses in the middle of the stream (mid-stream). 2
Revenge is sweet. 2
Every man has his price. 2
Don't put all your eggs in one basket. 2
A friend in need is a friend indeed. 1
The road to hell is paved with good intentions. 1
Diamond cuts diamond. 1
Haste makes waste. 1
Don't judge a book by its cover. 1

You can lead a horse to water, but you can't make him drink. 1
Never put off till tomorrow what you can do today. 1
When it rains, it pours. 1
As you sow, so shall you reap. 1
Discretion is the better part of valour. 1
Rome was not built in a day. 1
The road to hell is paved with good intentions. 1
Time and tide wait for no man. 1
There is no fool like an old fool. 1
When the cat's away, the mice play. 1

Paremiological Minimum of German (100, down to 95% of knowledge, by Chlostek Grzybek)

Der Klügere gibt nach.
Eine Hand wäscht de andere.
Es ist nicht alles Gold, was glänzt.
Es ist noch kein Meister vom Himmel gefallen.
Hunde, die bellen, beißen nicht.
In der Kürze liegt die Würze.

Man muß die Feste feiern, wie sie fallen.
Man soll den Tag nicht vor dem Abend loben.
Scherben bringen Glück.
Über den Geschmack läßt sich nicht streiten.

Übung macht den Meister.
Viele Köche verderben den Brei.
Was sich liebt, das neckt sich.
Wenn zwei sich streiten, freut sich der dritte.
Wer anderen eine Grube gräbt, fällt selbst hinein.
Wer A sagt, muß auch B sagen.
Wer nicht hören will, muß fühlen.
Wie gewonnen, so zerronnen.
Aller Anfang ist schwer.
Andere Länder, andere Sitten.

Aufgeschoben ist nicht aufgehoben.
Ausnahmen bestätigen die Regel.
Den Letzten beißen die Hunde.
Der Apfel fällt nicht weit vom Stamm.
Die Zeit heilt alle Wunden.
Doppelt hält besser.
Einem geschenkten Gaul sieht man nicht ins Maul.
Einmal ist keinmal.
Ein Unglück kommt selten allein.
Ende gut, alles gut.

Geld allein macht nicht glücklich.
Irren ist menschlich.
Kleider machen Leute.
Kommt Zeit, kommt Rat.
Lügen haben kurze Beine.
Man ist so alt, wie man sich fühlt.
Morgenstunde hat Gold im Munde.
Ohne Fleiß kein Preis.
Probieren geht über Studieren.
Reden ist Silber, Schweigen ist Gold.

Stille Wasser sind tief.
Von nichts kommt nichts.
Was du heute kannst besorgen, das verschiebe nicht auf morgen.
Was ich nicht weiß, macht mich nicht heiß.
Wer den Pfennig nicht ehrt, ist des Talers nicht wert.

Wer die Wahl hat, hat die Qual.
Wer rastet, der rostet.
Wer wagt, gewinnt.
Wer zuletzt lacht, lacht am besten.
Wie du mir, so ich dir.

Wie man in den Wald hineinruft, so schallt es wieder heraus.
Wo ein Wille ist, da ist auch ein Weg.
Alter schützt vor Torheit nicht.
Auf Regen folgt Sonnenschein.
Aus den Augen, aus dem Sinn.
Der Krug geht so lange zu Wasser (zum Brunnen), bis er bricht.
Der Ton macht die Musik.
Durch Schaden wird man klug.
Ehrlich währt am längsten.
Eigener Herd ist Goldes wert.

Eigenlob stinkt.
Ein blindes Huhn findet auch einmal ein Korn.
Ein Küßchen in Ehren kann niemand verwehren.
Erst die Arbeit, dann das Vergnügen.
Es ist noch nicht aller Tage Abend.
Frisch gewagt ist halb gewonnen.
Früh übt sich, was ein Meister werden will.
Gegensätze ziehen sich an.
Gelegenheit macht Diebe.
Kleinvieh macht auch Mist.

Selbsterkenntnis ist der erste Schritt zur Besserung.
Selbst ist der Mann.
Träume sind Schäume.
Wenn man dem Teufel den kleinen Finger gibt, so nimmt er die ganze Hand.
Wer zuerst kommt, mahlt zuerst.
Wie man sich bettet, so schläft man.
Wo gehobelt wird, fallen Späne.
Keine Antwort ist auch eine Antwort.
Lehrjahre sind keine Herrenjahre.
Mit Speck fängt man Mäuse.

Sich regen bringt Segen.
Vorbeugen ist besser als heilen.
Was lange währt, wird gut.
Alte Liebe rostet nicht.

Wer einmal lügt, dem glaubt man nicht, und wenn er auch die Wahrheit spricht.
Dem Glücklichen schlägt keine Stunde.
Des Menschen Wille ist sein Himmelreich.
Jedem Tierchen sein Pläsierchen.
Kleine Kinder — kleine Sorgen, große Kinder — große Sorgen.
Was Hänschen nicht lernt, lernt Hans nimmermehr.

Wenns am besten schmeckt. soll man aufhören.
Wer nicht kommt zur rechten Zeit, der muß sehen, was übrigbleibt.
Besser den Sperling in der Hand als die Taube auf dem Dach.
Man muß *das* Eisen schmieden, solange es heiß ist.
Morgen, morgen, nur nicht heute, sagen alle faulen Leute.
Rom ist (auch) nicht an einem Tag erbaut worden.
Aller guten Dinge sind drei.
Was man nicht im Kopf hat, muß man in den Beinen haben. Arbeit schändet nicht.
Dem Mutigen gehört die Welt.

SEMANTIC SPACE TAKEN BY THE CORE 20 PROVERBS IN CZECH, ENGLISH AND GERMAN

I SIMPLE

A Declarative Structures (ordered by the third component only).

HUMAN (man):
- **man better wins** • Kdo s koho. (*May the best man win.*)
- **man coming sooner gains the privilege/claim** • First come, first served.
- **man courageous is successful, man timid does not achieve result** • Odvážnýmu štěstí přeje. (*Fortune favours the brave/bold.*)
- **man inconspicuous surprises** • Still waters run deep.
- **man irrational wants two contrary things** • You cannot have your cakeand eat it too.
- **man rational settles for a result smaller (and does not risk), certainty is better than hope** • Lepší vrabec v hrsti než holub na střeše. (*A bird in the hand is worth two in the bush.*)
- **man refusing advice refuses help too** • Wer nich hören will, muss fühlen. (*'He who doesn't want to listen will have to experience.'*)
- **man threatening is not dangerous** • Hunde, die bellen, beissen nicht. (*His bark is worse than his bite., Barking dogs don't bite.*)
- **man wise terminates dispute** • Der klügere gibt nach. (*The wiser head gives in.*)
- **man forgets and does not think of people absent** • Out of sight, out of mind.

- **man is influenced by parents** • Jablko nepadne daleko od stromu. (*The apple never falls far from the tree.*)
- **man is punished for deed evil likewise** • Wer anderen eine Grube gräbt, fällt selbst hinein. (*'Who digs a pit for others falls into it himself.'*)
- **man learns/knows from experience** • Es ist noch kein Meister vom Himmel gefallen. (*Practice makes perfect.*)
- **man loses easily what he gained without effort/what he does not appreciate** • Wie gewonnen, so zerronnen. (*Light come light go.*)
- **man must deserve result, do not expect something free!** • There is no such thing as a free lunch.
- **man must finish thought consistently (despite consequences)** • Wer A sagt, muss auch B sagen. (*If you say A, you have to say B as well.*)
- **man must practice / to achieve for achieving perfection** • Üben macht den Meister. (*Practice makes perfect.*)
- **man profits from discord of other two•** Wenn zwei sich streiten, freut sich der dritte. (*'When two quarrel, the third rejoices.'*)
- **people have tastes different** • Über den Geschmack lässt sich nicht streiten. (*There is no accounting for taste.*)
- **people equal associate** • Birdsof a feather flock together.
- **people in group make man feel secure and confident** • There is safety in numbers.
- **I want to be alone, home is inviolable/untouchable** • Můj dům můj hrad. (*My house is my castle.*)
- **I will do it under condition** • Něco za něco. (*One good turn deserves another.*)
- **he talks much and does nothing** • Moc řečí a skutek utek. (*(be) all talk and no action.*)
- **they cover and support themselves** • Eine Hand wäscht die andere. (*You scratch my back and I'll scratch yours.*)
- **everyone looks for interests own** • Every man for himself.

ABSTRACT:

- **advice is easier than to do it** • Easier said than done.
- **appearance is deceptive, do not believe impression external!** • Zdání klame. (*Appearances may be deceptive.*)
- **appearance effective may be deceptive, it is deceptive** • Es ist nicht alles Gold, was glänzt. (*Not all that glitters is gold.*)
- **appearance tiny/fine is pleasant** • Small is beautiful.
- **beginning is difficult** • Aller Anfang ist schwer. (*All beginnings are difficult, Every beginning is hard.*)
- **deed evil/hostile is punished severely** • Oko za oko, zub za zub. (*An eye for an eye and a tooth for a tooth.*)
- **deed good requires master, team is irresponsible** • Viele Köche verderben den Brei. (*(Too) Many cooks spoil the broth.*)

- **end is decisive/decides** • Konec dobrý, všechno dobré. (*All's well that ends well.*)
- **experience unfavourable brings gain too** • Všechno zlý/zlé je k něčemu dobrý/dobré. (*Every cloud has a silver lining.*)
- **failure small brings good fortune/luck, you will be lucky** • Scherben bringen glück. (*Broken crockery brings you luck.*)
- **goal justifies use of crime also** • Účel světí prostředky. (*The end justifies the means.*)
- **it is necessary to proceed systematically** • First things first.
- **it is sign of danger** • No smoke without fire.
- **knowledge is weapon, information is advantage** • Knowledge is power.
- **love goes through discords, people close irritate themselves often** • Was sich liebt das neckt sich. (*The quarrel of lovers is the renewal of love.*)
- **mistake backfires, it will backfire** • Chickens come home to roost.
- **money decides/ is decisive** • Money talks.
- **morning is inspirational/brings inspiration, postpone it!** • Ráno moudřejší večera. (*Let's sleep on it.*)
- **place of hiding best is visible** • Pod svícnem bývá tma. (*Still waters run deep.*)
- **places different have customs different, do not be surprised and accept it!** • Jiný kraj jiný mrav. (*Other countries other manners.*)
- **situation bad has way out too** • Every cloudhas a silver lining.
- **thing best can be escalated/stepped up to unbearableness (and harmful effect)** • Všeho moc škodí. (*'Too much (of anything good) is harmful.'*)
- **three is lucky number** • Do třetice všeho dobrýho. (*Third time lucky.*)
- **waiting costs money, it is urgent** • Time is money.

RES (thing):
- **appearance tiny/fine is pleasant** • Small is beautiful.

TEMPORAL-LOCATIVE:

ANIMAL:
OTHER:

B *Imperative Structures*:

- **act with restraint!** • Všeho s mírou! (*Too much of one thing, good for nothing.*)
- **be brief!, talk briefly!** • In der Kürze liegt die Würze. (*Brevity is the soul of wit.*)
- **be cautious!, do not exult prematurely!** • Man soll den Tag nicht vor dem Abend Loben. (*One shouldn't praise the day before the evening.*)
- **do it by all means!, it is necessary to do it (even belatedly)** • Better late than never.
- **do not exaggerate!** • Všeho s mírou! (*Too much of one thing, good for nothing.*)
- **do not think of wrongs past!, do not worry about past!** • Forgive and forget!
- **fight using weapons/means of enemy!** • Fight fire with fire!

- **respect customs local!** • Andere Länder andere Sitten. (*Other countries, other customs, When in Rome, do as the Romans do.*)
- **speak with forethought!** • Nikdy neříkej nikdy! (*Never say die. Never say never!*)
- **use every opportunity!** • Man muss die Feste feiern, wie sie fallen. (*Christmas comes but once a year.*)

4. Proverbs: Linguistic and Lexicographic Approaches versus Ethnographic, Logical, Onomasiological and Other

In **Actas ICP 1, 2007**, 197–207, **Čermák Proverbs 2014**, 9–24.

Abstract

A linguistic or rather lexicographic description of proverbs is, basically, an inductive one while those of M. Kuusi, Ju. Permjakov and innumerable scholars of earlier centuries are, in contrast, of a deductive nature. It should not then be surprising that results of their treatment are so widely different. Moreover, while the latter are based on a long tradition and cumulative basis offering a wide range of results, however different, the former are scarce, having no tradition to base their descriptions on.

Trying to single out problems linguists, and specifically lexicographers, are faced with should an attempt be made at a dictionary description of proverbs, one has to take stock of both those that have been pointed out by paremiologists primarily, and those dictated by the requirements and expectations of users. It is evident that an ideal description of this kind should be theory-conformant and systematic on the one hand, and offer a useful coverage of form, meaning, and function of a standard, prototypical kind on the other. Due to the existence of modern corpora, some major problems, such as proverbs' formal variability, major functions and prototypical meaning can be pinned down and put to a definition. Other, such as proverbs' intonation, are still very much an open issue. Last but not least, due attention should just be paid to delimiting more sharply synchrony and diachrony here, too. This requirements stands in some contrast to many ethnographic approaches mixing up past and present times in their collections.

On the basis of a large Dictionary of Czech Idioms and Phrasemes whose last volume, covering all types of propositional idioms and phrasemes, includes all living proverbs of Czech, an attempt will be made to present a descriptive system of proverbs within a broader and unified framework. Some of the Czech data will be compared to the English.

1. INTRODUCTION

It seems that conveying systematically the meaning, function, and usage to the users has never been a priority with ethnographers and most paremiologists. Hence the scarcity of really good lexicographical descriptions which may be odd, say, to foreign students, and not only to those. Given the obvious differences, both minor and major, even between seemingly identical proverbs in two languages, having a reliable description of this kind would be an enormous help in encouraging further comparative and other types of study. The situation may not be surprising, however, if one considers problems and many alternative solutions used in current dictionaries concentrated on single word lexemes only.

The situation is further complicated by a long ethnographical tradition or, rather, obsession, to pigeonhole proverbs into some 10–20 categories that are so broad as to be virtually useless, far from giving an accurate picture of the proverb. Those few linguists or linguistically minded people, notably Jurij Permjakov and Matti Kuusi, have started, in their time, both to criticise and elaborate on this tradition coming up with their own systems. Yet, these, too, are far from being used in lexicographic practice whose descriptions could be used more widely. This trend, which could be developed and illustrated in more detail, involves, naturally, more than these two men who might unfortunately be unknown, such as the Czech logician Otakar Zich with his ingenious book *Czech Proverbs from the Logical Point of View* (1956, in Czech), etc.

In the following, both problems will be addressed here briefly, a lexicographic approach and an onomasiological one.

2. DESCRIPTIVE APPROACH OF SOME DICTIONARIES

Only an illustration of what is said about proverbs in some dictionaries and how this is said is possible here. However, the insight gained from this will hopefully lead to some serious conclusions. Hence, five familiar proverbs have been chosen in two English sources, one a handbook (Rideout, Whiting 1969 = R–W) and one standard dictionary offering explanations (NODE 1996 = *Node*), being a sufficient basis for seeing the lexicographic strategy used here and formulating some basic desiderata.

(1) Out of sight out of mind.
R–W: We cease to worry about anything that can no longer be seen. This includes people. Absent friends are soon forgotten.
Node: you soon forget people or things that are no longer visible or present.

(2) A bird in the hand is worth two in the bush.
R–W: If a hunter has shot one bird, he should be satisfied with that and not go off look-ing for the ones that flew away. We use the proverb to mean that it is better to accept something small than to reject it and hope to get more later on.
Node: it's better to be content with what you have than to risk losing everything by seeking to get more.

(3) Birds of a feather flock together.
R–W: People of the same (usually, unscrupulous) character associate together.
Node: people of the same sort or with the same tastes and interests will be found together.

(4) The road to hell is paved with good intentions.
R–W: When not followed by good deeds, good intentions are worse than useless, and the more often we fail to turn our good intentions into actuality, the worse the effect on our characters is...We become less and less able to keep our good resolutions and sink lower and lower in our downward course – the road that leads to hell.
The road to hell is paved with good intentions proverb, promises and plans must be put into action, otherwise they are useless.
Node: promises and plans must be put into action, otherwise they are useless.

(5) Never look a gift horse in the mouth.
R–W: Never be too critical of anything you have received as a gift. The condition of a horse's teeth is a good guide to its age...
Node: don't find fault with something that you have discovered or been given.

Imagining a man not knowing these five expressions, not even that these are proverbs, one has to question the information he/she is offered in the two sources quoted here and wonder whether it is sufficient. For him/her, all of these are definitely dialogical sentences and these, as such, require context. The problems involved here are twofold **(A)** those related to the **meaning** itself and **(B)** those involving the standard set-up and situation where these proverbs are used, i.e. the number and type of persons present, their relationship, the occasion prompting the proverb's use, and the reason why it is used, or, rather, its **function**, at least.

It is obvious that the first source does not care about how to express the meaning having, in fact, not made up its mind how to signal, e.g., the generality of use which might be signalled by the standardized type of the speaker and, in more general terms, by a uniform **metalanguage**, but it is not (cf. *We cease..., If a hunter has..., People..., Good intentions are..., Never be...*). The second source (NODE) seems to be doing only margin-ally better in this.

To come to the first point **(A)**, apart from a distinct short and more concise ap-proach of the second source, meanings of the proverbs seem to be covered here in the same way, with one difference in (3). While (R–W) obviously consider the proverb to refer to negativelly viewed people (*usually unscrupulously*), (NODE) seems to be quite neutral in this. Without sufficient data, I'd rather not go into such fine details as, for instance, wondering whether *anything* in the first definition of (1) is meant as really 'anything' or there might be some limitations, or whether *gift* in (5) is really any kind of it. The general quality of the proverb's meaning is, in fact, its prototypicality and that can be extended rather far in some cases. In fact, what one should be interested in more, is whether there is some usual or **prototypical set** of things, people (referents), etc., that proverbs are used of most.

It is the other type of problem (**B**) that is hardly ever mentioned, let alone solved, at least tentatively, namely function. In the absence of any knowledge of the five proverbs, presented in isolation without any context, one would inevitably have to ask, in all of the five cases, at least the following four questions:

(1) who uses the proverb and what are his/her characteristics, if any,
(2) who is being addressed by (1), what are his/her characteristics and relation to him/her,
(3) what does the proverb mean,
(4) why is the proverb used, or, what is the motivation for its use,
(5) when, on what occasion or under what circumstances is it used?
While the third question, as the only one, is basically identical with (A) above, it gets a different kind of answer for each proverb. The rest is different in that it may be generalized up to a degree. The generalization, which may take more than form (with the Czech solution being offered later on), is basically directly due to the specific and uniform function of proverbs as such. In other words, the answers to questions (1)–(2) and (4)–(5) may be viewed as prototypical, involving, prototypically:
(1) an older and experienced person,
(2) a younger and less experienced person, both of them knowing each other,
(3) reaction to a negative experience or failure, usually as a reminder,
(4) intervention before a problematic action intended, usually as an advice or warning,
To put things more schematically, the answers to (4) and (5) have been made to overlap and do not exactly correspond to the questions above.

It would seem then, that given all of this there is little scope left for anything else. From experience we know that there is a lot of finer and more specific details present when proverbs are actually used and, also, that their use does not conform to such a simplified functional skeleton exactly. However, the very **core of the proverb function** is made of more than one type including, next to *advice*, *warning* and *reminder*, a generalized *comment*, generalized *explanation*, often *appeal*, *apology*, etc., that has or may have its attributes and be further specified, such as a warning before something that is specified, advice to be wary or exercise some restraint, etc. For the Czech counterpart of the proverb (5) *Darovanému koni na zuby nehleď* one has to record, among other things, a distinct appeal to the listener to be grateful for the gift, too, a feature that does not seem to be present in English (see also Čermák 2001, 2004).

Apart from meaning and function, viewed in a compact framework of persons involved (one of them being the speaker), and a clearly defined situation and motivation for the use of the proverb, there are other features that are in need of a standardized description (see more in 4.). These include anything recurrent or notable for the particular proverb in question, cf. the first definition of the proverb (4) above. However clumsy it may seem, slipping unfortunately, into a metaphorical explanation, it does make its point in saying *'We become less and less able to keep our good resolutions and sink lower and lower in our downward course'*. This idea of repeated, gradual progress, not so clear from the first part, is rather important.

One of the general features never described in dictionaries is a specific intonation of proverbs, too, a feature handled in the forthcoming Czech dictionary.

3. On the Meaning and Function of Proverbs. An Onomasiological Approach

To facilitate a search in, say, one thousand proverbs one needs a rigorous and unambiguous system, not very much different from what is usually called a thesaurus on the level of words (such as Roget's Thesaurus). However, it must be different from it as well as from whatever Permjakov, Kuusi and others suggest, as it may not depend on a single word being able to capture the meaning and function of proverbs. Moreover, it must be data-conformant, suiting every single proverb in sufficient detail. Therefore, a formalized system has been devised, forming an *onomasiological* counterpart of the main alphabetical dictionary where one may be rather confident to find the sought-for proverb form corresponding to the initial meaning given in the alphabet. The initial meaning and function are being expressed in a slightly formalized but still basically natural language. Forcing the user to first learn any type of artificial logical system and language is out of the question, although it may look nice on the paper. One of the features of the solution adopted has been in setting up a stable order of word classes in the multi-word lemma, thus abolishing the free word order which is normal in Czech, placing all adjectives behind their nouns and adverbs behind verbs, etc. Thus the wording of the following class (printed in bold), showing how this is done, is slightly artificial in this sense (see next to a standard translation, the literal English translation in the parentheses, introduced by *lit.* which corresponds verbatim to Czech). This class label is followed, then, by one or more proverbs (introduced by •).

lidé stejní sdružují se (same people associate, *lit.* people same join).
• Vrána k vráně sedá, rovný rovného si hledá. (Birds of feather flock together).

This is both a system developed much earlier for all the other types of the Czech phraseology as it has been published in the previous three volumes in past (Čermák – Hronek – Machač 1983, 1988, 1994), and, at the same time, one that can accommodate here, next to proverbs, also all the other types of sentence-like idioms (Čermák 2004). In principle, the system is alphabetical, too, based on the alphabet of the first word (usually a noun which is **lidé** (people) in the example above) followed by the alphabet of the second word, then of the third word, etc. There had to be some other minor adjustments made, such as using the present tense as much as possible, etc. Thus, the prototypical metalinguistic form of the sentence denoting a class in this onomasiological dictionary is:

Subj(-Atr)-V-(O)-ADV, i.e. subject (adjectival attribute)-verb-(object)-adverb.

Surprisingly, no metalinguistic sentence needs more, i.e. a longer form. A minor type of proverb may be represented by a short imperative sentence, too, starting with a verb (see the Appendix). Sometimes, if a proverb may be given more than one alternative reading to be used as the name of the class, it is classed in both. The idea behind the metalanguage used is to have it as natural as possible as well as accessible to users as possible – it just has to be rather naturally and easily guessed at.

The full system of proverbs has been given, next to their standard *semasiological* dictionary treatment (form → meaning), this *onomasiological* label and classification (meaning → form) which forms a separate dictionary entry in the same volume. Some select cases of the onomasiological classes and proverbs belonging here are given in Appendix 2. All of the other items, i.e. non-proverbs, have been left out here, although they, too, fit into the same framework without any (major) problem.

In contrast to a more elaborate hierarchy in some word thesauri, none is considered here to be useful, so far, as there is no natural nor logical hierarchy available where the classes used here belong. No one has been able to offer a taxonomy of statements and propositions in general, as the system used here must be general enough to encompass any of the stable and fixed sentences (or, to put it more technically, propositional idioms and other types). It remains to be seen to what extent M. Kuusi's 13 general thematic classes could be used here, should a more elaborate taxonomical approach be needed. In a sense, since it has been, basically deductively, tailored to suit proverbs only, separating them from the rest of the propositional idioms, this seems doubtful. No need to say that a broader and uniform system advocated and in fact implemented here seems to be much more useful; it does not have to grapple, among other things, with the border-line between proverbs and non-proverbs which is questioned in many cases. Permjakov's set of some 800 binary classes seems definitely to be not suitable at all here.

4. A DESCRIPTIVE SOLUTION

In order to be able to cope with problems involved in a lexicographic description of statements, utterances, etc., i.e. full-fledged sentences usually endowed with a specific function and pragmatics, a uniform system had to be devised. It is based on a set-up of (1) four **partners** at most, the first one being identical with the speaker and the second one with the listener; for uniformity's sake the partners are, with the exception of the first one, numbered by ordinal numerals which may and often are further specified (see below *Experienced man*). (2) Their **relationship**, mutual

familiarity and attitudes is then given, followed by (**3**) a mutual **assessment and reactions** and, often, by (**4**) information on the **reason**, **cause or goal** of the pronouncement of the proverb where its function may be mentioned, too. In this way, a *general framework of the speech situation* is given, modified in details. To separate the situation covered in this way from the meaning proper, all of this information, being given in parentheses, precedes the meaning part. That is given outside the parentheses and is to be viewed as a necessary specification of the somewhat general framework of situation preceding it. Compare, then, the third English proverb (from NODE):

Birds of a feather flock together. *People of the same sort or with the same tastes and interests will be found together.*
with the descriptive version used in Czech for the same proverb (see the Appendix).

(Experienced man to a known second one, usually in a scornful commentary on a negatively assessed third and fourth ones, etc.) people with the same (negative) orientation and goals look for each other and get associated for mutual support, or have an understanding between themselves.

Obviously, this is only a simplified version of the array and multitude of descriptive techniques used in the Czech dictionary; a full version is to be printed in the dictionary, too. To put it in a nutshell, the following landmarks in the proverb's landscape or, rather, situation have to be made clear at least:

WHO to WHOM says WHAT WHEN/WHERE/HOW/WHY

5. Open Problems

There is a number of problems lurking behind this approach and some more may emerge later on. While the onomasiological treatment depends basically on the data and should be kept short and concise, the semasiological part, that of the lexicographical definitions proper may change more. Obviously, it very much depends on our knowledge of the proverb usage, available data and that is being gradually studied in large corpora only now. This may not be enough but it is many times better and more than the introspection and scanty manual excerpts of a time not so long ago.

Literature

ČELAKOVSKÝ, František Ladislav. 1852. *Mudrosloví národu slovanského v příslovích. Připojena jest sbírka prostonárodních českých pořekadel*, 3. vydání, 1949. Praha: Vyšehrad. (= Wisdom of the Slavonic Peoples. Attached is a Collection of Folk Czech Sayings)

ČERMÁK , František. 2009. České frazémy a idiomy propoziční,in *Slovník české frazeologie a idiomatiky. Výrazy větné.* Praha: Leda. (= Czech Proposional Phrasemes and Idioms)

ČERMÁK F., *Slovník české frazeologie a idiomatiky. Přirovnání., Výrazy neslovesné., Výrazy slovesné., Výrazy větné.* Leda (new ed., of 1983, 1988, 1994, 2009, with a team) (= A Dictionary of the Czech Phraseology and Idiomatics. Similes, Non-Verb Expressions, Verb Expressions, Sentence Expressions)

ČERMÁK František. 2003. "Onomaziologické systémy u propozic a proverbií." In *Parémie národů slovanských.* Sb. z konference v Ostravě 20.–21.2 u příležitosti 150. výročí úmrtí F. L. Čelakovského a jeho Mudrosloví, 47–54. Ostrava: Ostravská univerzita. (= Onomasiological Systems of Propositions and Proverbs)

ČERMÁK, František, HRONEK, Jiří, and MACHAČ, Jaroslav. 2009. *Slovník české frazeologie a idiomatiky. Výrazy větné.* Praha: Leda (= Dictionary of Czech Phraseology and Idiomatics. Sentence Expressions).

ČERMÁK, František, HRONEK, Jiří, MACHAČ, Jaroslav, eds. 1983. *Slovník české frazeologie a idiomatiky. Přirovnání.* Praha: Academia (= Dictionary of Czech Phraseology and Idiomatics. Similes).

ČERMÁK, František, HRONEK, Jiří, MACHAČ, Jaroslav, eds. 1988. *Slovník české frazeologie a idiomatiky. Výrazy neslovesné.* Praha: Academia (= (Dictionary of Czech Phraseology and Idiomatics. Non-Verbal Expressions)

ČERMÁK, František, HRONEK, Jiří, MACHAČ, Jaroslav, eds. 1994. *Slovník české frazeologie a idiomatiky. Výrazy slovesné. A-P, R-Ž.* Praha: Academia. (Dictionary of Czech Phraseology and Idiomatics. Verb Expressions)

ČERMÁK, František. 1982. *Idiomatika a frazeologie češtiny.* Praha: Univerzita Karlova (= Idiomatics and Phraseology of Czech)

ČERMÁK, František. 1994. "Idiomatics." In *The Prague School of Structural and Functional Linguistics,* edited by P. A. Luelsdorff, 185–195. Amsterdam/Philadelphia: J. Benjamins.

ČERMÁK, František. 1998a. "Identificación de las expresiones idiomáticas." In *Léxico y fraseología,* edited by J. de Dios L. Durán and A. Pamies Bertrán, 1–18. Granada: Método Ediciones.

ČERMÁK, František. 1998b. "Idiomatismos y lexicografía: en busca de criterios." In *Léxico y fraseología,* edited by J. de Dios L. Durán and A. Pamies Bertrán, 133–138. Granada: Método Ediciones.

ČERMÁK, František. 1998c. "Usage of Proverbs: What the Czech National Corpus Shows." In *Europhras ,97,* edited by P. Ďurčo, 37–59. Bratislava: Akadémia PZ.

ČERMÁK, František. 2001. "Dictionary of Czech Phraseology and Idiomatics." *La lessicographia storica e i grandi dizionari delle lingue europee. Atti della Giornata di studi Firenze,* Villa Rele di Castello, 10 luglio 2000, Bolletino dell'Opera del Vocabolario Italiano. Supplemento 1, 77–86.

ČERMÁK, František. 2001. "Substance of Idioms: Perennial problems, Lack of data or Theory?" *Internatuional Journal of Lexicography* 14 (1): 1–20.

ČERMÁK, František. 2001b. "Propoziční frazémy a idiomy v češtině." In *Frazeografia słowiańska,* edited by M. Balowski and W. Chlebda, 93–101. Opole: Uniwersytet Opolski. (= Propositional Phrasemes and Idioms in Czech)

ČERMÁK, František. 2003. "Paremiological Minimum of Czech: The Corpus Evidence." In *Flut von Texten - Vielvalt der Kulturen. Ascona 2001 zur Methodologie und Kulturspezifik der Phraseologie,* edited by H. Burger, A. Häcki Bufofer, and G. Greciano, 15–31. Hohengehren: Schneider Verlag.

ČERMÁK, František. 2004. "Propositional Idioms." In *Europhras 2000,* edited by Ch. Palm-Meister, 15–31. Tübingen: Stauffenberg Verlag.

KUUSI, Matti. 1972. "Towards an International Type-System of Proverbs." *Proverbium* 19: 699-736.

LAUHAKANGAS Outi. 2001. *The Matti Kuusi international type system of proverbs.* Helsinki: Suomalainen Tiedeakatemia.

PEARSALL, Judy and HANKS, Patrick, eds. 1998. *The New Oxford Dictionary of English.* Oxford – New York: Oxford University Press, i-Finger version 2004

PERMJAKOV Grigorij L'vovič. 2000. *Die Grammatik der sprichwörtlichen Weisheit.* Hohengehren: Schneider Verlag.

RIDEOUT, Ronald and WITTING, Clifford. 1969. *English Proverbs Explained.* London: Pan Books.

SCHINDLER F. 1993. *Das Sprichwort in heutigen Tschechischen: Empirische Untersuchung and Semantische Beschreibung,* Műnchen: Otto Sagner.

SIMPSON, John, ed. 1993. *Concise Oxford Dictionary of Proverbs* (paperback ed.). Oxford – New York: Oxford University.

ZICH, Otakar. 1956. *Lidová přísloví z logického hlediska*. Praha: NČSAV. (= Czech Proverbs from the Logical Point of View)

APPENDIX 1

A Lexicographic Treatment of the Czech Proverbs
(in *Slovník české frazeologie a idiomatiky. Výrazy větné*, 2009).

(1) Sejde z očí, sejde z mysli. (Čl. zkušeně v připomínce, radě n. vysvětlující omluvě vůči druhému zvl. o svém vztahu k nepřítomnému třetímu po jeho odchodu, vzdálené n. odstraněné věci, popř. i už neurgentnímu problému ap.:) člověk na nepřítomného n. nepřítomné tolik, popř. (po čase) už vůbec nemyslí, nezabývá se jím, tím n. si kvůli němu, tomu nedělá starosti, popř. se proto pak dál netrápí; člověk po čase na něj, to zapomene.

(2) Lepší vrabec v hrsti než holub na střeše. (Čl. zkušený vůči druhému v radě n. varování před jeho těžko dosažitelným cílem ap.:) je lepší zvolit sice menší, ale jistý zisk, než zisk vyšší, ale velmi nejistý či spojený s riziky; buď skromný a spokoj se s tím prospěchem, co je jistý!

(3) Vrána k vráně sedá, rovný rovného si hledá. (Čl. zkušený vůči známému druhému obv. v opovržlivém komentáři na negativně hodnoceného třetího a čtvrtého ap.:) lidí stejného (záporného) zaměření a cílů se pro vzájemnou podporu vyhledávají a sdružují se n. mají pro sebe porozumění.

(4) Cesta do pekla je dlážděna dobrými úmysly. (Čl. zkušený varovně vůči druhému a jeho dobrému, šlechetnému úmyslu, přehnané obětavosti ap.:) **1.** lepší je se obejít bez dobrých předsevzetí, protože jejich obvyklé nedodržení vede k dalším a radikálnějším dobrým úmyslům a následně k ještě větším prohřeškům; sliby je třeba plnit; **2.** není dobré být příliš obětavý k druhým lidem, protože to může místo vděku vyvolat závist a nenávist.

(5) Darovanému koni na zuby nehleď. (Čl. zkušený zvl. v radě druhému a jeho příliš kritickému vztahu k daru, přidělené možnosti ap.:) buď (trochu) vděčný a nekritizuj jen!; člověk má být za každý dar, pomoc vděčný n. být s ním spokojený, a to bez ohledu na jeho (někdy horší) kvalitu n. vzhled, potřebu apod.

APPENDIX 2

blázen může říkat pravdu (fool may tell the truth)
· Blázni a děti mluví/mají pravdu.
buď opatrný! (be careful!)
Cave canem.
Čert nikdy nespí.
Nechval dne před večerem.
Důvěřuj, ale/a prověřuj!
Každá hůl má dva konce/svůj konec.
Z malý/malé jiskry velkej/velký oheň/voheň (bývá/bejvá).
Pamatuj na zadní kolečka!
Pamatuj na starý/stará kolena!
Kdo nedává bacha, ten se vždycky zmáchá.
Nikdy neříkej nikdy.
Malý oheň velký les spálí.
Opatrnost (je) matka moudrosti.
Opatrnosti nikdy nezbývá/není nikdy dost.
Rozumu (není) nikdy nazbyt.
Kdo sliby živ, zbohatne-li, bude div.
Pamatuj na strejčka Příhodu!
Svěř se tetě, roznese tě po všem světě.
Všem věř, nikomu nedůvěřuj!
Videant/caveant consules, ne quid detrimenti res publica capiat.
Mysli na zadní vrátka!
První vyhrání z kapsy vyhání.
Nekupuj zajíce v pytli.
buď vděčný! (be grateful!)
· Darovanému koni na zuby nehleď!
čl. bez moci není nebezpečný (a powerless man is not dangerous, *lit.* man without power is not dangerous)
· Mrtvej pes nekouše.
čl. dělá věci nečestné v nouzi (in need man does ignoble things, *lit.* man does things ignoble in need)
Hlad je špatný rádce.
Hlad žene vlka z lesa.
čl. dělá věci neobvyklé v nouzi (in need man does unusual things, *lit.* man does things unusual in need)
V nouzi čert i mouchy lapá.
Nouze láme železo.
čl. dělá věci příznačně (man does typical things, *lit.* man does things typical)
· Člověka po věci, bylinu po vůni (poznáš).

čl. zapomíná (one forgets, *lit.* man forgets).

• Sejde z očí, sejde z mysli.

děti potřebují péči pořád (children require care all the time)

• Malý/malé děti kaši jedí a velký/velké děti srdce užírají.

děti prozradí všechno (children give away everything)

• Děti nejspíše pravdu povědí.

lidé stejní sdružují se (same people form company, *lit.* people same join)

• Vrána k vráně sedá, rovný rovného si hledá.

jídlo dobré podporuje lásku (good food supports love, *lit.* food good supports love)

• Láska prochází žaludkem.

žena komplikuje situaci (woman complicates situation)

• Kam čert nemuže, tam nastrčí bábu.

život je proměnlivý (life is changeable)

• Dneska tlusto a zejtra pusto.

• Nil homini certum est.

B
PROVERB USE AND PRAGMATICS

Proverbs are used in some specific types of text, though not much in scientific texts. Their use in fiction and elsewhere (in Part B, here) often goes hand in hand with expressions of evaluation, i.e. pragmatics of the text. Ways how they can be used is illustrated in an exhaustive study on a single proverb. Proverbs are often used by a specific signal, an introducer.

5. WHAT ONE CAN DO WITH PROVERBS IN TEXT

In *Phraseologie disziplinar und interdisziplinar*, C. Földes (ed.), Gunter Narr Verlag, Tübingen, 2009, 307–321, **Čermák Proverbs 2014**, 25–46.

ABSTRACT

The stability of idioms is always a compromise based on variants offered by development. Without giving it much thought, many people believe that proverbs are among the most stable types of idioms, especially old and famous ones. Also, it is often taken for granted that proverbs are self-contained units, with little or no connection to or dependence on the text (context). Upon closer look, it is readily seen that neither is quite true.

In the following, a comprehensive analysis of a single English proverb (mostly, Every cloud has a silver lining) is offered and, against a general background, every single aspect of the proverb's form (variants, both paradigmatic and syntagmatic, including improvised extensions) and function (including its position in a paragraph, relation to what it refers to, attitude of the speaker, evaluation of it, etc.) is scrutinized so that a detailed portrait of the proverb can be offered.

Thus, this case study reconnoitering (surveying) the terrain and outlining possibilities of an analytical corpus-based approach to proverbs is meant both as a model and as a representative map of one prominent item of the field.

1. INTRODUCTION

Variability, stability and identity of language units are those aspects that are closely interconnected, yet we still know very little of the relationships and limits that they are based on. How far a variant may go, how much it can batter, destroy the initial form, and to what extent the identity of this form is still basically preserved, might be one of the central questions one might ask here.

In an attempt to delve into the nature and behaviour of proverbs in a complex way, a single English proverb *Every cloud has a silver lining* has been examined on the basis of what a corpus shows (see also Grzybek (1984)). In the following, all of its relevant formal, semantic and functional aspects will be briefly discussed.

2. FORMAL ASPECTS

2.1 FORMAL USES AND TYPES AND THE METHOD USED

The proverb *Every cloud has a silver lining* is one of the most frequent in English, attested in the 100 million words of British National Corpus by its 52 occurrences. It has to be made clear, however, that, surprisingly, this frequent proverb is found in many different forms, where only a minority is represented by its full form. It has been its variability lying behind this that is one of the reasons why the proverb has been chosen and is scrutinized here.

Proverbs come in various sizes, ranging from two to some ten or more words. Obviously, the longer a really stable and familiar proverb is, the more possibility and space for its variability is there to arise. Due to their fixed and stable form, proverbs serve as a suitable basis for many sorts of textual creativity (in newspapers, fiction, etc.), where what may be left out is refixed by association thanks to the proverb's firm place in one's memory. It is its full form one remembers underlying all of its uses. It seems that a safe and rough limit of the variability could be that it should not include more than 50 percent of the proverb's form. Thus, *Every cloud has a silver lining* seems to be of average length and, accordingly, its scope for variation is average, too. Yet, in the case of this particular proverb a notable exception to this 'size' rule is encountered, as it is found in a much shorter than 50% form of *silver lining*, too. In general, it is to be expected, of course, that variability, by far not infrequent with proverbs, implies, to a varying degree, other types and shades of meaning and function than the original one, where by 'original' that one is meant that conveys general truth, often accompanied by advice.

In the following, only **contextual variability** and variants are studied, since our data show that this proverb does not have any stable variants, remembered out of context, i.e. with, perhaps, a single exception (see below). Hence, two types of the proverb **usage** are distinguished here, **reproduction**, i.e. a case where it is used unchanged, and **modification**, based on a kind of partial change and, accordingly, a variant. It seems that in the former, the proverb is not anchored formally in the text at all (this is taken care of by meaning only), while the latter is, due to new parts of the variant.

Proverbs are sentences and, accordingly, they are **propositions** (propositional idioms, Čermák 2001a,b, 2004), too. Yet they are often modified, due to various transformations, into variants, many of these acquiring a non-sentential (non-propositional) status. In the case of *Every cloud has a silver lining* only slightly more than one third of its uses retains its sentential character, while almost two thirds function as non-sentences, resembling **collocational idioms** of many types, such as ...*few could see the silver lining*. It may be surprising that out of all uses only 4 (i.e. 7.7%) are exact reproductions, amounting to unmodified uses, while the overwhelming majority (over 92%) is made up of variants. Moreover, most of these seem to prefer a changed, non-sentential status, where the ratio of non-sentential variants to sentential ones is 34 : 14 (65.4% : 27%).

The **position** of the proverb in the text seems to be rather simple. Due to the particular nature of its meaning, this type of proverb tends to occur more often **after** whatever is being commented on by the proverb. This means that first a mention of something wrong or hopeless event is made that is followed by the proverb signalling some hope or possibility of improvement (see the concordance below). Nevertheless, rare cases of this order being reversed, at least in part, are to be found, too, such as in

(6) **If there is any silver lining to their dark cloud**, *it is the dubious one that the super--regional banks for most of the 1980s the successes of American banking also are on their way down (or, like Bank of New England, out).*

However, the kind of the position of the proverb cannot be determined in cases where variants have not retained the sentential form, or have been transformed into a proper noun or are used as reproductions, i.e. as pure quotations.
As for the search of the corpus and **methodology** of the approach: this started with a *silver lining* query only; among the 52 attested forms there has been found a single case of a homonym, too, where the *silver lining* form is used literally, as in

(1) *...where the last outgoing wavelet left them; the grassy knolls girding the hollow of the bay, and the rock promontories, whose darker tones gave force to* **the silver lining of the breaking wavelet**.

The search method used here, namely *silver lining*, is based on a prominent part of the proverb, though it may be difficult to define it in general and say what it exactly consists of. Yet, it produced the 52 results and is, at the same time, proof that a different method popular with some field researchers, namely using the first half of the proverbs and expecting the respondents to provide the missing second half, may be misleading. Thus, BNC has been also searched using the initial *Every cloud* which has, however, produced only 14 relevant concordance lines, i.e. much less. Most of these do overlap with the *silver lining* method, however, which has not been able to capture only one occurrence, namely *Every cloud, as they say*. This casts a shadow over the other method and supports the original *silver lining* method chosen here.

It should be noted that BNC does not contain any evidence for another, rather a drastic variant, namely *silver line*. For reasons still to be explored, the English language seems to leave this line of language creativity unemployed.

2.2 Distribution of the Proverb in Types of Text

It is now generally recognized that proverbs are not limited to a single text domain only, although there might be a tendency for them to occur more often in some. What one may only presume so far, is a different and perhaps higher use and distribution in the spoken language. In the case of this particular proverb, BNC gives the following domains where it has been used:

Periodical (*The Economist, Bookseller, Guitarist*, etc.) ≅ 40% (20)
Newspaper (*Independent, The Guardian, Daily Telegraph*, etc.) ≅ 20% (10)
Novel (fiction) ≅ 10% (6)
Book (nonfiction) ≅ 10% (6)
Miscellaneous (*Trade Union Congress, Leeds United e-mail list*, pamphlets, Radio/TV programmes, etc.) ≅ 20% (10)

The proverb has not been found in technical and other specialized or scientific texts, but its rather low turnout in fiction may be surprising. It may not be surprising, however, that the highest rate of occurrence is due to periodicals and newspapers, which may be due to the proportions in which BNC is made up, at least partly.

2.3 Variation and Variants

All of the variation manifested in variants and recorded here is entirely due to the authors who have used the proverb and express thus their intention to give it some additional shade of meaning. Obviously, it also depends on their ability to do so, since it is not so common to coin an acceptable change of the form of such a stable language unit as proverb and not everybody can do it. In a broad sense, the latter may be viewed as a kind of language creativity.

In what follows, no difference will be made between **variants proper** (Čermák 2004a), i.e. those forms that basically preserve the proverb's identity, meaning and function, and **transformations**, i.e. those where a more substantial change made the proverb into a structurally and functionally different entity. An example of the latter is to be found in a two-word variant *silver lining* (see the line 23 below in the concordance), where the resulting form is no longer the proverb, as it has lost its sentential character altogether.

Variants of form may generally be viewed as being of two types, basically, syntagmatic and paradigmatic ones. These, then, either retain the proverb's structural function (i.e. the propositional one) or change it (see more in 3.2).

The **syntagmatic** type is based on the proverb's linear character. It is, however, almost exclusively (as in this case) based on reduction or addition, the resulting form being thus shorter or longer than the starting one, such as:

(2) *When parts of Hampton Court were damaged in a fire two years ago, few could* **see the silver lining**.

While reduction is common with this kind of variant, it is, however, debatable if the initial form of the proverb can be made longer. In any case it seems to occur very seldom. In

(3) *But whatever the truth, the NASA team insists that the* **Pinatubo cloud does have one silver lining.**

the total length of the proverb is retained, in fact, as the inserted form *Pinatubo* is a replacement (of *Every*), not an enlargement. The only addition, being, however, of a grammatical nature only stressing the proverb's validity, is the form *does* and that may belong, at the same time, to the following type of variation.

The other type is **paradigmatic**, based on a substitution (of a word, morpheme, etc.) and is made up of replacements of some forms or their parts by others. This has already been referred to in the preceding case. Other cases of this type may be seen in variation of tense form, as in

(4) *In the seventies life was rosy for all trade unions and everyone within the organization felt secure.* **Every cloud had a silver lining**.

The pure paradigmatic variation preserving the full form of the proverb is rare here, however; it does occur with shorter forms more. As we have already seen, **both types of variation** may be found at the same time quite often and even a cumulation of several subtypes in a single proverb is possible. For example,

(5) *If the sheer quantity of information about 1992 is* **clouding** *your vision,* **look no further for the silver lining**.

The proverb has been considerably shortened here but also some words have been added, this corresponding to a syntagmatic change, while a variation on *cloud*, namely *clouding*, corresponds to a paradigmatic change and a variant, followed by a substantial shift of meaning. A different type fits, not surprisingly, the proverb into the common existential construction *There is/was*, such as in:

(6) **But there was a silver lining to the cloud**, *those first natural contacts with the West paradoxically inspired groups to search out their own roots and national identification.*

A variant which, due to its recurrence, may seem to suggest an alternative stable form to the basic form of this proverb is **But there's always a silver lining**, as in:

(7) *I can see a number of roads up ahead for you, 'Mavis was saying.' Whichever you take will be rough and rocky.* **But there's always a silver lining**, *isn't there*, **dear?**

Since in the 52 forms attested, this has been found three times (Nos 15, 25, 26 in the Appendix) it is obviously too little to base such a suggestion on. On the other hand, this *there is/was* form is the only prominent variant which is found repeatedly.

Apart from words added by the speaker to convey a meaning he/she just intends to add, syntagmatic variants may be accompanied by some standard **introducers**, too, having a different role from that of a mere variant, namely modal or structural (see Čermák 2004b), such as *even, but, they say* or *there is*, etc., cf.

(8) *...so maybe it's true what* **they say about every silver lining having a cloud**, or

(9) **Mind you, every cloud had a silver lining**. *The brothels were free, the ladies of the night well rested and more than prepared to accept sustenance, a loaf or a jug of wine, instead of silver.*

In more than half of the cases, the proverb has been found to have lost its sentential character and is used either in a **verb construction** or a **nominal one**. The verb constructions include such verbs as *have, find, search* or *present*. They all nicely retain and support the core meaning of a rescue, help or improvement to look or hope for, sometimes in an emphasized form, such as in:

(10) *AMERICA'S recession may* **have a silver lining**,
(11) *I got a bit upset, but soon* **found a silver lining**,
(12) *Kenneth Clarke, usually a man* **to find a silver lining in the blackest cloud**, *admitted that the government was in a dreadful hole*,
(13) *We need another Harry Cross and Ralph* **to present a silver lining to** *the ever present* **cloud of** *worthwhile issues*,
(14) *Head east, young man, and* **search for the silver lining**.

Let us now return back to the size and form of the nominal variant *silver lining* which is much shorter than anything else. One has to wonder why this very form, of all possibilities, is the shortest variant of all. Because of so few occurrences of this proverb, one can only speculate. Is it because this appeals to the user as the most likely core of the form, retaining, at the same time, its core meaning? Why can this and other forms be so drastically shortened? An indirect semantic support of this choice is found in the single case, attested in the BNC, where *silver lining* has a literal meaning, which may seem to be marginal and extremely rare in language.

An analysis of this basic nominal variant *silver lining* shows that it is viewed as stable (to the extent that some might view it as an independent idiom now) and thus provides for the possibility of further modification. Here, only some further variants based on it have a bearing on the canonical sentential form, while others seem to have a life of its own, related to the nominal form only. It may be interesting to observe ways how the nominal form is further developed and modified. Compare:

(15) *In 1905, something happened;* **a silver lining on the cloud** *of doom,*
(16) *The* **tiny bit of silver lining on the cloud** *is a new application by National Wind Power,*
(17) *I do hope that the* **proverbial silver lining** *becomes more apparent for you now,*
(18) **The cloud in this particular silver lining** *is progestogen, a synthetic form of the hormone progesterone,*
(19) **Silver lining bonus** *in slow crawl to recovery.*

In all, there are at least 10 purely paradigmatic variants (Nos 2, 6, 15, 25, 26, 28, 29, 32, 37, 46 in the Appendix) to be found here and twice as many, i.e. 20 syntagmatic ones (Nos 4, 5, 7, 11, 12, 13, 18, 21, 23, 24, 34, 38, 39, 40, 43, 44, 47, 48, 50, 51). Naturally, variants may go together forming at least 11 mixed cases (Nos 1, 2, 3, 6, 8, 16, 19, 20,22, 35, 49, see the Appendix).

Semantic variants, which may be due to and accompanied by a change of form, are more difficult to pin down, but some of these will be commented on in 3.

3. Meaning, Function, and Use

The basic and prototypical meaning and function of a proverb is generally recognized; although, this may get a different wording in popular use and even general-reference sources. Thus, ENCYCLOPEDIA BRITANNICA (1997) defines it as:

succinct and pithy saying in general use, **expressing commonly held ideas and beliefs**, while NEW OXFORD DICTIONARY OF ENGLISH (NODE) views the proverb as **a short pithy saying in general use**, **stating a general truth or piece of advice**.

The latter, i.e. general statement expressing accepted truth and shared experience (see also Čermák 1998, 2001b, 2004), agrees more with a linguistic approach stressing the proverb's didactic, edifying nature and function, sometimes culminating into a recommendation or suggestion. Our particular proverb *Every cloud has a silver lining* is defined in NODE as:

every difficult or sad situation has a comforting or more hopeful aspect, even though this may not be immediately apparent.

3.1 Types of Meaning of the Proverb

Obviously, the basic, **prototypical meaning** of proverbs is the one that corresponds to its reproduction use (see above in 2.1), i.e. one where the proverb is quoted unchanged or with a minor change of its form only, cf.

(7) *Mr McEd was acting pretty cagey about it for one thing and, when pressed, would only come up with the reassuring phrases:* **Every cloud has a silver lining**.

All of the (major) formal modifications and variants seem to correspond, accordingly, to a modified, though usually derived meaning, based on the prototypical one. There are various types of meaning found here, based on this formal modification.

The largest type may be called **HOPE** and ways of its expression, where the proverb is used as a signal that a bad situation may be changed for a better one and at least some hope is justified there (case Nos 10, 11?, 13, 14?, 20, 23, 24, 25, 28, 29, 34, 37, 40, 45, 46, 47, 48, 49, 50, 51). This nicely fits the core meaning of the proverb that has been mentioned above. See, for example,

(20) **The only silver lining** *is the fact Strach could step right in.*

However, the proverb may be used in other senses, too, whereby the speaker **limits** or **counters** the proverb's basic function (adversative use), such as in:

(21) *If the sheer quantity of information about 1992 is clouding your vision,* **look no further for the silver lining**.
or he/she may take a more **reserved attitude** to the proverb's validity, such as in:

(22) *It won't be very good for the petrol companies that I've been visiting here today,* **but every cloud tends to have it's silver lining**.

There are yet other and more different uses found. Thus, conspicuous **semantic modifications** may employ the basic meaning to **stress** inherent **opposition** (23) and to contextually **specify** what might also be meant by the word *cloud* (24), as in:

(23) *But as he inspected the size of the Tories' losses on May 6th, even the home secretary, Kenneth Clarke, usually a man* **to find a silver lining in the blackest cloud**, *admitted that the government was in a dreadful hole.*
(24) *We need another Harry Cross and Ralph* **to present a silver lining to** *the ever present* **cloud of** *worthwhile issues which can be quite a daunting thing to watch, especially the 90-minute Saturday omnibus edition.*

A more or less open attempt to move the listener to wish to improve his/her situation is to be seen in
(25) *Head east, young man, and* **search for the silver lining**.

The use of the proverb, in fact of a variant, may also suggest the train of the speaker's thought and his search for words. From the example below, it is obvious that the speaker finally prefers the proverb to a simple verbal expression using *hope* or similar words and one may wonder why. In a sense this may be evidence that idioms, including proverbs, are not necessarily secondary to words, which a primitive, false and rather wide-spread assumption holds. Observe now the example:

(26) *Death. Well, I wouldn't put it quite like that. But* **it's** *certainly how can I put it –* **the silver lining**.

Surprisingly, even with so few cases attested for a single proverb, there are other and minor shades or interpretations of meaning to be found here, too, such as emphasis in the examples above (12, 23), etc.

3.2 FUNCTIONS OF THE PROVERB

Though basic meaning and underlying everything, is not identical with function, however. Here, three basic **textual functions** (or structural functions, out of 51) may be distinguished:

A-propositional (34.6%, i.e. 18 out of 52)

B-collocational (65.4%): -verbal (some 21)

-nominal (at least 12)

When the proverb has its propositional function (see above, in 2.1) it amounts to a sentence; when it does not amount to a sentence, but is part of it only or stands alone, this function may be called collocational. If the proverb is used in a verbal function (i.e. it is used broadly, as a verb), then its nominal core *silver lining* is linked with verbs such as *have, see, look for, hope for, search, find*, etc. (see above in examples of formal variation (10)–(14)), as in:

(27) *When parts of Hampton Court were damaged in a fire two years ago, few could* **see the silver lining**.

The nominal function is almost always related to the prototypical core form of *silver lining* and its core meaning, too.

(28) *I do hope that the* **proverbial silver lining** *becomes more apparent for you now; surely it's about time.*

However, some of these functions can take a peculiar shape, such as in:

(29) **The cloud in this particular silver lining** *is progestogen, a synthetic form of the hormone progesterone.*

where the proverb has a nominal shape and function but it manages to retain *the cloud* which is often omitted.

A special use and function is to be found in those cases where the proverb, usually transformed into its nominal core, is used as **proper name** or part of it (Nos 10, 14, 40, 45), such as in:

(30) *Organisations range from Brownies, Cub-Scouts, Scouts and Guides to the **Silver Lining Club** for the Senile Citizens, as they tend to be called locally.*

Due to the polysemy or rather homonymy of *silver lining*, there is also a scope for some **punning** to be created, based on contrasting the idiomatic and literal meaning, such as in

(31) ***The Silver Lining Pillow Company** based in Middlesbrough used the show to launch a travelling version of their orthopaedic pillow*, or:

(32) *It seems that **even the toxic cloud** that rose over Seveso in 1976 **has had a silver lining**.* At the same time, this last case is a fine example of a simultaneous mix of both the literal and proverbial meaning. A case of punning is to be seen also in the example (5) above.

In contradistinction to these formal textual functions, the proverb in its full form always has a **communicative function** as well (Čermák, 2001, 2004). It has a factual or directive function, or, more usually, a combination of both in the sense that it states a fact and, to a varying degree, suggests an action or possibility of an action that might or should be taken. Statements of fact are usually easy to detect, as in

(33) *Traditional peg tiles have been in great demand since the storms of the past few years, so for Tenterden tile makers Spicer, **the clouds had a silver lining**.*

But suggesting a hope, that is a possibility to await or, perhaps, contribute to it, may become more obvious in other cases, as in:

(34) *Mr McEd was acting pretty cagey about it for one thing and, when pressed, would only come up with the reassuring phrases: **Every cloud has a silver lining.** Edor Don't worry son, you father's not such an old fool as he looks.*

Naturally, in the sense that the choice and use of the proverb is motivated by the speaker's knowledge and evaluation of the particular situation in question, virtually all of the standard uses of the proverb have an **evaluative**, **pragmatic function**, too. In the following example, the speaker (Mavis) evaluates the future course of things, which may not be too easy, but suggests also, evidently due to her experience, that the solution will be successful and whoever is being addressed will eventually be lucky. Thus, the overtone is one of reassuring the listener.

(35) *I can see a number of roads up ahead for you, 'Mavis was saying.' Whichever you take will be rough and rocky. **But there's always a silver lining**, isn't there, dear?*

4. Conclusions

From the multitude of aspects, briefly discussed here, at least two may be worth finally stressing. Formally and contrary to expectation, perhaps, proverbs, as seen in the case examined here, do display a rather unusually high degree of variability. Semantically and functionally, proverbs appear to be far from the accepted view that they primarily or exclusively convey an accepted truth used in a prominently didactic way, prototypically by elders to youngsters. Thus, to return to the title of this contribution, it is evident that one can do a lot of things *with* and *to* a proverb.

Literature

ČERMÁK František. 2004. "Propositional Idioms". In *Europhras 2000*, edited by Ch. Palm-Meister, 15–23. Tübingen: Stauffenberg Verlag.

ČERMÁK, František. 1998. "Usage of Proverbs: What the Czech National Corpus Shows." In *Europhras '97*, edited by P. Ďurčo, 37–59. Bratislava: Akadémia PZ.

ČERMÁK, František. 2001a. "Substance of Idioms: Perennial problems, Lack of data or Theory?" *International Journal of Lexicography* 14 (1): 1–20.

ČERMÁK, František. 2001b. "Propoziční frazémy a idiomy v češtině." In *Frazeografia słowiańska*, edited by M. Balowski and W. Chlebda, 93–101. Opole: Uniwersytet Opolski. (= Propositional Phrasemes and Idioms in Czech)

ČERMÁK, František. 2003. "Paremiological Minimum of Czech: The Corpus Evidence." In *Flut von Texten - Vielvalt der Kulturen. Ascona 2001 zur Methodologie und Kulturspezifik der Phraseologie*, edited by H. Burger, A. Häcki Bufofer, and G. Greciano, 15–31. Hohengehren: Schneider Verlag.

ČERMÁK, František. 2004a. "Jazyková variabilita: případ přísloví." In *Čeština - Universalia a specifika 5*, edited by Z. Hladká and P. Karlík, 99–109. Praha: NLN. (= Language Variability: the Case of Proverbs).

ČERMÁK, František. 2004b. "Text Introducers of Proverbs and Other Idioms." In *Phraseologismen als Gegenstand sprach- und kulturwissenschaftlicher Forschung*, edited by C. Földes and J. Wirrer, 27–46. Hohengren: Schneider Verlag.

ĎURČO, Peter. 2005. *Sprichwörter in der Gegenwartssprache*. Trnava: Univerzita Sv. Cyrila a Metoda v Trnave

GRZYBEK, Peter. 1984. "How to Do Things with Some Proverbs: Zur Frage eines parömi(ologi)schen Minimums." In *Semiotische Studien zum Sprichwort, Simple Forms Reconsidered I*, edited by P. Grzybek and W. Eismann, 351–358. Tübingen: Günter Narr.

GRZYBEK, Peter. 1995. "Foundations of Semiotic Proverb Study." *De Proverbio, An Electronic Journal of International Proverb Studies* 1(1). http://info.utas.edu.au/docs/flonta/

MIEDER, Wolfgang. 1982, 1990, 1993. *International Proverb Scholarship. An Annotated Bibliography*. 4 Vols. New York: Garland Publishing New York; 2001. New York: Peter Lang.

MIEDER, Wolfgang. 1995. "Paremiological Minimum and Cultural Literacy." *De Proverbio* 1 (1). http://info.utas.edu.au/docs/flonta/

MIEDER, Wolfgang. 1999. *Sprichwörter/Redensarten - Parömiologie*. Heidelberg: J. Gross Verlag.

MIEDER, Wolfgang. 2004. *Proverbs. A Handbook*. London: Greenwood Press Westport.

MOON, Rosamund. 1998. *Fixed Expressions and Idioms in English. A Corpus-Based Approach*. Oxford: Oxford University Press.

SEARLE, John R. 1979. *Expression and Meaning: Studies in the Theory of Speech Acts*. Cambridge: Cambridge University Press.

WHITING, Bartlett Jere. 1989. *Modern Proverbs and Proverbial Sayings*. Cambridge, Mass.: Harvard University Press.

APPENDIX

Concordance of the Proverb *Every cloud has a silver lining.*
(British National Corpus, modified). Search: **silver lining**.

1 When parts of Hampton Court were damaged in a fire two years ago, few could **see the silver lining**.

2 Traditional peg tiles have been in great demand since the storms of the past few years, so for Tenterden tile makers Spicer, **the clouds had a silver lining**.

3 The good news, meanwhile, is that reformed shopaholics almost always **speak of a silver lining to the cloud** which hung over their lives (and bank accounts).

4 Bite One: The Secretary of State **told us about the silver lining** he told us nothing about the *dark clouds on the horizon.*

5 AMERICA'S recession may **have a silver lining**.

6 **If there is any silver lining to their dark cloud**, it is the dubious one that the super-regional banks for most of the 1980s the successes of American banking also are on their way down (or, like Bank of New England, out).

7 Head east, young man, and **search for the silver lining**. With top City firms forced to ask some of their young accountants to take unpaid leave, CHRISTOPHER FILDES advises a nephew on profitable ways of utilising his time off.

8 In 1905, something happened; **a silver lining on the cloud** of doom.

9 There was so much of loveliness in every scene, my mind was surfeited with joys: how the far-spreading bay, with its expanse of white shell-sand, was girded by a sea which placidly reflected the blue of heaven; and how the seaweeds left their markings in curious lines just where the last outgoing wavelet left them; the grassy knolls girding the hollow of the bay, and the rock promontories, whose darker tones gave force to **the silver lining of the breaking wavelet**.

10 Organisations range from Brownies, Cub-Scouts, Scouts and Guides to the **Silver Lining Club** for the Senile Citizens, as they tend to be called locally.

11 The most appropriate technology for many people will be one that helps a country to organise a postal system so that stamps are available, to bring radio within everyone's reach and that holds out the possibility of early telephone links. **Silver lining?**

12 It seems that **even the toxic cloud** that rose over Seveso in 1976 **has had a silver lining**.

13 So I suppose I shall have to **rely for my silver lining** upon Carrie Schlegel of Capistrano Beach, California, who was kind enough to write to this magazine to say that I was God.

14 For instance, Jeff Beck's **hit Hi Ho Silver Lining** had a bit in the middle where he double-tracked the guitar and, just for a moment, it breaks into harmony.

15 CHRISTOPHER COLUMBUS: THE DISCOVERYTOM SELLECK as the King of Spain! Rachel Ward as his missus! Marlon Brando as Marlon Brando! Crap editing! Crap acting! Crap script! **But there's always a silver lining**.

16 The **cloud** that engulfed the market on Black Wednesday **had a silver lining** for electric gadgets maker Kenwood.

17 Mr. McEd was acting pretty cagey about it for one thing and, when pressed, would only come up with the reassuring phrases: **Every cloud has a silver lining**. Edor Don't worry son, you father's not such an old fool as he looks.

18 I got a bit upset, but soon **found a silver lining**.

19 But whatever the truth, the NASA team insists that the **Pinatubo cloud does have one silver lining**.

20 The **tiny bit of silver lining on the cloud** is a new application by National Wind Power they want to reduce the number of proposed turbines from 15 to 12.

21 But as he inspected the size of the Tories' losses on May 6th even the home secretary, Kenneth Clarke, *usually* a man **to find a silver lining in the blackest cloud**, admitted that the government was in a dreadful hole.

22 But the worst local-election result ever? The Tory performance was in fact one and a half percentage points better in The Economist's regular sample of provincial English districts than it was three years ago, at the height of the rebellion against Mrs Thatcher's poll tax (see table 1). However, in 1990 **there was a silver lining**.

23 Those attending the Börsenverein's Frankfurt seminar gave many examples of numbers received which were not compatible with country codes. **Silver lining**. But there is a bright side.

24 I may no longer be the best thing that Limerick has yet produced. That's why. STUDIO UPDATE HIGH HOPES. **SILVER LINING.** JACKIE HAYDEN TAKES *A LOOK AT THE BLACK CLOUD* CURRENTLY OVER THE MUSIC INDUSTRY HERE, BUT OFFERS HOPE OF A BRIGHTER FUTURE.

25 **But there was a silver lining to the cloud** those first natural contacts with the West paradoxically inspired groups to search out their own roots and national identification.

26 I can see a number of roads up ahead for you, 'Mavis was saying.' Whichever you take will be rough and rocky. **But there's always a silver lining**, isn't there, dear?

27 ...when pressed, he would only come up with the reassuring phrases: **Every cloud has a silver lining**, Ed or Don't worry son, you father's not such an old fool as he looks.

28 The ultimate PR coup, Celia said harshly. Death. Well, I wouldn't put it quite like that. But **it's** certainly how can I put it – **the silver lining**.

29 I do hope that the **proverbial silver lining** becomes more apparent for you now; surely it's about time.

30 3 to give practice in changes in intonation: Teacher A bird in the hand. Student A bird in the hand? Teacher To live from hand to mouth. Student To live from hand to mouth? Teacher **Every cloud has a silver lining**.

31 Teacher Every cloud has silver lining. Student **Every cloud has a silver lining?**

32 In the seventies life was rosy for all trade unions and everyone within the organization felt secure. **Every cloud had a silver lining**.

33 He's offered to go away and come up with incriminating evidence, Robert. Facts and figures about unethical disbursement of club funds and that kind of thing. Christ! You better make sure he doesn't get murdered as well. Although it would be a help in reducing the number of suspects by one, I suppose. **Every cloud has a silver lining, what!**

34 I'm trying to decide if reducing it to four **is a silver lining**, said Amiss.

35 But that did mean she was also between me and Prentice, who was hovering trying to cut off my retreat as well, so *maybe it's true what* **they say** about every silver lining having a cloud.

36 ...life was hard in Paris. Yuletide and Twelfth Night passed with only the occasional carols in church, for no one dared to go out at night. **Mind you**, **every cloud had a silver lining**. The brothels were free, the ladies of the night well rested and more than prepared to accept sustenance, a loaf or a jug of wine, instead of silver.

37 **The only silver lining** is the fact Strach could step right in.

38 AREN'T YOU SICK OF IT Worried About Being Taken Over? Competitors Threatening Your Market?...**Every Cloud Has a Silver Lining Croner's Europe**! Some publishers are making heavy weather of 1992.

39 If the sheer quantity of information about 1992 is clouding your vision, **look no further for the silver lining**.

40 If you're feeling under the weather as yet more 1992 bumf lands on your desk, **order the silver lining**, CRONER'S EUROPE on 10 days free approval now.

41 How's the boy who was run over? Driving us nuts. His foot's still elevated, so he can't fidget about, and that's tough on a little boy.... Oh, well, **they say every cloud has a silver lining**. How's the little chap on the railings? Jeremy? He's fine. Going home tomorrow.

42 And you know what **they say about every cloud having a silver lining**, well could young Joey Beecham be United's ray of hope?

43 The sun was shining at the Manor Ground but Oxford finished under **a cloud the silver lining was the form of** some of the young players especially Matthew Keble who was making his debut.

44 We need another Harry Cross and Ralph **to present a silver liningto** the ever present **cloud of** worthwhile issues which can be quite a daunting thing to watch especially the 90-minute Saturday omnibus edition.

45 **The Silver Lining Pillow Company** based in Middlesbrough used the show to launch a travelling version of their orthopaedic pillow.

46 **The cloud in this particular silver lining** is progestogen, a synthetic form of the hormone progesterone.

47 This is the 10th year the Celebrities Guild has presented its Unsung Heroes Awards to people who help the disadvantaged for no personal reward. Forest flyer puts Blues in cup mood Happy Howie **sees silver lining** HOWARD KENDALL is ready to keep faith with the men.

48 Ex-Red **hopes for silver lining** to injury disaster.

49 **Silver lining bonus** in slow crawl to recovery.

50 The current difficulties may **have a silver lining**, added Mr Bootle.

51 **It's a silver lining** the Chancellor desperately needs amidst the current spate of doom and gloom, most recently this weekend C B I report showing industry in recession.

52 It won't be very good for the petrol companies that I've been visiting here today, **but every cloud tends to have it's silver lining**, and I, I think I can say with some confidence that the last factor that we're considering is pouring over the revenues and wondering how much is coming in, that, that really hasn't much come into it.

6. TEXT INTRODUCERS OF PROVERBS AND OTHER IDIOMS

In *Phraseologismen als Gegenstand sprach- und kulturwissenschaftlicher Forschung*, C. Földes, J. Wirrer (eds.), Schneider Verlag, Hohengren 2004, 27–46, **Čermák Proverbs 2014**, 157–183.

ABSTRACT

Empirically, it has been observed that many idioms and proverbs are used in text by speakers which stress and signal their introductory role by using a limited set of typical phrases. On the basis of corpus research, these introducers have been assembled for English and Czech and classified both formally and semantically.

1. INTRODUCTION: INTRODUCERS

Sometimes, speakers may feel it necessary to introduce, whatever they are going to say next, with a word or combination of words in order to signal that it is coming. Accordingly, whatever is used in this function may be called the **(text) introducer**. There are, generally, at least two types of such situation where introducers are used. In the first, one may not be sure about his or her choice of words (or may be in search of it), such as the English phrase *so to speak* or the equivalent Czech one *abych tak řekl*. In the second, it is, oddly enough, many idioms and phrasemes (in a very broad sense) that are being introduced by certain phrases or words. It is this latter field of introducers, which seems to be general for languages, that I will be concerned with here in some detail. An attempt has been made here to arrive at as balanced a coverage of the field as possible, using a combination of approaches, and drawing data from two very large corpora of the same size, namely the *British National Corpus* (http://info.ox.ac.uk/bnc) and the *Czech National Corpus* (http://ucnk.ff.cuni.cz), each being a representative corpus of 100 million words. Upon closer look, introducers occur both before and sometimes after the expression they introduce; for practical reasons, both are viewed here as a single phenomenon.

Though the question where else in the language recognizable and standard introducers are to be found remains open, a preliminary conclusion seems to point at phraseology and idiomatics as a primary and prominent field. The prototypical use of **linguistic terms** proper, such as *idiom* or *proverb*, these being among the candidates for the introducers examined here, is in linguistic analysis, of course, while the use of idioms is rather different from that. Yet, there is an evident link between the use of idiom introducers and using linguistic analysis terms, namely their **metalinguistic** character.

Despite the analysis having been limited to two languages here, namely English and Czech, one may easily recall other languages using equivalent expressions, such as German **sprichwörtlich**: *Ihr Glück ist schon sprichwörtlich, Ich habe, **wie man sagt**, in allen Ecken und Winkeln gesucht*, or French **Comme on dit**, or **comme l'on dit**, *le renard cache sa queue*, or Russian **как гласит народная мудрость** or, **как в народе говорится** *Дареному коню в зубы не смотрят*, or Finnish **Kuten sanotaan**, *oma maa mansikka, muu maa mustikka*, etc. Thus, it seems that the phenomenon of introducers is widespread.

Although it still remains to be specified when and to what extent J. R. Searle's neo-Gricean maxim 'speak idiomatically unless there is some special reason not to' (Searle 1979, 50) holds, one may, in broad terms, accept it. Provided that by *speaking idiomatically* Searle really means using idioms, too, and that he suggests that their use is thus a standard norm, one must wonder, however, why these, when used, should often be signalled by special devices, namely introducers. Are these to signal some less known idioms, perhaps, and prepare, tune the listener to what is coming or are idioms so special in language as to be in need of being specifically signalled? A more general question, linked to this, is how do we know in fact that something is an idiom when we come across one? On the other hand, it is definitely not true that use of introducers is compulsory. Hopefully, some hints as to how to answer these questions will emerge in the course of my analysis.

In 1998 (Čermák 1998), in my corpus-based analysis of proverbial usage in Czech, I have been able to distinguish some of the basics of proverb behaviour for that language. While some 80% of proverbial use may be viewed as *prototypical* in the sense that proverbs are used here as general statements expressing accepted truth and shared experience and, in fact, linguistically resuming somehow an event, action, etc., mentioned before, some 18% belong to *non-prototypical* instances of use, such as argumentation, adversative use, etc. I hope to show that the use of introducers goes across this distinction and is to be found in both types of use. Moreover, it has also been shown that, for Czech, the standard, prototypical position of the proverb is its postposition relative to what it is related to, i.e. an event, action, etc. This is best illustrated by, e.g., the following sentence: *Evil communications corrupt good manners, **says a Greek proverb**, and in the polarised world we live in it is not surprising that good manners and etiquette have gone by the board.* Since introducers (here bold-faced **says a Greek proverb**) tend to occur in a certain position relative to the idiom, one may wonder whether there is some kind of correlation between the two, i.e. the position of the introducer and that of the idiom or, rather, proverb. In contrast to proverbs, non-sentential idioms do not, as a rule, proverbially resume the contents of the text to any significant degree. This distinction and a significant number of forms and occurrences of introducers have been taken up and used in this analysis (for German, see also Ďurčo 2002).

In the following, the distinction between collocational idioms and proverbs, one of the subtypes of sentential or propositional idioms (for the distinction, see Čermák 2001), will be observed and both types of idioms will be examined as to their co-occurrence with introducers.

2. Idioms and Their Introducers

As a starting point, various sources of idioms and proverbs have been used (including Čermák 2003, 2007, Collins Cobuild Dictionary of Idioms 1995, Ferguson 1983, Moon 1998, and Whiting 1989). Where possible, indications of the frequency of their use have been taken up as criterion for the choice of an idiom's or proverb's inclusion in the list tested. The test deciding on the final inclusion has been based on the frequency in both large corpora. Although all four lists, i.e. of 20 collocational idioms (for short, collocations, 2.11–2.113) and 20 proverbs (2.12–2.123) in both languages, may not be quite balanced, which might be particularly true of English where, in contrast to Czech (Čermák 2003), no minimum frequency list exists, all of the items eventually included do cover the **core of the idiom usage**. Thus, there is an obvious bias towards the core of the field here, where more details of the use of the items selected are to be found than in the low-frequency periphery. That, however, still remains to be explored in more detail.

2.1 Searching Idioms in Text

Generally, all those forms accompanying idiom items in text have been recorded, which may be considered to be an extraneous element in the text, drawing attention to the idiom used. Both their appearance and non-appearance is of importance. However, the number of items recorded is too small and should be viewed as a preliminary probe only. In what follows, different functional types of idioms have been selected for inspection.

2.1.1 Collocational Idioms in Text and Their Introducers

2.1.1.1 English Collocation Introducers in Text

The list of 20 English idioms examined in the BNC includes the following:

BNC Frequency Introducers

head and shoulders	218	0
come to a head	114	0
be in the doldrums	73	0
before one's very eyes	39	0
the nooks and crannies	32	0
lead/go astray	29	0
place in the sun	28	0
like a drowning man	22	0
tough as old boots	8	0
be at daggers drawn	7	0
catch so with his pants down	7	0
mad as hatter	6	0
go to pot 5	0	
fresh as a daisy	5	0
let the grass grow under one's feet	5	0
cry wolf	5	0
dog in the manger	4	2
work like a Trojan	3	0
keep his hand in	2	0
out of a clear blue sky	2	0

The results of this search have been rather disappointing. Against expectations, only one English idiom had been signalled twice by some sort of introducer, namely **dog in the manger** accompanied by *a kind of* and *really: I think the idea of having numbers from each firm is **really** a dog in the manger attitude*, stressing and fortifying here the validity and typicality of the phenomenon named by the idiom. That suggests a very low preliminary ratio of 2 introducers per 586 occurrences (1: 293). Obviously the status of *really* might be questionable from a certain point of view, a point I will not go into here.

2.1.1.2 Czech Collocation Introducers in Text

Frequency Introducers

vzít si do hlavy	1,315	0	(take it into one's head to do)
černá ovce	323	0	(black sheep)
hodit/házet flinta do žita	277	0	(throw in the towel)
nechat někoho naholičkách	139	0	(leave sb in the lurch)
prubířský kámen	75	3	(the acid test)
nebrat si servítky	74	0	(not to mince one's words)

mít vystaráno	73	0	(no longer need to worry)
vzít nohy na ramena	63	0	(take to one's heels)
bejt padlej na hlavu	33	0	(be off one's head)
kapka v moři	32	5	(a drop in the ocean)
mít nahnáno	25	0	(have the wind up)
dát někomu co proto	17	0	(give sb a ticking off)
prásknout do bot	14	0	(take to one's heels)
mít za ušima	12	0	(be up to all the dodges)
mít hlad jako vlk	11	0	(be as hungry as a hunter)
dobrák od kosti	13	0	(the salt of the earth)
neslaný nemastný	6	0	(wishy-washy)
ptáček v kleci	4	0	(sb. under lock and key)
mít kachní žaludek	2	0	(have a cast-iron digestion)
růže mezi trním	1	0	(a rose among the thorns)

Doing somewhat better than English, Czech employs here, as introducers, two types of non-specific words, all of them being of high frequency in the language. These include adjectives and adverbs *hotový* (*veritable, downright*), *pravý* (*real, genuine*, **pravý** *prubířský kámen*), *doslova* (*literally*), *přímo* (*virtually, squarely*), the particles *přece* (–), *vždyť* (–); and noticeably, 4 times, the adjective *pověstný* (*legendary, renowned*). Apart from the last case, there is no tendency to be observed here. All of the forms found here are used as typical intensifiers in general language, however, directing the attention to what is obvious and familiar. The 8 : 3,796 introducer to proverb ratio (i.e. 1 : 474.5) suggests a double, if compared to English.

2.1.1.3 COLLOCATION INTRODUCERS IN TEXT: A SUMMARY

Obviously, the number of idiom occurrences observed in both languages is different, Czech scoring, perhaps surprisingly, about 4 times more idioms in text than English. In view of lack of comparable frequency dictionaries, it is not possible to draw any obvious and serious conclusions, however. Yet, comparing the relative figures for both languages, a remarkable difference is to be observed, namely twice more introducers per comparable number of collocational idioms in Czech as against English.

2.1.2 PROVERBS IN TEXT AND THEIR INTRODUCERS

An attempt has been made here to research only those proverbs with the highest frequency, based, in the Czech case, on another research (Čermák 2003). Also here, 20 proverbs have been chosen.

2.1.2.1 ENGLISH PROVERB INTRODUCERS

BNC Frequency Introducers

1 You can't have your cake and eat it	42	2
2 There is no such thing as free lunch	36	5
3 Prevention is better than cure	36	15
4 Chickens come home to roost	31	6
5 Every cloud has a silver lining	22	10
6 Better late than never	18	4
7 Discretion is best part of valour	15	9
8 All's well that ends well	14	1
9 Forewarned is forearmed	13	3
10 A bird in the hand is worth two in the bush	13	2
11 Let bygones be bygones	12	1
12 Practice makes perfect	12	5
13 Don't look a gift horse in the mouth	12	1
14 Like father like son	11	1
15 An eye for an eye	11	3
16 An apple a day keeps the doctor away	11	4
17 Once bitten twice shy	9	2
18 Two heads are better than one	8	2
19 Charity begins at home	8	2
20 Too many cooks spoil the broth	8	2

Without any *a priori* discrimination, there are, basically, four broad classes of introducers to be found here:

(a) nouns, such as *axiom, proverb, maxim, adage, saying, rule, principle, fact, message, conviction, phrase, argument, cliché* (often followed by *that*, e.g., *message **that***)

(b) verbs, such as *remember, conclude, comment, decide, assert, point out, counter*

(c) phrases, such as *as they say, mind you, so it is said, they say that, on the basis/premise that, to quote X*, or

(d) other, mostly adverbs or conjunctions, such as *always, really, but, though, if – then, definitely, well, so*

Obviously, in some cases, the introducers are to be found in various forms or with an additional word, such as *commenting, he decided, coining the phrase, the grim fact that.., but the idea was that...* Some of more interesting full examples:

*Contrasting **proverbs** with ponderous prose offers a way in: 'too many cooks spoil the broth' is a far more expressive way of saying: Over-maximization of the work force is counter-productive because it inhibits the realization of a satisfactory outcome. The **saying** 'An apple a day keeps the doctor away' contains some truth., the golden **rule** of banking is..., **If**,* *however, you get elected and you then have to carry out your policies,* **then** *of course you face the real world and then you can't have your cake and eat it problem.,* The old **adage** *that holds prevention is better than cure...,* **Deciding** *that discretion is best part of valour Davidson began...*

Sometimes, reference to the proverb is rather a subtle one, if only a hint at the proverb is present, such as in *'Once bitten and things of that* **nature**,' *smiled Tuppe.* The proverb might be signalled, however, by referring to the author who has become an authority, such as in *All's well that ends well,* **to quote Shakespeare.** Or it may be veiled as a simile, such as in *This seems* **like** *looking a gift horse in the mouth but these things do occur.* If unknown, however, it is almost impossible to recognize a proverb, if used as a quotation, in direct speech, such as: *Then, through a loudspeaker, the mother told cheering neighbours in Palermo, Sicily: 'An eye for an eye, a tooth for a tooth and nudity for nudity'.*

Despite their small frequency and number of items, some introducers exhibit a tendency for repetition, suggesting that they might be fixed in language. The top 5 introducers here include *saying* (7×), *always* (7×), *they say that* (5×), *decide* (5×), *principle* (4×). A limiting influence on the choice and appearance of introducers may be attributed to occasional proverb transformations into something else, such as *silver lining*, being a nominalization. This, rather exceptionally, was found to be the case in 17 out of 22 occurrences of this particular proverb. For reasons to be yet explored, it seems that the semantics of proverbs may influence the choice of introducers in some cases. Thus, the co-occurrence of the verb *decide* (in various forms) with the proverb *Discretion is the better part of valour* in almost 50 percent does not seem to be due to chance only.

It is worth observing that the obvious candidate, being a direct name English has here, namely *proverb*, has only a marginal frequency (1×), being superceded by *saying* (7×), or, to a lesser extent, by *maxim* (2×), *adage* (2×), *axiom* (2×), and the like. This seems to confirm that normal users cannot always identify the type and function with its proper label, or, simply want to avoid it for some other reason, which is not clear here, however. The low frequency of the *proverb* here is somewhat improved by a double occurrence of the adjective *proverbial*, however. In trying to pin down types of proverbs used with introducers, no firm conclusion can be made. Due to the fact that the *free lunch* proverb uses an introducer five times, it seems that there is no evident link between the introducer and the metaphorical quality of the proverb.

The 20 English proverbs that have been recorded in BNC occurred 351 times, having 69 introducers altogether (19.65%). All English proverbs examined do have at least one introducer to accompany it.

2.1.2.2 Czech Proverb Introducers

CNC Frequency Introducers

1 Účel světí prostředky	89	44	(The end justifies the means)
2 Nic není zadarmo	88	28	(Nothing is for free)

3 Oko za oko, zub za zub	76	24	(An eye for an eye and a tooth for a tooth)
4 Mnoho povyku pro nic	71	0	(Much ado about nothing)
5 Pravda vítězí	50	15	(Truth will prevail)
6 Vlk se nažral a koza zůstala celá	48	16	(The wolf has eaten and the goat remained whole)
7 Naděje umírá poslední	44	9	(Hope dies last)
8 Všechno zlé je k něčemu dobré	40	10	(Every cloud has a silver lining)
9 Za málo peněz málo muziky	40	5	(You get what you pay)
10 Boží mlýny melou pomalu, ale jistě	39	6	(The mills of God grind slowly, but they grind small)
11 Když dělají dva totéž, není to totéž	39	15	(No two people do anything quite alike)
12 Stará láska nerezaví	39	5	(Old love is never forgotten)
13 Sliby chyby	37	12	(Fine words butter no parsnips)
14 Čas jsou peníze	35	21	(Time is money)
15 Kdo umí, umí	34	5	(He is certainly good at it)
16 S jídlem roste chuť	33	11	(The more one has the more one wants)
17 Kdo hledá, najde	33	5	(Search and you shall find)
18 Pozdě bycha honit	32	3	(It is late to shut the stable door after the mare is gone)
19 Šaty dělají člověka	32	10	(Fine feathers make fine birds)
20 Všude dobře, doma nejlíp	32	10	(There is no place like home)

As in English, four basic classes of introducers have been found here also:

(a) nouns, such as *axiom* (*a*), *heslo* (*motto*), *pořekadlo* (*saying*), *pravidlo* (*rule*), *přikázání* (*commandment*), *přísloví* (*proverb*), *rčení* (*locution*). *krédo* (*creed*), *skutečnost že* (*fact that*), *slogan* (*slogan*), *úsloví* (*phrase*), *zásada* (*principle*), *zákon* (*law*);

(b) verbs, such as *dbát toho že* (*heed*), *dokazovat že* (*prove that*), *platit že* (*hold*), *potvrzovat* (*confirm*), *říkat si* (*tell to oneself*), *u/věřit* (*believe*), *vědět že* (*know*);

(c) phrases, such as *dá se říct že* (*it may be said*), *jak je vidět/jak vidíš* (*as seen/as you see*), *jak se říká* (*as they say*), *jak už to bývá* (*as is usual*), *je známo že* (*it is known that*), *jak známo, říká se / říkává se* (*it is said*);

(d) other, mostly adverbs, particles or conjunctions, such as *ale* (*but*), *holt* (*just*), *jenže* (*nevertheless*), *koneckonců* (*after all*), *neboť* (*since*), *ovšem* (*of course*), *protože* (*because*), *však* (*however*).

Some introducers, especially nominal ones, appear with an additional modifier, expressing an attitude of the speaker or fortifying, stressing its validity, such as *immoral slogan* (*nemravné heslo*), *cynical view* (*cynický názor*), *a newly fashionably slogan* (*dnes opět módní heslo*), *it holds relatively* (*platí jen relativně*), *it should hold/be true* (*mělo by platit*).

Some of the full examples: *V moderní dopravě* **platí** *víc než jinde, že čas jsou peníze.*,*Znám jedno* **přísloví**, **co praví**, *že stará láska nerezaví a v tom je asi celá vada...*, *Jádro jeho myšlenkového arzenálu tvoří právě* **zásada** *účel světí prostředky, Dělá to šalamounsky* **podle hesla**, *aby se vlk nažral a koza zůstala celá. Ťukala jsem na stroji* **metodou** *Kdo hledá najde.*, *Po letech putování jsem však* **dospěl k tomu**, **že** *všude dobře doma nejlíp.*

The folk or popular and, hence, anonymous, authority of the proverb may be somewhat changed and fortified at the same time if a famous person is mentioned using the proverb, such as *citát z Masaryka* (quote from Masaryk), *Husova slova* (John Huss' words), *podle biblického/starozákonního X* (according to the biblical X). Reference to the Bible in the use of *přikázání* (commandment) is obvious and belongs to this group, too. It is worth observing that there has been only a single Czech proverb which did not have any introducer to accompany it in any of its appearances.

Also here, it is the repetition of certain introducers which suggests some regularity and fixity. The top 5 Czech introducers, which have been found here, include *heslo* (slogan 30×), *přísloví* (proverb 16 ×), *platit* (hold 14 ×), *ale* (but 14 ×), *zásada* (12 ×).

However, Czech speakers do not seem to have such difficulty in identifying a proverb and its linguistic label as English speakers do.

Altogether, 20 Czech proverbs have been recorded having been used 931 times in the CNC, out of which 254 (over 27%) have been accompanied by some kind of introducer. There has been the total of 104 distinct introducers found, this rather large number suggesting both a tendency for improvisation and only a small number of those which might be considered to be stable and fixed.

2.1.2.3 PROVERB INTRODUCERS IN TEXT: A SUMMARY

The total number of English proverbs is much smaller than that of the Czech ones. Disregarding this, it is also the ratio of the introducers to the number of proverb occurrences that is somewhat smaller in English than in Czech, namely 19.6% : 27.3%. Given that proverbs of roughly equal familiarity are chosen, further research might address a possible correlation of the use of introducers and of their stability (variability). As for the choice of the form of introducers, one might wonder what the general tendency is: a sentential form of the proverb does not necessarily vouch for the use of a sentential type of introducer. However, the results suggest an obvious dominance of nominal introducers over anything else, this being mostly due to that there is no verb, in either language, which might be associated with the use of proverbs. Although a germ of such tendency might be seen in the use of the Czech verb *platit*, *platí* (it holds), its English equivalent *hold* is marginal only. While the choice of verbs is rather diverse and does not point to any preference applied, it is the nouns which exhibit a preference to be used in quite a few cases, this being reflected in their frequency. At the same time, noun introducers are somewhat different as to their meaning: apart from purely formal ones (see 2.3); it seems, for example, that English users are not very fond of stressing such meanings as *truth, wisdom, slogan, rule* as the Czech ones are. A minor difference is to be observed in the use of some modifiers here, too. While English may prefer the attribute *old* (*old adage, old saying,* 4×), stressing thus the time quality, Czech resorts to the preferential use of the adjective *známý* (*renowned, known, familiar, známé přísloví,* 8×), stressing thus the generality aspect of the proverb used.

2.2 SEARCHING INTRODUCERS IN TEXT

Having had a look at the introducers through the prism of selected idioms of both types above, it is worth considering their independent analysis in both corpora. In doing that, an attempt will be made to pin down those introducers that might be viewed as stable and pertinent for both fields of collocational and proverbial idioms. Basically, only some of those introducers, having been found before (in 2.1), have been examined as to their co-occurrence with (collocational) idioms here, namely *proverbial, proverbially* for English, and their Czech equivalents *příslovečný, příslovečně*.

2.2.1 COLLOCATION INTRODUCERS (ENGLISH AND CZECH)

BNC/CNC Frequency With Idioms

proverbial	161	61
proverbially	19	1
příslovečný	343	101
příslovečně	21	1

Surprisingly, the results obtained here completely reverse the impression one might have from the preceding approach (2.111–2), which did not yield a single stable introducer for English and very few for Czech. Obviously, the greatest and most surprising difference is to be seen here in the simple frequency of Czech using its adjectival introducer more than twice more than English (343 : 161) in 100 million words. On the other hand, the ratio of their use with idioms is almost identical in both languages. In practical terms, every third use of these adjectival introducers is bound with an idiom, roughly, this being a noticeable tendency which has to be stressed. Not surprisingly, adverbial introducers *proverbially, příslovečně* are quite marginal and unimportant in both languages. Possible candidates for a further research might be other adjectives, too, such as the Czech *pověstný* (legendary, renowned) or the English *traditional*.

There is, however, a more theoretical point to be raised here. In the case of *proverbial* and *příslovečný*, both languages have here frequent **metalinguistic** means and their use does generally belong to analysis in the sense that by mentioning them one employs a tool to point at an idiom or its part. Thus, these natural metalinguistic tools and their use should not be confused with idioms' decomposition into component parts, this being a favourite argument of those linguists who wish to show that the idiom's meaning, as well as its form, is decomposable, 'analysable'. It is not, and the very existence and use of *proverbial* and *příslovečný* does point to the contrary, since these belong to both a different level and function in the language (Čermák 2001). If these introducers are viewed as textual metalinguistic pointers, it is, then, not surprising that these are solely allowed to seemingly break the idiom's formal integrity.

Examples: (1) *This, of course, may be the* **proverbial** *'chicken and the egg situation'. Resembling the* **proverbial** *Cheshire Cat, SDR General Manager Richard Elliott commented...* (2) *We* **proverbially** *think of tossing a penny at random,* (3) *Je to handrkování o* **příslovečný** *kozí chlup., Velmi snadno ostatním ukážete* **příslovečná** *záda,* (4) *90% ledovce, které nejsou* **příslovečně** *nikdy vidět.*

2.2.2 PROVERB INTRODUCERS

Using introducers found mostly above (in 2.12), the corpora have been searched for their co-occurrence with proverbs, which is being compared with their overall frequency. Since many introducers, being of a general nature, are found very often in either BNC or CNC, only limited random samples could be used for analysis, in such cases. If proverbs have been found in the sample, their estimated number for the whole corpus has been calculated (marked by *). As a preliminary filtering of Czech introducers has already been made in an earlier paper (Čermák 1998), only those found to function prominently in the field have been used for analysis here. This explains a much larger input list of potential introducers searched, analysed and, ultimately, filtered for English here. Non-introducer functions of these forms have not been analysed, however interesting they might be.

2.2.2.1 ENGLISH PROVERB INTRODUCERS

BNC Frequency With Proverbs

you know	42,477	0
remember	18,456	0
saying	17,958	200*
principle	8,106	225*
truth	7,935	0
expression	7,226	0
they say	3,087	62*
phrase	3,044	20*
wisdom	1,542	0*
mind you	1,382	10*
it is said	566	0*

slogan	463	0
it is known	340	0
so to speak	353	0
motto	336	1
idiom	270	0
as they say	232	8
it is claimed	195	0
adage	115	44
(it is) common knowledge	102	0
proverb	99	62
catchphrase	53	0

These results both partially corroborate and modify what has been suggested in a sample of only 20 proverbs (2.121). If recalculated, the list of introducers which tend to accompany English proverbs rather often would be the following (in%):
proverb 62.6, **adage** 38.3, **as they say** 3.4, **principle** 2.8, **they say** 2, **saying** 1.1, **mind you** 0.72, and **phrase** 0.65. It is evident that it is only *proverb* and *adage* that are relevant as stable and standard introducers and the rest is only marginal, standing next to accidental and improvised coinage and use.

2.2.2.2 CZECH PROVERB INTRODUCERS

CNC Frequency With Proverbs

heslo	5,128	45*
přísloví	978	398
pořekadlo	117	40
jak známo	703	27
jak se říká	439	20

Slightly different figures from those for English have been obtained for Czech, the list including the following introducers (in%): *přísloví* (4.7), *pořekadlo* (34.,2), *jak se říká* (4.6), *jak známo* (3.8), and *heslo* (0.9). Obviously, only the first two are of any relevance as candidates for stable proverb introducers, the rest being rather marginal. It may come as a surprise that the introducer: proverb ratio is somewhat higher in English than in Czech (62.6% : 40.7%).

2.3 CLASSIFICATION OF PROVERB INTRODUCERS

Taking into account all of the introducers found in both corpora, including their textual behaviour and support by additional modifiers, an attempt may be made at classification. A number of distinctions, observed above in passing, has to be applied, such as their form/meaning, non/stableness (non/systematic character), non/standard use, etc. Here, primarily the data from the text use of the most frequent proverbs (as in 2.1.2) has been analysed.

2.3.1 FORMAL INTRODUCERS

By formal, those introducers are meant that, by the use of a specific form, signal that a proverb is being used. Obviously, formal introducers do not point to any type or shade of the proverb's meaning.

A Standard Introducers

These are set and stable standard words and phrases which accompany proverbs more often than by chance. There is evidently a problem in their being properly targeted at proverbs. Hence some competition and alternative forms may be found here. These include *adage, proverb, maxim, saying, (as) they say* and, for Czech, *přísloví (proverb), pořekadlo (saying), heslo (slogan, motto), jak se říká (as they say)*, and *jak známo (as it is known)*. Unlike in English, considerable frequency has been found for the Czech verb *platí* (it holds). There are, however, other differences to be observed here.

a-Type: As for their type, it is primarily nouns which are used here in this capacity, followed by verbal phrases. **Přísloví**, *že šaty dělají člověka, platí jenom relativně.So maybe it's true what* **they say** *about every silver lining having a cloud. Jsou lidé, pro které* **platí**, *že účel světí prostředky.*

b-Position: The introducers are both found before the proverb in text and, as a comment, after it (though sometimes inside a proverb, too). *The* **old adage** *'practice makes perfect' must be kept in mind when one begins to despair. In 1905, something happened; a silver lining on the cloud of doom. 'Forewarned is forearmed',* **as they say**, *and the defeat of the murderous invaders proved easy. Sliby jsou chyby –* **praví české přísloví**. **Říká se** *sliby – chyby*. The last two cases illustrate the same proverb being used in both positions, before and after the proverb.

B Non-standard formal Introducers

These include all sorts of other and less common words or phrases the speaker may feel appropriate to use in this function. Though there is some obvious improvisation possible here, the variety and class of formal labels to be chosen from is definitely not unlimited, cf. *rule, idea, policy, notion* or, for Czech, *zásada (principle), teze (thesis), taktika (tactics), filozofie (philosophy), potvrdit (confirm), věřit (believe)*, etc. It seems that English does not prefer verbs here to the extent that Czech does (the last two examples). Obviously, only much greater research might eventually be able to answer the question of the reasons for the choice of this or that form. The limited freedom of choice may be indicated explicitly, such as in: *He is widely credited with* **coining the phrase** *'There ain't no such thing as a free lunch'.*

a-Type: The variety of forms used here is much larger, employing, next to nouns and phrases, some other verbs, but, noticeably in the Czech case, also particles and conjunctions. *Louis Gerstner clearly* **decided** *that discretion was the better part of valour when it came to facing the blue rinse brigade.* **Ovšem** *sliby jsou chyby.*

b-Position: Also here introducers take up both positions, i.e. before and after the proverb, cf. *Nikdy ani na vteřinu* **nezapochybuje**, *že účel světí prostředky. Účel světí prostředky – praví lidová* **moudrost**... This type may show some overlap with semantic introducers, however (2.3.2).

2.3.2 Semantic Introducers

In contrast to the formal group of introducers, these are viewed from the point of their validity and attitude the speaker wishes thereby to express. Hence, it is the proverb's meaning that is brought into focus here. Mostly, but not always, this is done by using an introducer from the first group and by an additional attribute or phrase.

A Expression of Attitude
a-Standard Use:
In standard use, general validity of the proverb is meant and confirmed which is presented in a number of ways. Thus, mere acceptation of the proverb might be involved, this being, by far, the commonest and most neutral case. Alternatively, one might signal that he or she uses the proverb for standardisation of an event by fitting it under the familiar label. One might also wish to project one's esteem to the authority behind the proverb, or even try to persuade the listener about the value of the proverb, etc., cf. **They say** *two heads are better than one,* **Ne nadarmo se říká**: *Kdo hledá, najde. 'So all's well that ends well,* **to quote Shakespeare**,*' she said cheerfully.* **Husova slova** *'Pravda vítězí' kráčejí dějinami a odmítají uznávat hranice.* One might even resort to an appeal, recommendation or reminder: **Remember**: *Practice makes perfect.* **It is worth remembering** *that 'practice makes perfect',* **Nenapadá vás**, *že všude dobře doma nejlíp?* Direct confirmation is suggested by the following two cases: *This dual approach often works,* **proving** *that two heads are better than one. S jídlem roste chuť o tomto* **přísloví** *jsme se opět mohli* **přesvědčit**. Validity of the proverb may also be stressed, such as in *Whatever the truth, the NASA team* **insists** *that the Pinatubo cloud does have one silver lining.*

Rather, a special case of use is signalled if the proverb's validity is presented as being prototypical and model-like, this mediated by its use in a comparison (simile), cf. *Now she feels it's a bit* **like** *looking a gift horse in the mouth.*

b-Modified Use:
A proverb's validity may not, however, be accepted entirely and the speaker may wish to dispute or weaken it, such as in: *It won't be very good for the petrol companies,* **but** *every cloud* **tends** *to have it's silver lining; 'Better late than never' being his* **unoriginal version of the truth**.

In some cases, it may be refuted (negated) and the converse may be indicated, such as in: *Pravda* **zkrátka přestala** *vítězit* (In short, the truth ceased to prevail). **Nemohl přijmout**, *že účel světí prostředky za každou cenu.*

B Argumentation/Manipulation

Finally, using an introducer may indicate that the speaker, basically accepting the proverb's truth, uses it in a more sophisticated way to support his or her own argument, as a generally accepted reason or motive for action, or even as the very target of the speaker's action or behaviour.

a-Argument proper: **On the basis that** *'forewarned is forearmed' the fundamental principle underlying the Companies Acts has been that of disclosure. But perhaps a better title might be how to prevent things going wrong,* **on the argument** *you know that prevention is better than cure.* **Protože** *čas jsou peníze, v kapitalismu by se to stávat nemělo.*

b-Causality: **Even if** *a money cost can't be put on it, then prevention is better than cure...* *Charity begins at home, she* **concluded**...

c-Other: A goal (aim) of one's action may be seen in the Czech case *To se* **má dělat tak,** **aby** *se vlk nažral a koza zůstala celá.* (One should do it in such a way, that the wolf has eaten and the goat remained whole). Still other type of use (a circumstantial one, introducing a possibility) may be seen in **When it comes to** *women, Clint Eastwood likes to have his cake and eat it, too.*

2.3.3 MIXED INTRODUCERS (FORMAL-SEMANTIC)

Obviously, both types, the formal and semantic one, may co-exist, as it may be seen from some of the examples above. Let us consider, briefly, two more cases. **Hodí se** *na to* **české přísloví** *– jako* **třeba** *Sliby, chyby. But* **as the old saying goes**, *it's better late than never,* **and** *better* **never late!** The Czech one manages to select the proverb (*třeba* for instance), name it (*české přísloví* Czech proverb) and suggest its appropriateness (*hodí se* it suits) at the same time. The English one, suggesting formally, though not properly, that there is a proverb involved (*as the old saying goes*), employs the proverb as a basis for a further modification, stressing its validity, too (*and better never late*).

3. CONCLUSIONS

However inspiring and revealing, the results of this limited probe, presented so far, do require further research, based on more data. Nevertheless, a few more concluding remarks might be relevant.

While, on the one hand, no single introducer has been found to fulfill its role uniquely, having, thus, a monopoly on the introducing function; some of the introducers, on the other hand, do show a pronounced tendency for this.

Semantically and pragmatically, proverbs express truth (a view stated over and over again) which is general, typical and, often, accepted as normative, while being, formally, familiar to most users. What has not been investigated here and what is thus merely accepted as true is the type of situation in which proverbs are used. Most probably, this might prototypically be seen as one between two partners knowing each other, where there is the distinction of older-younger and experienced-less experienced to be observed. The use of introducers seems to confirm this. Since speakers ideally belong to the older and more experienced of the two, introducers and proverbs are used by them. Accordingly, the prevalent use of both proverbs and their introducers should be in direct speech, while no such conclusion is true of collocational idioms. Yet in practice, the distinction between direct and indirect speech is rather blurred and it is often difficult to distinguish between them.

Though different in their frequency and variety of forms found, there seems to be no basic difference in meaning and function between introducers used with the collocation and proverb idioms.

Functionally, proverbs might be viewed as belonging, primarily, to two major classes, the factual one (committing the speaker to the truth) and voluntative or directive one (aiming at producing some effect on the listener, see Čermák 2000). Hence, it is in the semantic types of introducers where one might discern this, but no specific indication of this has been made here.

Next to the obvious metalinguistic function of the introducers (see 1., 2.21), elements of the phatic communicative function (or communion, following Malinowski and Jakobson) can be found with some introducers, too. Thus, using such introducers as *as they say* obviously establishes a desirable atmosphere or maintains social contact, which is what the phatic function is about.

There is a number of minor differences between both languages, observed above, some of which (as the Czech tendency to use verbs for the introducers) might be attributed to the different typological status of these languages.

To sum up the results from both the search of proverbs and introducers, each having been used as a different starting point, an ordered synopsis of both types may be presented for proverbs (**x** standing for a marked difference and : for a similarity).

Proverb → Introducer Introducer → Proverb

    (Frequency in Nos)   (Frequency in %)

1	saying	7	x	1.1	**-5**
2	principle	4	x	2.8	**-4**
3-7	phrase	2			
	adage	2	x	38.3	**-2**
	axiom	2			
	maxim	2			
	(as) they say	5		5.4	**-3**
8-9	cliché	1			

it is said	1			
proverb	0	x	62.6	-1
1 heslo	30	x	0.9	**-5**
2 přísloví	17		40.7	**-1**
3 zásada	13			
4 platí	13			
5 říká se	8			
6 rčení	5			
7 jak se říká	3	:	4.6	**-3**
8 úsloví	3			
9 jak známo	2	:	3.8	**-4**
10 pořekadlo	2	x	34.2	**-2**

LITERATURE

ČERMÁK, František. 1998. "Usage of Proverbs: What the Czech National Corpus Shows." In *Europhras '97*, edited by P. Ďurčo, 37–59. Bratislava: Akadémia PZ.

ČERMÁK, František. 2001. "Substance of Idioms: Perennial problems, Lack of data or Theory?" *Internatuional Journal of Lexicography* 14 (1): 1–20.

ČERMÁK, František. 2003. "Paremiological Minimum of Czech: The Corpus Evidence". In *Flut von texten – Vielvalt der Kulturen. Ascona 2001 zur Methodologie und Kulturspezifik der Phrazeologie*, edited by H. Burger, A. Häcki-Buhofer, G. Greciano, 15–31. Hohengehren: Schneider Verlag.

ČERMÁK, František. 2004. "Propositional Idioms". In *Europhras 2000*, edited by Ch. Palm-Meister, 15–31. Tübingen: Stanffenberg Verlag.

ĎURČO Peter. 2002. Parömiologische Konnektoren *oder* 'Wie der Volksmund so schön sagt'. In *Phraseologie in Raum und Zeit*, edited by E. Piirainen and I. P. Piirainen, 203–212. Hohengehren: Schneider Verlag.

FERGUSSON, Rosalind. 1983. *The Penguin Dictionary of Proverbs*. Harmondsworth: Penguin Books.

MOON, Rosamund. 1998. *Fixed Expressions and Idioms in English. A Corpus-Based Approach*. Oxford: Clarendon Press.

SEARLE, John R. 1979. *Expression and Meaning: Studies in the Theory of Speech Acts*. Cambridge: Cambridge University Press.

SINCLAIR, John, FOX, Gwyneth, and MOON, Rosamund, eds. 1995. *Collins Cobuild Dictionary of Idioms*. London: Harper-Collins.

WHITING, Bartlett Jere. 1989. *Modern Proverbs and Proverbial Sayings*. Cambridge, Mass.: Harvard University Press.

7. Usage of Proverbs in Today's Czech language: What Czech National Corpus Seems to Suggest

In *Europhras '97 Proceedings*, 1998, 37–59, **Čermák Proverbs 2014**, 111–132

Abstract

An analysis of the corpus shows that proverbs are used in several ways, mostly in a prototypical way, but also in a nonprototypical way. Examples of both, split into minor subtypes, amply illustrated by contextual use are offered below. At the same time, a common core of use can be outlined. It has been established that, due to a lot of repetition, the corpus may be related to many lexical forms, namely: 1 proverb : 80,986 word forms.

1. Introduction: Paremiological Minimum of Czech and Corpus Evidence

Since 1993, there is a paremiological minimum for the Czech language available, containing 99 proverbs, based on well-founded research. By his *Das Sprichwort im heutigen Tschechischen. Empirische Untersuchung und semantische Beschreibung* (O. Sagner München) and other contributions, its author, Franz Schindler, has made the results of his extensive questionnaire-based demographic research public in a book form. The obvious question, then, is how do his results, oriented at finding out the real **knowledge** of proverbs, compare with the actual **usage** of proverbs.

To be able to do this and also to gain some more general insights into the usage, a step that has not been possible until recently, it was decided to use the interim material of *The Czech National Corpus*, which is being built up at the Institute of the Czech National Corpus, Faculty of Philosophy, Charles University in Prague (which, in part, is also publicly accessible via the Internet at the address *http://ucnk.ff.cuni.cz/cnc*). Although its present state is far from being balanced and representative, some 23 million text words which it had at the time of the analysis (spring 1997) are far more than anything else that has ever been available; most of the texts are taken from recent volumes of nation-wide journals and non-specialized magazines with some books of modern fiction as they were available at the time. Despite the preliminary character of the findings presented here, I hope to be able to use these as a strong and well-supported indication of some recent tendencies of proverbial usage, at least; in the span of a few years, the data, when made more representative and numerous, will be able to bring the necessary corrective, too; a new and revised list of proverbs found in the Czech National Corpus (further *Corpus*) can be offered then.

As there is as yet no discovery procedure or even software programme available enabling one to find proverbs in a corpus, whether it is annotated or not, it has been decided to use what offered itself, i.e. Schindler's List representing a proposed *Proverb Minimum of Czech*. The starting point has been to find out if Schindler's List (of proverbs) is, in fact, represented in the Corpus, and if it is, what is the extent and quality of this representation. There have been some surprises, indeed. For instance, out of the total of his 99 proverbs, there are 16 that seem not to be contained in the Corpus at all. There have been other differences found, too, such as in form, but to deal with them here would go beyond the scope of the proposed goal of this paper.

For those proverbs that have been found to be represented, i.e. some 83% of Schindler's proverbs, all of their contexts and variants have been extracted and analysed. This contribution deals with some points of the structural and formal analysis of the proverbs found but its main preoccupation is with **types of meaning and function** that these proverbs seem to have today.

Let us start with some general preliminaries. It may be of some interest to query first what the real frequency of proverbs in *The Czech National Corpus* is at present. The figure is rather unique in that it has not been available for any language, so far: in total, there are some 284 proverb occurrences in over 23 million words, which gives the **frequency of 1 proverb per more than 80,000 words,** shedding some light onto the hitherto general and vague statement saying that proverbs are rarely used. There are undoubtedly other proverbs in the corpus that Schindler's List does not have, but their overall frequency may not be very high; hence, the real figure does not have to be very far from that which has been found.

Sociologically, any usage research should take into account the ratio of two basic factors, that of production and reception (Biber 1988). In our case, this is to be seen as the relation of a few (authors, producers) to very many (receivers, presumably as general as possible); or, more precisely, as the intention of the few to address as broad a public as possible. This is, however, not to be identified with the representative sample, however small, which has been used for Schindler's questionnaire techniques. How to match both sets of results is still very much an open question; yet a working presumption and hypothesis may be made that these are roughly comparable somehow, and that, since the producers of the Corpus texts are, generally, well-educated, the proverbial production here might be even somewhat broader than the sociological average would be. To sum up, in contrast to Schindler's results, listing 99 proverbs as the paremiological minimum for the Czech language, which was knowledge-oriented (and of the reception type), the results based on the corpus, which are frequency-oriented (and more of the production type), are somewhat different and due to the enormous size of data, also more reliable, in a sense.

2. Usage of Proverbs in the Corpus

Semiotically, there is no denying that proverbs, if used prototypically in text, always denote a **generalized situation** which is of a somewhat **categorial** and more abstract character than the situation in the text, i.e. set-up of denotata, to which it is related. This is to be seen in a simple newspaper example, such as the following:

(1) *Dvojí projednávání zákona, byť v politicky identických sborech, by mohlo naplňovat poža-*
davek rčení **'Dvakrát měř, jednou řež'**, (*A double discussion of the bill, though in the poli-*
tically identical bodies, could meet the demand of the saying **'Look twice before you leap'**).

where the proverb, being called here 'saying (*rčení*)', is not actually recognized by the writer as a proverb but its categorial value is; it is called '*the demand (požadavek)*' here. The linguistic situation naming a legislative act introduced here is recognized by the author as having recurrent features resembling very many other similar situations that can and have been usually summarized by the proverb; this is why it is followed by a proverb, too.

Now, the kind of problems here which are not **semiotically** recognized in any unanimous way, is what is exactly the relation between the simple **mentioning of the situation** (i.e. the legislative act) and **the proverb** itself. Is it a simple relation or a complex one? Are all the proverbs, if used prototypically, of the same kind or are there more semiotic types? In trying to discern some possibilities which might seem to be looming here one might point, for instance, to an obvious difference between the kind of proverb just mentioned, which is in the imperative form, and one which is in the indicative form, such as, for instance

(2)*...to bylo ekologické sdružení, jež místo rozumných argumentů volilo útok na emoce. Víte,*
my jsme podobnou kampaň dělali poprvé a **tonoucí se stébla chytá**. (...*it was the ecological*
association which instead of reasonable arguments has chosen an attack at emotions. You see,
it was for the first time that we prepared such a campaign and **a drowning man clutches**
at a straw).

Given the alleged instructional or normative quality of the proverb, it is obvious that the former type represents a more direct appeal to the reader than the latter, which means that the latter, next to the appeal component, also contains some other features that veil the urgency of the former and make it sound more general at the same time.

Is there a real **difference in generality** involved in both types, too? If there is, how can we determine it? These are some of the questions that are rarely asked, let alone answered. Admittedly, the current semiotic theories do not offer very much here by way of both criteria and classifications, i.e. in the sphere of sentential types of signs. In fact, it seems that proverbs may not be recognized unanimously by all theoreticians as standard language nominations which, despite these doubts, is the position I would like to take in my present remarks on proverbs. Hence I view proverbs to be both a special type of fixed nominations, i.e. on a par with other types of idioms, and having, at the same time, a kind of function which is different from the rest of idioms.

In Jakobsonian terms, proverbs are provided, generally, with the obvious **directive function** (**connative** or **Appel** in Bühler's terminology) which is mixed with some degree of the **expressive function**. In other words, the speaker or writer wants to direct or positively influence his or her listener or reader. Should we delve a bit further into these rather general terms, which is not a particularly frequent case, we must ask the same type of questions as before: is the force of directive as well as expressive function the same in both proverbs? Obviously not, but here, once again, we are up against a lack of criteria enabling us to distinguish the difference in degree and in quality, too. I am afraid that reframing this problem by the terms of the speech acts is not of much help, either: proverbs seem to be notorious **perlocutionary acts** (with no performative role to play, obviously) which are of a **directive type** (here, also Searle's and Austin's term coincides with that of Jakobson) and that's it; this kind of statement is so general that it does not really say much. What might, perhaps, be more revealing is, given the **conversational implicature** of cooperation between the author and the user, to investify the type of **felicity conditions** present when a proverb is used. Clearly, there must be a different motivation and choice of a proverb depending on the varying degree of the user's or addressee's respect or esteem towards the author or producer of the proverb.

Things being the way they are, what should the procedure analyzing proverbs be? Obviously, there are two primary points to be clarified, namely:

(1) **not all** proverbs or what is formally viewed as proverbs are used **prototypically**, i.e. as proverbs,
(2) the almost stable and constant qualification of proverbs as expressing **generality** must be questioned and some sort of a further split-up of this monolithic quality should be attempted.

As an additional minor problem, such points deserve to be raised as the validity of Permjakov's view of the proverb as a **sign of situation** (1979, 306), whatever that might mean semiotically (extra-linguistic reality and/or a model, etc?); this is not made particularly clearer by Grzybek's reinterpretation as 'interaction situation' (1995, 4) since that would suggest some kind of exchange of (extralinguistic) actions. If one does not choose to be counter-intuitive in using one's terms (which is what Permjakov does), it is difficult to see what proverbs are really used for as names for situations. On the contrary, the proverb is very often a name for a dynamic extralinguistic complex, made up of several acts or phases, for an event, incident etc., i.e. of a complex and changing set of denotata (with their referents being stable neither in identity nor in number, sometimes). Or the proverb may denote even a more complex human doing that is, perhaps, best termed in literature as a story, which is either viewed in its progress or as being concluded, often with some sort of **result calling for proverbial comment by someone else**. To put it bluntly, a story cannot be fitted into a single situation only.

Clearly, generally accepted terms are not available, but I do not want to go into any semantic classification of this field, which for all sorts of reasons I believe is impossible; what I merely wish to do is to make the point that the basically static term **situation** is far from being well-chosen and it is misleading to adhere to it.

2.1 NON-PROTOTYPICAL USAGE OF PROVERBS

Let us return to the two basic questions raised above. An analysis of the contextual use of 265 occurrences of the proverbs in question found in the whole corpus has been undertaken using very large concordances, usually far beyond the boundary of a single sentence; out of the total of 284 occurrences 19 occurrences of a far from simple case of *sůl nad zlato 'the salt is above gold'*, with a multiple overlapping with other expressions, had to be excluded (although they were used for other counts wherever it was possible).

It is rather significant to note that almost 17 percent (48) of cases are those belonging to **non-prototypical use**, where the proverbs found do not function as proverbs. These are made up of two types. One consists of the:

A(a) use of proverbs as **titles**, **captions**, **headings** (including subtitles) of various pieces of the text itself (there are 6 articles using a proverb as a heading) or, in the other case, they are:
A(b) used in giving **names for films** (4 cases), TV programmes (6, mostly films, too, presumably).

There is also one specimen of the use where a **book** is called this way and also an **opera**. As far as films are concerned, their proverb names were usually found next to other, more standard film names in lists of film programmes given for the city for a particular period of time. Altogether, there were 20 occurrences of this **title-function** found.

The second group of non-prototypical use of proverbs consists of their being made:

B topic of various types of quiz

The general type of such **quiz** would be to list a small number of proverbs and introduce it by some such question as 'What is your creed in interpersonal relations?' or, rather, more simply, such as giving a list of a small number of proverbs introduced by an appeal to the reader of the type 'Which of the following proverbs do you like?'. In some cases, the readers were asked whether they believed in the given proverb being true (such as *Láska prochází žaludkem* lit. 'Love goes through one's stomach') with some alternatives given, such as being true in general, true for men only, etc. But there were also more sophisticated ways, such as confronting the reader with the Latin proverb *Carpe diem* and several potential Czech proverbial equivalents from which he or she was supposed to choose one, a formidable task nowadays with Latin being so poorly understood. Altogether, there were almost 10 percent (9.86%, 28 cases) of this **quiz--function** recorded in the corpus.

One may just wonder about a third potential type of this kind of usage, namely in **advertisements;** there have not been any, however, which may raise one's curiosity. Perhaps, a still larger and more versatile material will be needed to offer some kind of result here, too.

2.2 PROTOTYPICAL USAGE OF PROVERBSAS GENERAL STATEMENTS: TWO MARGINS

It is not surprising that some 83% (83.1%) of all the uses attested and studied belong to what might be called **protypical usage**, i.e. instances where proverbs do function as proverbs in the text as one expects them to. In trying to offer some kind of solution to the second question above (2), i.e. what types of generality (general-experience type) one can find here, some preliminaries have to be mentioned first. These include two special types of the general usage.

A part of this **general-experience type of the proverbial usage** is special in its being either in a **different position** in the text or in its use as a **direct quotation**. Out of all the uses of proverbs examined (265), over 8 percent (8.3%, i.e. 22 uses) are found in the **anteposition**, i.e. as expressions introducing the actual explanation of the action, scene or situation which follows it and which is, as a rule, presented either as a specimen (one of many) or illustration of the general truth stated before, or as a special type of entailment of what has been generally implied before. As, for example, in

(3) *Neštěstí nechodí po horách, ale po lidech*. *Kanadská krasobruslařka Jaqueline Petrová při tréninku nešťastně upadla...* (**It never rains but it pours.** [lit. Misfortune never visits mountains, but people]. During her training, the Canadian skater Jaqueline Petr has fallen down so unfortunately...).

The standard and fully prototypical use of proverbs is characteristically and typically one where the proverb is found at the end of the relevant piece of text, 'summing up', as it were, what has preceded it (**postposition**). Here, however, in clear contrast to this, this usual order is reversed and the proverb precedes everything else. In fact, it is sometimes quite difficult to distinguish this case from what has been called the title-function above. This, in turn, leads to the crucial question of the degree or quality of generality, general value of such proverb in this position. Is it really the same as that of the proverb found in its typical 'postposition', i.e. in reference to its relevant (antepositional) piece of text? And if there is a difference, how can it be measured or verified? In fact, examples like that, or the next one, prompt one to ask yet another question. Let us have an illustration of this first:

(4) *...zahraničních studentů. Ti byli vždy předmětem živého zájmu tajné policie. Někteří pod-*
lehli, jiní ne a další podepsali třeba proto, aby jim povolili sňatek. Pak **sešli s očí i z mysli.**
('...foreign students. These have always been subject of a keen interest of the secret
police. Some have succumbed, some have not and others have signed perhaps because
they wanted that their marriage be permitted. Then **they went both out of sight and
mind**, too').

The question to be asked is then this:
is there any basic difference in the generality of value between any other text nomina-
tion (there are several of them in the example above), especially if these are to be found
in a series or chain of names following one another, and the proverb that behaves here
just like any other idiom?

As it is used to name a specific phase in the sequence of events, it is hard to see any
special general quality about it. Does this possible weakening or loss of the general
validity of the proverb have to do with its position, with its being in a series of other
nominations or with something else? This is yet another doubt and potential limitation
of the true value of the proverbial usage, once the proverb is not strictly part of the
prototypical use.

The second special type of general usage of the proverb is its **quotation use** which
borders on the title-function and the quiz-function of the proverb referred to above.
Without going into details, if any piece of text, including a proverb, is used in a strictly
quotational manner (i.e. accompanied by inverted commas, colon, etc.), it introduces
a piece of a different, second text into the present one which amounts to mixing two
texts together. And that is not exactly the same as the proverb being incorporated into
a text as its integral part. One of the integrating devices for this standard use of proverbs is often found in the employment of special introductory phrases (**introducers**)
which I shall take up presently. But this does not solve the problem mentioned, which
is left, largely, open.

2.3 PROTOTYPICAL USE OF PROVERBS AS GENERAL STATEMENTS: THE CORE

Let us take up again the proverb in the example No (2) illustrating its most prototypical
use, i.e. that of a statement concluding description of happened or someone else dis
and adding a reminder of the generally accepted truth:

(2)...*to bylo ekologické sdružení, jež místo rozumných argumentů volilo útok na emoce. 'Víte,*
my jsme podobnou kampaň dělali poprvé a **tonoucí se stébla chytá.**' (*...it was the ecological*
association which instead of reasonable arguments has chosen an attact at emotions. 'You see,
it was for the first time that we prepared such a campaign and **a drowning man clutches
at a straw**').

If we compare this proverb with a few of other ones, some other typical uses of proverbs in their protypical function are revealed:

(5) *Říkali jsme si: když s námi nejednají férově,* **na hrubý pytel patří hrubá záplata.** (*We said to each other: if they are not fair to us,* **rudeness is met with rudeness**.)

In (5), a type of argumentation may be observed where the proverb *Na hrubý pytel hrubá záplata* is used to explain the reason for the action (not mentioned in the context), without losing the general value and truth of the proverb. In fact, the proverb, which stands in a sort of causal relation to its antecedent (where the commentor and the doer are, basically, identical), is the source of the wisdom here and justification of whatever followed (= **argumentation use** including motivation or even goal, etc.). On a closer look, however, it is also possible to see the example (2) as belonging here, since it is, in fact, very difficult to distinguish semantically a mere generalized comment use from the argumentation use, despite the basic difference in the identity of the doer and commentor (as in 2) and its absence (as in 5). Hence, in the following, no attempt to distinguish these two will be made and the argumentation type will be viewed as a subtype of the prototypical generalization (general statement) function.

(6) *Vlkodlak žije sedm let, ale když se mu spálí lidský oděv, je odsouzen k vlčímu bytí na zbytek života, takže babky ve zdejším kraji se domnívají, že pomůže hodit na vlkodlaka klobouk nebo zástěru,* **jako by šaty dělaly člověka.** (*Werewolf lives seven years, but if you burn its human clothes down, it is condemned to live as a wolf for the rest of its life and this is why old wives of this region believe that it is a help if you throw a hat or an apron over the werewolf* **as if clothes make a man.**)

Let us note that in (6), there is, by the use of the proverb, a considerable doubt cast upon the wisdom and value of both the act described and the proverb itself (= **adversative use**). In fact, this kind of refusal, weakening or the speaker's distancing himself from the proverb's validity is not exactly peripheral and it might, in itself, constitute an interesting line of research to pursue, checking the age of proverbs against the time of their use. Note also, that this **distancing function** of the proverb is mediated by the use of a compound conjunction *as if* (*jako by*).

(7) *Jsem přesvědčena, že kdo vysílá dobro, tak se mu dobro vrací. Kdo vysílá zlo, tak se mu vrací taky. A pak také existuje známé přísloví* **Pro dobrotu na žebrotu.** (*I am convinced that he who sends out the good also receives some good. But then there is also the well-known proverb* –**Too much goodness makes one a beggar**).

The last case (7) is different from the preceding one (6) in that it is the ambivalence of the action which is taken up here, and the wisdom of it is being contrasted with the wisdom of the proverb used. Thus, it is not the truth of the proverb that is contested here, but of the action alone. In other words, the speaker suggests that the solution taken here is not the only and best one and a different approach may be imagined, too (= **contrastive use**).

This type of **prototypical use** (whose core is, strictly speaking, represented by No (2) only) is attested in some 70% (70.1%) of the attested proverb occurrences altogether (186 cases, with some overlapping) which clearly demonstrates that the previous generally intuitive presumptions, often mentioned by various scholars, basically correspond to the real usage, but not quite.

A full breakdown of the total figure in subclasses observed offers the following survey:

Generalization Type Use: 70.1% of the total (186)
a-**Contrast use**: 4.8% in this type only (9)
b-**Adversative use**: 2.2% in this type only (4)
c-**Argumentation use**: 12.9% in this type only (24)

Some additional remarks are due here, introducing some other minor points or those that have not been, for various reasons, further analysed. Within the generalization type of usage, some 22 **direct quotations of proverbs**, used in a typical quotation manner and situation, have been singled out. Problems of their boundary have been mentioned above.

Another **formal** aspect, having its semantic and functional side, i.e. various **transformations** of the proverbs, has been left unattended here (see 3). Out of the total of 15 transformations of various types (5.6% of all the proverbs) most tend to have a **nominal character**. For the sake of brevity, these have been functionally treated as retaining their generality type of use, even though it may not, on a closer look, be always so.

Finally, the role of the **question form** a proverb might take should be raised. Against the prevailing Indicative and Imperative Mood used for the proverbs if employed in text, a mere 3 occurrences of proverbs in the question form (1.1%) might seem very marginal, indeed. Yet the very possibility that this form may occur is of consequence. With more data available, relations and affinities to the adversative or contrast type of use could be studied, taking into account the auxiliary presence of the Conditional Mood and so on.

3. FORMAL ASPECTS OF PROVERBS REPRESENTED IN THE CORPUS

Let us briefly sum up some of the most salient aspects of the proverb usage in the corpus analyzed. First, a summary of the generalized representation. Out of the 284 proverb occurrences, 1,012 word forms belong to the proverb having their frequency higher than 2, while 322 word forms belong to those with the frequency of 2 or 1 which amounts to a tendency that some words are inclined to be repeated. Together, over 12-hundred word forms (1,324) make the total span of proverb 'texts' found in the Corpus. Since the average length of a proverb is 4–6 word forms (= 1,324 : 284), it is evident, then, that the proverb use is rather rare, being expressed by the correlation

1 proverb : 80 986 word forms

Some 19% of the proverbs used (18.9%) belong to the no verb type, i.e. belonging to a purely nominal or mixed type with some other parts of speech, excluding the verb. It might be of some interest to correlate this with their type of dominant function, however. As far as clause distribution is concerned, 56.75% of the proverbs have been found to form a single clause while the rest, almost a half, belongs to a two-clause type, out of which the subordinating subtype is used slightly more (27%, i.e. 10 proverbs), the coordinating being less (16.2 = , i.e. 6).

If we try to distinguish variation and transformation (which is frequently confused with each other in various approaches), some interesting figures shed light on both the stability of the proverbs and a potential for a creative use of them. More than one quarter of the proverbs used (27.7 = , i.e. 78) have been found to vary and differ from the canonical form found in Schindler's minimum list. Out of this, generally, syntagmatic variation of more than one type has been found to be slightly more prominent than paradigmatic one (46 : 32). All of the variants have been considered special instances of their canonical forms. The transformatins of the proverbs, which in contrast to variants have a different text function, i.e. with the alteration performed upon them being much more profound and innovative, come up in 5.6% (15).

Finally, a brief note should be made about the **introducers**, mentioned above, i.e. text expressions that the writer uses to introduce the proverb, signalling thus its introduction in the text and function. A partial analysis has shown some interesting facts here, and a more detailed analysis is definitely required.

Almost half of the proverbs have some sort of introductory expression preceding them, spanning from a single word to a clause (47.5%, i.e. 135 occurrences). Another surprising fact is that there is obviously no tendency to use any standard way to introduce proverbs in a text, as there is only a very low and varied repetition found of some expressions only (whose total is 114). On the other hand, there are other tendencies that have been observed here, too. There is, clearly, both in the category of verbs and nouns (to simplify the picture somewhat):

(A) a tendency to use specialized words for naming the linguistic **form** of the proverb,
(B) a complementary tendency to signal, on the other hand, rather the proverb **content or function**.

This is best illustrated by a different choice of nouns for (A) and (B). In the first case, the most appropriate word, i.e. *přísloví* (proverb), has been used 28 times to introduce the proverb itself, followed, however, by other expressions, too, such as *heslo* (slogan,

11×), *pořekadlo* (saying, 5×), and so on. In the second case (B), however, quite different nouns have been found, although with a much lower frequency of repetition, such as *zásada* (principle, 4×), *pravda* (truth, 3×), *pravidlo* (rule), *idea,*and so on. Even these few findings raise a number of questions and topics for further research, such as the kind of textual need to use these introducers, the (non)obviousness of the proverbs which may be related to the degree of their familiarity, strengthening or weakening of the proverbs' force and function by their use and the like. The reason for the choice of either (A) or (B) is, however, not quite clear.

4. CONCLUDING REMARKS

To sum up briefly. The present research into a really large-scale usage has both shown some hitherto new insights and a necessity, apparent from numerous questions raised here, to expand it and follow up various aspects in more detail. Leaving out subtypes dealt with above and one special case, the overall summary of the proverb types found and examined is the following:

Prototypical Generalization Type of Use: 70.1% of the total (186)
Non-Prototypical Type of Use: 18.1% (48)
Anteposition Type of Use: 8.3% (22)
Transformation Type of Use: 5.5% (15)

With this approach being a linguistic one primarily, many of the proverb aspects could hardly be tackled because they seemingly do not belong here, though some could, such as those that might, at least partly, be viewed as linguistic, too. This contrasts with the current practice of the field, strongly emphasized by Permjakov and others, that semiotical aspects are different from linguistic ones. Well, they are not, at least not in many points. It is, in fact, not difficult to translate many of the above results into semiotical terms; these are, however, often rather vague or absent, and the wisdom of such an undertaking is dubious. There is, definitely, a sort of correlation to be established between semiotic types of functions, if any, and the linguistic difference of the postpositive and antepositive use, between prototypical and non-prototypical use and the like. A point seldom raised is the expected semiotic difference between a proverb from a system point of view (which has been the predominant approach, so far) and from the point of view of text where all sorts of changes in the function and class memberships take place. This approach is, basically, the same as the one used in lexicology where the distinction **type – token** has been used, with all of its implications, for a long time. The proverb is, after all, a sort of **lexeme**, too.

To be able to say, finally, more about what has been repeatedly stressed but never really done, namely about a formal analysis of the **type of situation** where the proverb is used (e.g., Mieder 1955), one must, as yet, develop exact methodologies for this. Here again, although text contexts for such an analysis must be much larger than those used for the present study, a corpus is indispensable.

APPENDIX

A Frequency List of Proverbs Based on Czech National Corpus

Note: lit. = litteral translation, cf. = non-cognate proverb, = cognate proverb

1. Pozdě bycha honit. 11×
   cf. It is late to shut the stable door after the mare is gone.
2. Lepší vrabec v hrsti než holub na střeše. 11×
   = A bird in hand is worth two in the bush.
3. Není šprochu, aby na něm nebylo pravdy trochu. 11×
   cf. There is no smoke without a fire.
4. Vlk se nažral a koza zůstala celá. 10×
   lit. The wolf has eaten and the goat remained whole.
5. Boží mlýny melou pomalu, ale jistě. 9×
   = The mills of God grind slowly, but they grind small.
6. Pod svícnem bývá tma. 9×
   cf. There are often low goings-on in high places.
7. Ráno moudřejší večera. 7×
   = Morning brings counsel.
8. Bližší košile než kabát. 6×
   = Nearest my coat, but nearer my skin (shirt).
9. Kdo jinému jámu kopá, sám do ní padá. 6×
   cf. He that mischief hatches, mischief catches.
10. Kdo chce psa bít, hůl si najde. 6×
    = Any stick is good enough to beat the dog.
11. Láska prochází žaludkem. 6×
    cf. The way to a man's heart is his stomach.
12. Není všechno zlato, co se třpytí. 6×
    = All that glitters is not gold.
13. Podej někomu prst a chce celou ruku. 6×
    cf. Give him an inch and he will take a mile.
14. Šaty dělají člověka. 6×
    cf. Fine feather make fine birds.
15. Zakázané ovoce nejvíc chutná. 6×
    = Forbidden fruit tastes best.
16. Dvakrát měř, jednou řež. 5×
    cf. Look twice before you leap.

17 Kdo chce kam, pomozme mu tam. 5×
lit. Let us help him who wants [to get] somewhere.

18 Moudřejší ustoupí. 5×
cf. Discretion is better part of valour.

19 Padla kosa na kámen. 5×
cf. Diamond cut diamond, He has met his equal.

20 Z cizího krev neteče. 5×
cf. Yours is not mine.

21 Žádný učený z nebe nespadl. 5×
cf. If at first you don't succeed, try, try and try again.

22 I mistr tesař se utne. 4×
cf. Homer sometimes nods.

23 Kdo nic nedělá, nic nezkazí. 4×
lit. He who does nothing, spoils nothing.

24 Navrch huj, vespod fuj. 4×
* Pretty face and foul inside.

25 Pro dobrotu na žebrotu. 4×
= One's kindness of heart makes one beggar.

26 Sejde z očí, sejde z mysli. 4×
= Out of sight, out of mind.

27 Stará láska nerezaví. 4×
* Old love doesn't rust.

28 Žádná kaše se nejí tak horká, jak se uvaří. 4×
cf. Things are never as black as they look

29 Bez práce nejsou koláče. 3×
cf. No work, no reward.

30 Čí chleba jíš, toho píseň zpívej. 3×
cf. Don't quarrel with your bread.

31 Jablko nepadne daleko od stromu. 3×
cf. Like father, like son, He is a chip off the old block.

32 Kdo hledá, najde. 3×
= Search and you shall find.

33 Kdo s čím zachází, tím také schází. 3×
cf. What a man takes over a job, the job takes over the man.

34 Komu není rady, tomu není pomoci. 3×
lit. He who won't take an advice, cannot be helped.

35 Láska hory přenáší. 3×
cf. Love will find a way.

36 Na hrubý pytel hrubá záplata. 3×
lit. On a rough sack, a rough lap belongs, Rudeness is met with rudeness.

37 Tonoucí se stébla chytá. 3×
lit. Drowning man clutches at a straw.

Note: Proverbs with Frequency 2–1 are not included. However, they can be found from the comparative lists in B. Forms of the Proverbs given here are the canonical ones, i.e. without sometimes numerous variants.

B Paremiological Minimum of Czech (Schindler's List) **versus CNC Frequency List**

A 100–95% knowledge: No of Occurrences:

1   Bez práce nejsou koláče. 3
2   Jak si usteleš, tak si lehneš. 2
3   Pro dobrotu na žebrotu. 4
4   Co Čech, to muzikant. 2
5   Jak se do lesa volá, tak se z lesa ozývá. 1
6   Komu se nelení, tomu se zelení. 2
7   Komu není rady, tomu není pomoci. 3
8   Práce kvapná, málo platná. 1
9   Láska hory přenáší. 3
10 Všude dobře, doma nejlíp. –
11 Pozdě bycha honit. 11
12 Lehce nabyl, lehce pozbyl. 1
13 Padla kosa na kámen. 5
14 Stará láska nerezaví. 4
15 Dvakrát měř, jednou řež. 5
16 Ranní ptáče dál doskáče. 1
17 S poctivostí nejdál dojdeš. 1
18 Co se v mládí naučíš, ve stáří jako když najdeš. 1
19 Kdo šetří, má za tři. 1
20 Pro jedno kvítí slunce nesvítí. –
21 Jablko nepadne daleko od stromu. 3
22 Není všechno zlato, co se třpytí. 6
23 Kdo dřív přijde, ten dřív mele. 2
24 Kdo chce kam, pomozme mu tam. 5
25 Sejde s očí, sejde s mysli. 4
26 Jak k jídlu, tak k dílu. –
27 Dočkej času jako husa klasu. 1
28 Co na srdci, to na jazyku. 2
29 Kdo jinému jámu kopá, sám do ní padá. 6
30 Vrána k vráně sedá. 1
31 Co se doma uvaří, to se doma sní. 2
32 Neříkej hop, dokud nepřeskočíš. –
33 Kdo se směje naposled, ten se směje nejlíp. 1
34 Ani kuře zadarmo nehrabe. –

35 Lež má krátké nohy. 2
36 Nové koště dobře mete. 2
37 Šaty dělají člověka. 6
38 Tichá voda břehy mele. 1
39 Každý chvilku tahá pilku. –
40 Práce šlechtí člověka. –
41 Co jest šeptem, to je čertem. –
42 Bez peněz do hospody nelez. 1
43 I mistr tesař se utne. 4
44 Kdo lže, ten krade. 2
45 Když ptáčka lapají, pěkně mu zpívají. 2
46 Láska prochází žaludkem. 6
47 Nechval dne před večerem. 1
48 Žádný učený z nebe nespadl. 5
49 Kdo maže, ten jede. 1
50 Odvážnému štěstí přeje. –
51 Kuj železo, dokud je žhavé. 2
52 Kdo se bojí, nesmí do lesa. 1
53 Dobrá hospodyňka pro pírko přes plot skočí. –
54 Boží mlýny melou pomalu, ale jistě. 9
55 Kdo nic nedělá, nic nezkazí. 4
56 Dej a bude ti dáno. 1
57 Čert nikdy nespí. 1
58 Darovanému koni na zuby nekoukej. 1
59 Nehas, co tě nepálí. 2
60 Neštěstí nechodí po horách, ale po lidech. 2
61 Čistota půl zdraví. 1
62 Kdo pozdě chodí, sám sobě škodí. –
63 Jeden za osmnáct, druhý bez dvou za dvacet. –
64 Na hrubý pytel, hrubá záplata. 3
65 Líná huba, holé neštěstí. –
66 Zakázané ovoce nejvíc chutná. 6
67 Kdo hledá, najde. 3
68 Každý svého štěstí strůjcem. 2
69 Jak ty mně, tak já tobě. 2

B Knowledge under 95%:

70 Dvěma pánům nelze sloužit. 78.5% 1
71 Kam nechodí slunce, tam chodí lékař. 87.75% 2
72 Mluviti stříbro, mlčeti zlato. 91.2% 1
73 Stromek se musí ohýbat, dokud je mladý. 91.5% 1
74 Ráno moudřejší večera. 90.0% 7

75 Pes, který štěká, nekouše. 91.5% 2
76 Moudřejší ustoupí. 92.4% 5
77 Sůl nad zlato. 93.6% 19
78 Čí chleba jíš, toho píseň zpívej. 92.1% 3
79 Bližší košile než kabát. 92.1% 6
80 Sytý hladovému nevěří. 90.2% 2
81 Tonoucí se stébla chytá. 93.0% 3
82 Kdo s čím zachází, tím také schází. 93.4% 3
83 Kdo chce psa bít, hůl si najde. 90.4% 6
84 Není šprochu, aby na něm nebylo pravdy trochu. 92.4% 11
85 Kam čert nemůže, nastrčí bábu. 92.4% 1
86 Vlk se nažral a koza zůstala celá. 94.0% 10
87 Dlouhé vlasy, krátký rozum. 94.9% –
88 Kam vítr, tam plášť. 93.7% 1
89 Lepší vrabec v hrsti, než holub na střeše. 92.7% 11
90 Mráz kopřivu nespálí. 94.9% 1
91 Pod svícnem bývá tma. 94.6% 9
92 Všude je chleba o dvou kůrkách. 94.9% 1
93 Žádná kaše se nejí tak horká, jak se uvaří. 94.6% 4
94 Z cizího krev neteče. 93.6% 5
95 Navrch huj, vespod fuj. 93.7% 4
96 Co se vleče, neuteče. 92.8% –
97 Co sis nadrobil, to si sněz. 93.4% 2
98 Co můžeš učinit dnes, neodkládej na zítřek. 93.6% –
99 Podej někomu prst a chce celou ruku. 94.4% 6

8. Pragmatics of Proverbs: Basic Types of Evaluation

In **Actas ICP 7, 2014**, 259–266, **Čermák Proverbs 2014**, 147–156.

Abstract

The prescriptive, instructive or educational nature of proverbs as a whole may and should be viewed as pragmatic since proverbs usually express traditional social norms. Hence, in their use, they serve as specific means of traditional and largely objective evaluation of behaviour, attitudes and human doing. Within this general character of proverbs, not always explicit, there is a group, notably those containing adjectives good and bad, that serve as an explicit expression of evaluation attitude such as in Good girls go to Heaven, bad girls go everywhere. Gold can make a good man bad. On the basis of an analysis of all proverbs of this type (in the Routledge dictionary) an analysis of proverbs from many languages is made and some conclusions drawn indicating the participation of two adjectives, good and bad, along with other means, in the totality of the proverb meaning and pragmatics of their specific, either positive or negative, character. Hopefully, this approach might be viewed as a kind of core of evaluative function of proverbs.
Many aspects of this contribution overlap with the one called Frequent Proverbs and Their Meaning (3 above).

1. Pragmatics and Evaluation of Proverbs: General Remarks

Most words are considered to be neutral, or, perhaps, ambivalent, as to the specific goal that they are used for. Take the word *knife* in a simplified view as a tool determined for ether cutting or stabbing, or work and killing and *indirectly valued* as such. Others, such as *betray* or *help* carry a pronounced, *direct pragmatic feature of* either negative or positive *evaluation*. Although the pragmatic feature of evaluation linked to single words is very common in one's utterances, on a higher level one finds just a few sentences that have the evaluative function as a whole predominantly. A notorious source of stable evaluation in language, basically either positive or negative, is linked with proverbs. The types of evaluation here are many, some more pronounced, some subtle, but the whole field of proverbs always falls into this category, once the proverb's general function is realized and one becomes aware of it, namely to render traditional experience of past generations to new ones, i.e. to teach it, remind people of its existence, reprimand them, etc. The basic aim of standard proverb usage is, then, to show what has turned out as good or bad and should be followed or avoided. Should these types of proverb usage be called prescriptive, instructive or educational is not to be taken up for discussion here, since, generally, proverbs always express traditional social norms and their correlation with real life invokes realization that has or has not been followed or adhered to. In other words, human action, seen against this experiential background, is always viewed as either basically good or bad, to put it very simply.

This is the case of such proverbs as (1) *Cats hide their claws* or *Still waters become stagnant*, whose meaning and pragmatics is known due to our experience where no single part or word of the proverb hints at any specific evaluation of something being good or bad. These, forming a majority, might be called proverbs with **implicit evaluative function** where evaluation is linked to the *totality of the proverb*.

A much simpler case, however, is to be found in (2) such proverbs that contain *as their part a familiar word* that is always linked with a positive or negative pragmatic attitude. The very core of this case is to be found in proverbs having the prototypically pragmatic words such as *good* and *bad* and their derivatives. These, being much less frequent (despite high frequency of *good* and *bad*, etc.) might be called proverbs with **explicit valuative function**, i.e. those rendered by the adjectives or adverbs in the following (see marginally Battistella 1990).

It may be of some interest to note, though, that verbs, such as *appreciate*, *evaluate*, *assess*, *view as*, etc., are rarely used with proverbs, if at all.

The goal being thus concentrated on the seven words given below and enabling explicit evaluation, one may ask at least two questions here:

1 What is the proportion of proverbs with implicit evaluative function?
2 What is the proportion of positive versus negative evaluation mediated by the seven words?

2. EVALUATION: ROLE OF BASIC ADJECTIVES AND ADVERBS

In Čermák (2012) we have dealt with the role of lexical foundations of proverbs as they are found in an international collection of proverbs (Routledge dictionary) which consists of some 17 000 proverbs from many languages. Analyzing this proverb data as a corpus, it was found that it consists of 149 648 words which, due to repetition of some, amount to 9425 different word types. Narrowing our attention to the few words expressing evaluation, let us have a look at their role played in evaluative proverbs. These seven words are the following adjectives and adverbs provided with absolute frequency figures:

Good 938 (0.63%)
Better 533 (0.35%)
Best 253 (0.17%)
Bad 312 (0.21%)
Worse 68 (0.05%)
Worst 43 (0.03%)
Well 244 (0.18%)
Total: 2,391

Thus, they represent altogether 2,391 forms expressing evaluative function. To be quite accurate, let us mention that marginal words, such as *goodness* (9×), *badly* (18×), or *evil* being primarily nouns and an adverb are left out while the meaning 'water source' of *well* (37×) has been detracted.

Altogether, proverbs having a positive evaluation due to the presence of *good, better, best* and *well* amount to some 80% of all occurrences, while only about 20% having *bad, worse,* and *worst,* form negatively evaluative proverbs.

It is to be noted that these words belong to the top adjectives and adverbs found in the proverb corpus. For example, the five most frequent adjectives in proverbs here are *good, better, old, great,* and *bad,* offering thus an insight into their importance in proverbs and words chosen for the inspection.

3. FORMS AND STRUCTURES OF GOOD-BAD EVALUATIVE PROVERBS

The seven evaluative adjectives and adverbs have a traditional distribution, i.e. standing before a noun, or after a predicative verb such as *to be* (this holds for adjectives, 1 and 2), or follow a verb usually (this holds for adverbs, 3). Examples:

Good **wages**, good **work. Give a dog a** bad **name and it will begin to stink**.
(2) If you can't be good, **be carefu**l.
(3) Better to do well **than to say** well.

In actual proverbs, the ways in which these words are used are special for each. After a brief formal characterisation of each of these and its use, some insight will be offered into its semantics as this is to be seen in typical collocations showing how these adjectives and adverbs are used.

3.1 GOOD-PROVERBS

Good (frequency 938): This relatively high frequency adjective shows its standard use in the attribute:
A good horse is worth its fodder.
while it is rather rare in the predicate (the case 2 above), as in:
*If you follow the good, you will become **good**. The ungrateful return evil for **good**.*
Yet, surprisingly, also the phrase *It is good* is rather marginal and infrequent, cf.
***It is not** always **good** to be wise, **It is** a **good** horse that draws its own cart.*

Structures using *good* include:
a comparative construction: ***is as good as***, such as in *nothing **is as good as** forbidden fruit, the first blow **is as good as** two, a man forewarned **is as good as two*** (altogether 23 items);
good for *(nothing, flight, the soul, three days, the eyes, 26)*;
it is a good *horse **that** draws its own cart* (only 4).

A rather frequent separate construction has an explicit verb following it (34 cases), such as ***it is good to*** *know the truth* where *good* is related to a noun, however.

The frequency of *good* is shown by its most ***frequent collocations***: (*good*): *advice* (5), *company* (5), *counsel* (6), *deed/s* (18), *fortune* (12), *friend/s* (8), *horse* (14), *luck* (23), *man* (26), *men* (14), *name* (16), *neighbor* (10), *thing/s* (22), *wife* (8), and *wine* (13); these being, in practical terms, all entities that proverbs consider to be good as models mentioning them and illustrating its typical use.

3.2 BAD-PROVERBS

Bad (frequency 312) is much lower in its frequency. It is very rarely used in *It is bad*, cf.
It is bad to have a servant, but worse to have a master, neither it is really found in *X is bad*;
see exceptions: *An empty purse is bad, Not to know is bad, Nothing bad is all bad, Self-love is bad.*
Its predominant use is almost always attributive, however, eg. *Bad advice is always fatal.*

Structures:
There is one expressing a comparison of two equal things: *Three removals are **as** bad **as** a fire* (16×).
It is a bad X, eg.,*it is a bad child who does not take advice, a bad thing to be poor* (5×).

The frequency of *bad* indicates its real use here, primarily through major ***collocations***, again in alphabetical order: (**bad:**) *advice/counsel* (3), *company* (5), *egg* (4), *fortune* (2), *friend* (2), *luck* (15), *man* (7), *name* (4), *neighbor* (6), *news* (12), *thing/s* (6), and *wife* (6).

A comparison of *good* and *bad* (see examples above) shows that these are not often viewed as opposites. It makes one wonder why *egg* is mentioned only with *bad* and never *good* but this would lead to a much different line of thought.

Apart from differences it may be of some interest to note **pragmatically ambivalent nouns** occurring with both *good* and *bad*: *advice, company, counsel, fortune, friend(s), luck, man, name, neighbor, thing(s), wife*. As ambivalent, i.e. evaluated (viewed) both as *good* and *bad*, it is *luck* that is dominant in *good luck* and *bad luck*, these being also independent phrasemes.

3.3 Related Positives *Better, Best, Well*

The rest of the positively evaluative proverbs is based on the presence of *better, best, well*, with frequencies of 533, 253, and 244 respectively. *Better* is used in comparisons such as *Better envy than pity, Better a good enemy than a bad friend*.

Two common ways how **better** is used are with the initial phrase *it is better X than*, cf. *It is better to lose than lose more*. The second, rather frequent way, has *better* at the very beginning of the proverb, such *as Better one-eyed than no-eyed. Better late than never*. This represents about one half of the use of *better* in proverbs.

The rest includes attributive uses, such as *The gray mare is the better horse*.

Peripheral **best** is mostly used in the attribute, but 52 cases are found in the predicate, too, cf. *In time of test, family is best*. Typical structure is *It is best*, such as in *It is best to profit by the madness of others*.

The adverb **well** invariably follows the verb that it qualifies, such as in *All's well that ends well, He lives twice who lives well* and it does not exhibit any special preference for a structure or construction.

3.4 Related Negatives *Worse, Worst*

The frequencies of the remaining negatively evaluative proverbs built on *worse* and *worst* is much lower, namely 68 and 43, respectively.

Oddly enough, **worse** is only rarely used in comparisons, i.e. constructions *X is worse than*, cf. *Feigned love is worse than hatred*, there being no use at all recorded of the initial *It is worse* while this is exceptionally found only in a second clause, such as *When an angel turns bad, it is worse than the Devil*.

Occasionally, however, the initial *Nothing is worse* is to be found, such as in **Nothing** *is worse than being accustomed to good fortune*.

Worst has the smalles trepresentation of all evaluative words of the group. Next to the attributive use, cf. *Aman's discontent is his worst evil*, it is also found (10x) in the predicate, too, such as *Dissensions among equals are the worst. Better the best of the worst than the worst of the best*.

4. Semantics of Evaluative Good, Bad, etc. in Proverbs

Except for the evaluative function, no attempt has been made here to explore the lexical meaning of the seven adjectives and adverbs in detail, such as *good* in the sense of 'useful, reliable, desirable, beneficial, salubrious, profitable', etc. The evaluative function, often mixed up with the meaning proper, has been singled out here as a unifying feature belonging to pragmatics rather than semantics and viewed as a generally accepted feature of what it is used about, i.e. irrespective of the context that semantics always depends on.

There is, however, one more solitary adjective, namely **worth**, often expressing a positive evaluation, too; used in a special type of comparison, cf. *A picture is worth a thousand words*. Because of its special situation it has been left out of any consideration.

5. Comparison and Contrast

Above, a strong feature common to all seven words inspected has been mentioned, namely that of comparison. Mostly, a normal use of *good*, *bad*, etc., is linked by an implicit comparison to a commonly accepted standard, such as *good wine*, *good news*. This use is often found in contrast to something or somebody converse to it whereby the very use of good, bad, etc., is clarified and strengthened. Cf. examples:

The bad gardener quarrels with his rake.
Good fruit never comes from a bad tree.
Good girls go to Heaven, bad girls go everywhere.
Gold can make a good man bad.
Good news knocks louder than bad.
Good wine ruins the purse, and makes the stomach bad.
Good words and bad acts deceive both wise and simple.

On the other hand, specific and more explicit is the use of formal comparison including comparative and superlative forms exemplified above, such as *Better a red face than a black heart*.

6. Concluding Notes

The five adjectives and adverbs, namely *good-bad*, *better-worse*, *best-worst* and *well* have been inspected in a proverb corpus as explicit bearers of evaluative function that all proverbs express in general, though mostly in an implicit way. It has been shown that these seven lexemes are far from symmetrical, some of them entering specific construction such as *It is better X than*. In inspecting their use, the most frequent collocations show fields where these words are applied most often, illustrating thus their main usage and semantics.

To answer the two questions in (1), it seems that about 14% of proverbs have the explicit evaluative function, researched here, while proportion of positive versus negative evaluative function of proverbs, i.e. going by the presence of these seven words only, is about 4 : 1.

LITERATURE

BATTISTELLA, Edwin L. 1990. *Markedness: The Evaluative Superstructure of Language*. Albany, NY: State University of New York Press.

ČERMÁK, František. 2012. "Lexicon and Proverbs: Basics and Foundations." In *5th Interdisciplinary Colloquium on Proverbs*, edited by R. B. Soares and O. Lauhakangas, 203–217. Lisbon: AIP-IAP

HUNSTON, Susan and THOMPSON, Geoff. 2006. *Evaluation in Text*. Oxford: University Press Oxford.

KUUSI, Matti. 1972. *Towards an International Type-System of Proverbs*. Helsinki: Academia Scientiarum Fennica.

LAUHAKANGAS, Outi. 2001. *The Matti Kuusi international type system of proverbs*. Helsinki: Suomalainen Tiedeakatemia.

C
LEXICAL AND PROVERB CLASSES IN LEXICON

Proverbs appear in language not distributed in an even way, but most of them tend to be used rather often. This feature (here, in Part C) has led to recognition of corpus-based proverb minima, the one for Czech and English being presented here. An exhaustive study of BNC for English has produced proverb frequencies, variation, semantic annotation, etc. Proverb minima are presented here in more detail. Also, a general framework of propositional idioms showing where proverbs fit in the language system, next to other types of expression is offered.

9. Propositional Idioms

In *Europhras 2000 Proceedigs*, Ch. Palm-Meister (ed.), Stauffenberg Verlag, Tübingen 2004, 15–23.

Abstract

Propositional idioms are idioms with a sentential function and form a special subsystem of the idiom system.

1. Propositional Idioms: Do They Exist?

There has never been much doubt about the core of idioms or phrasemes. In their search for it, practically all research has uniformly pointed to typical combinations of word forms on a non-sentential level, more particularly to verbal idioms, such as *spill the beans, make it up for somebody*. However, the problem of periphery and, in fact, the boundaries of the scope of idioms, including more than one level, has been addressed only rarely and there are precious few approaches tackling the whole of the field. For a number of reasons, such a multitude of views is not surprising and, on the other hand, there are even doubts about such combinations as *pay attention* and their being part of the idiomatic core of a language. Perhaps the most important reason for this situation has been a lack of consensus as to what idioms really are. The insistence by many to approach idioms semantically, to look for metaphors and images conveyed by them prevents one from considering many semantically composite or almost composite types of combinations as idioms.

Very few theoreticians are aware of and admit that there are idioms on the sentence level and beyond. Since it is proposition (in a broader sense) that the sentence is mostly based on, these idioms might be called **propositional idioms**. It may come as a surprise to many that they form one of the two most numerous fields of idioms at all (an estimate for the Czech language, based on a database collected over more than

10 years lists around 10 000 items). With a single notable exception, namely that of proverbs, which have been under scrutiny for centuries, it is disconcerting to see, on the one hand, the sheer vastness of the field and the degree of descriptive neglect on the other hand. Dictionaries never tell that a particular combination has a sentential, discoursal function to be distinguished from other types of idioms, even if a particular propositional idiom is recorded, which is often not the case.

There is every reason to use for the **identification** of this type of idioms the same test based on the anomalous and unique character of its components as in the case of other types of idioms (see, e.g., Čermák 1982, 1988). The idiom is, by definition, *such a unique and fixed combination of at least two elements for which it holds that at least some of these do not function, in the same way, in any other combination or combinations of the kind, or occur in a highly restricted number of them, or in a single one only*. As this definition can be converted into an operational test of commutation of the idiom's components, it is readily seen that it does work along the following lines. Thus, in the case of *Count your blessings!* it is, for example, impossible to substitute the component of *count* with any other having the same broad function, i.e.with neither *number, ennumerate, tell, name* or such like. It is obvious that a further refinement is possible here.

Traditional names, language labels, given to this type of idioms are often missing. Consider, for example, the act of *encouragement* having no proper linguistic label (it is a content word) in many languages. Those names (one must hesitate to call them terms because of their vagueness in most cases) which do exist, have been coined with a rather different motivation in various languages and are not particularly telling as far as their character is concerned. It is definitely not possible to include all the types under a single heading, such as proverb, as they are too diverse and varied.

Labels, such as *sayings, proverbs, formulae, greetings, slogans, watchwords, motto's, maxims, aphorisms, riddles, axioms, adages, apophthegms, wellerisms, catchwords, familiar quotations, gambits, counting-out rhymes*, and other, seem to point in various directions in what they suggest. Upon closer inspection, it is a varied and inconsequential series pointing in their particular definitions, alternatively, to their form, effect, content, instruction, belief or contact involved, goal or usage. It may seem that there is no consistency here and, accordingly, that there is no classification, based on unifying criteria, possible.

Another way to handle these idioms is to give them descriptive labels pointing to what they do. Such is the approach of A. Makkai for English, using such names as *idioms of institutionalized politeness, of detachment or indirectness, of proposals encoded as questions or proverbial idioms with a moral*, etc. (Makkai 1972, 172n.). For a number of reasons including that of the ad hoc character of them, it seems that it is not a particularly suitable way to proceed. Such labels do not point to any common denominator and one can never be sure how many of them would be necessary to use until the whole scope is covered. Makkai does, however, try to find a common term for all types and calls it **sememic idioms**, a term which is firmly embedded in the tradition of Sydney M. Lamb's stratificational theory. In his view, somewhat difficult to understand without any a priori knowledge, such a sememic idiom is a *polylexemic construction whose aggre-*

gate literal meaning derived from its constituent lexemes functions additionally as the realization of an unpredictable sememic network. Yet he does not offer much tangible criteria
enabling the identification of such propositional idioms.

This approach of no clear definition criteria for identification and delimitation of
the whole field prevails elsewhere. R. Moon in her recent survey of phraseology and
idiomatics (Moon 1998) is aware of the multitude of approaches and views and opts
for a cover term. Accordingly, she calls the whole of the field **fixed expressions and
idioms** (FEI), although she admits that **fixed expressions as** a label may not be satisfactory (p. 2) and that idioms are in fact subsumed under it. The obvious advantage of
fixed expression used as a term, however, is no bias or further limitation. Hence, no
specific types of combinations, either on word or sentence level, are discarded a priori. Propositional idioms mostly come under her pragmatic type of FEI which she calls
formulae (p. 20, 62ff), but in fact no clear boundary line is drawn and no distinction
is made between propositional idioms, i.e. idioms on a sentence level, and other type
of idioms. The formulae are rather loosely subclassified by her into simple formulae,
sayings, proverbs and similes, although similes seem to belong, more specifically, to
her class of collocations.

2. Problems in Their Analysis

Traditionally, the bulk of the propositional idioms seems too varied to offer any obvious unitary feature that could be used for their identification, except that of their
sentence character. A number of features, though not all, can be seen in definitions,
however loose, of the traditional types, like sayings, proverbs, catchwords, and formulae, enumerated above. Obviously, next to features (1) shared with the collocational and
lexical idioms, they must have a number of hitherto unexplored (2) features due to specific types of situation, discourse and speech act in which they are used. Here, various
sorts of interactions and transactions of interlocutors, their motivation and attitudes
as well as observance of social rituals and rules, such as politeness and cooperation
principles, will have to be taken into account. Most of these latter aspects, if observed
at all, go under the heading of **pragmatics** now. Hence a necessity for a multiple but
mutually consistent approach on more than one level.

While along more traditional lines their **anomalous** character (a redefined
ill-formedness) seems to prevail in all idiom types (see the definition and the test
above), one can hardly rely on a stable presence of **metaphor**, so much stressed by
many traditional phraseologists. With the advent of corpora it is increasingly evident
that even the very notion of **fixedness** (stableness) is at stake and researchers often do
not know whether a particular combination may be viewed as fixed or not. It depends,
ultimately, on the sheer number of occurrences and their repetition which in the case
of the spoken language is still so difficult to come by. Since this is still very much an
open question, there is no clear awareness of the boundaries, if any, of the field and,

accordingly, of membership of, for example, axioms and principles of mathematics and physics.

3. Some Tentative Types of Propositional Idioms

There might be more than one way to view or classify this type of idioms, each offering a different insight. In the following, I will briefly take up three approaches, formal, functional, and pragmatic.

3.1 Formal Types of Propositional Idioms

As to their **form**, propositional idioms could tentatively be classified into two broad classes, (1) **propositional idioms** proper and (2) **polypropositional** ones, which are based on more than one clause, such as:

(1) *The penny has dropped, Fortune favours fools*, and
(2) *Don't count your chicken before they're hatched, You'd forget your head if it wasn't screwed on.*

The latter class may be further subdivided according to the number of speakers involved whereby one deals with in the latter case in dialogue. An idiom having characteristically two different subjects, such as greetings and witty, facetious reactions to some remarks ((*It's coming, e.g., a tram*)– *So is Christmas*), might be called:

(2a) **intersubjective polypropositional idiom** while the one with one subject only would be called
(2b) **monosubjective**, see, e.g., (1) above.

This way, also a broader question is addressed, namely that of the borderline between idiomatics and minor text forms, larger in form, such as riddles, apophthegm, folk-tale, anecdote, joke, etc. However, this question has never been satisfactorily solved so far (for such forms see Koch). It is also worth noting that a further formal distinction could be brought into play by introducing the difference between question and statement. However, there are rather few propositional idioms in question form, such as *Head or tails? A já jsem vosk?*, the majority being in statement or exclamation form, hence the distinction may not be of much use.

Similarly, the presence or absence of negation could be made relevant for a subsequent classification.

From a more traditional and less revealing view, types of sentences involved could be used for another, rather a broad classification. Thus, four types based mostly on the presence or absence of the verb could be distinguished including:

1 Interjectional type: *But of course!, Dead right! Jak by ne?, To je fakt.*
2 Nominal type: *Once a fool, always a fool. Heads or tails?*
Hlupák zůstane hlupákem. Hlava nebo panna?
3 Imperative type: *Go on, kick yourself! Dej si facku, nikdo se nekouká.*
4 Predicative type: *It's in the thing. To teď frčí.*

3.2 FUNCTIONAL TYPES OF PROPOSITIONAL IDIOMS

For the purposes of a true **functional** approach unfortunately no typology of larger structural units is available in which and against which an appropriate place and function of these idioms could be examined. In lack of this, however, a well-known functional point of view, i.e. of communicative functions, proposed by Jakobson, can be used for classification (Jakobson). On this basis, at least four broad functional types of propositional idioms can be discerned, *including vocative, contact, thematic, and metalinguistic.*

A Vocative type includes both the expressive and conative/appeal function on the axis Speaker-Hearer. A finer subdivision into minor types would include three subclasses, interjective, imperative, and categorizing, i.e. according to their obvious character, cf.
(a) Interjective (emotional reactions and attitudes): *Vida ho!, To mi může bejt ukradený!, You must be joking!*
(b) Imperative (volitional influence upon the hearer): *Koukej mazat!, Mě vynech!, Steer clear of me!*
(c) Categorizing: this last subtype merges with the categorizing subtype of the thematic class (Cd below).

B Contact type includes the phatic function whereby the contact between the Speaker and Hearer is maintained or modified. The **Contact** proper (phase and type of contact) often consists of greetings: *Zdař bůh!, Tak se měj!, See you later!, Bon appétit!,* or *Dobrou chuť!*

C Thematic type refers to the referential function of the Speaker in relation to the topic (theme), i.e. what the communication is about. It could be subclassified into:
(a) Descriptive (simple statement and description): *Vzduch je čistý, Zatmělo se mu před očima, The penny has dropped.*
(b) Attitudinal (expression of evaluation and point of view): *To zrovna!, Opatrnosti nikdy nezbývá, Not on your life!, Dead right!*
(c) Connective (links between sections or phases of the topic): *Bylo, nebylo..., Jak se věci mají..., Once upon a time....*
Categorizing (identification with a familiar type): *To je slovo do pranice, He is a voice crying in the wilderness.*

D Metalinguistic type refers to the metalinguistic function of Jakobson's which covers the relationship between the Speaker and the code or means of communication, i.e. language; it loosely and in part corresponds to Halliday's textual function: *Na tom si zlomíš jazyk, It's a bit of a mouthful.*

3.3 Pragmatic Types of Propositional Idioms

Finally, **pragmatic aspects** of the propositional idioms can be used for their classification. Since these seem to be prominent, they might turn out, after further refinement, to belong among the most rewarding, too. Although these might rather overlap with speech act types, speech acts cannot be used directly as their basis. The main reason is that many propositional idioms do not constitute a speech act per se, they rather form a part of it. Moreover, some idioms seem to find no corresponding and suitable speech act as these acts are viewed rather too narrowly and a revision would be required. On the other hand, there seem to be few or no idioms corresponding to commisive acts.

Instead, five broad basic pragmatic classes, different from speech acts, are distinguished, namely, the factual, voluntative, expressive, emotive, and declarative ones while two more, evaluative and intensificational ones, serving mostly as their extensions, will also be considered. Below, a preliminary survey includes a selection of idioms used for the last volume of the *Czech Dictionary of Idioms. Propositional Idioms*, and the English equivalents that are to be considered for inclusion.

1 Factual class of idioms (F) commits the Speaker to the truth of the proposition and its various shades and degrees. There is a number of subclasses:

a **statement**, **possibility/necessity**, **in/definiteness**, **existence**
b **un/certainty**, **truth/falsity**
c **im/probability**
d **in/dependence**, **un/conditionality**
e **limitation/expansion/change of validity**, **generality**
f **categorizing**, **classification**, **typology**

Cf. *It's beginning to dawn on him* (a), *That's nice of you, but…, He's got a bee in his bonnet* (Fa/Exi), *He won't lose any sleep over that* (Fc/Exg), *…and Bob's your uncle* (Fa-e/Emc), *We've had it* (Fa/Emc), *It'll take some doing* (Fa/Emf);
V hlavě mu už svítá (a), *To je vod tebe sice hezký, ale…, Straší mu to v hlavě* (Fa/Exi), *Hlava ho pro to nebolí* (Fc/Exg), *…a je po ftákách* (Fa-e/Emc), *To je v háji* (Fa/Emc), *To dá fušku* (Fa/Emf).

An extension of factual class may be seen in the **metalinguistic** subtype, cf. *It's on the tip of my tongue, Mám to na jazyku* (Fa).

2 Voluntative (directive) class of idioms (V) aims at producing some effect through action on the Hearer (such as proverbs do). It includes a number of subclasses, such as:

a order, request
b dis/approval, acceptance/refusal, agreement
c threat, warning, reprimand
d assurance, reassurement, assuagement, palliative, encouragement
e indifference, resignation
f advice, appeal
g wish
h persuasion, recommendation
i support

Cf. *So many men, so many opinions* (Vf), *Count your blessings!* (Vd), *Cheer up!* (Vd), *Go to hell!* (Vb/Emc), *That's not on* (Vb-d/Fa), *He should use his head and save his legs* (Vh/Emh), *You must be joking* (Vb/Emc/Ex), *Go on, kick yourself* (Vb/Emc);
Kolik hlav, tolik rozumu (Vf), *Buď rád, že seš rád* (Vd), *Nevěš hlavu!* (Vd), *Di do háje!* (Vb/Emc), *To je hloupý* (Vd/Fa), *Když je hlava blbá, trpí celý tělo* (Fa/Vh/Emh), *Ještě to tak!* (Vb/Emc), *Dej si facku, nikdo se nekouká* (Vb/Emc).

3 Expressive class of idioms (Ex) makes known the Speaker's attitude towards the state of affairs. Its subclasses are made up of the following:

a congratulation
b thanks
c apology
d doubt
e sympathy
f belief/disbelief
g blaming, reproach
h forgiving
i jocularity
j puzzlement, avoidance

Cf. *I wonder!* (Exd), *I take my hat off to him* (Exa), *You can have three guesses* (Va/Exi-j), *That's a long story* (Fa/Exj);
Jen aby! (Exd), *Klobouk dolů!* (Exa), *Hádej, můžeš třikrát* (Va/Exi-j), *To je dlouhá historie* (Fa/Exj).

A further extension of this class may be seen in **polite wish** as represented by conventional greetings, cf. *Bon appétit!, Many happy returns!, Dobrou chuť!, Všechno nejlepší!*

4 Emotional class of idioms (Em) makes known Speaker's emotional reaction. The subclasses include:

a **surprise, astonishment**
b **admiration, praise**
c **dis/pleasure, aversion, dislike**
d **envy**
e **satisfaction, disappointment, regret**
f **apprehension/fear, equanimity, trust**
g **anger**
h **ridicule**

Cf. *It's a sight for sore eyes* (Ema-d), *Just the man I wanted!* (Eme), *That's quite something* (Emb), *The colour drained out of his cheeks* (Emf/Va);
Srdce se na to směje (Ema-d), *Dobře že deš* (Eme), *To je ale kus!* (Emb), *Krve by se v něm nedořezal* (Emf/Va).

5 Declarative class of idioms (D) brings about a new state of affairs which is being declared. This is a minor class, closely copying the traditional speech act and including such subclasses as:

a **dismissing, excommunication**
b **naming, appointing**
c **sentencing**
d **realization**

Cf. *Heave-ho!*, *Hej rup!* (Va/Dd)

It is only seldom that two other potential classes, the **Evaluative** (E) and **Intensificational** (I) ones, stand alone, cf. *...so much that his head is spinning* (I). Rather, they accompany the basic five classes as a kind of modifier. It is, in fact, almost impossible to find, for example, an emotional propositional idiom which could not be, at the same time, evaluative, i.e. expressing a personal attitude which is basically either broadly positive or negative. Accordingly, an idiom such as *That's quite something!* expresses not only admiration but a positive evaluation, etc.

4. Lexicographic Notes

Lexicographically, there has, so far, been no attempt to cover the propositional idioms properly. If they are recorded at all, which is a serious problem by its own right, one finds them interspersed with other types of idioms and collocations with a far-from-satisfactory kind of brief remark. It is very difficult to find evidence for them in even very large corpora and data-banks since they mostly belong to speech and their written records are very sparse.

Evidently, to be able to put this situation right, one has to have very large **spoken corpora** at one's disposal and to cope with a number of new or different issues. These, briefly, involve the incorporation of both the **functional and pragmatic classes and properties**, although their form may be still very much a matter of debate. There is also no doubt about the necessity to cover their **intonation**, as that is their inherent feature, a frequent stumbling-block for foreign learners. The spoken corpora will become a basis for determination of an optimum type of **illustration of use**, which is undoubtedly of a dialogic character as most of these idioms are reactions to something that has been said or what has happened before. It appears that most of these features have already been incorporated into the *Czech Idiom Dictionary* (see Čermák 1994a, Čermák – Hronek – Machač 1983, 1988, 1994).

10. Basic English Proverbs: Their Variability and Corpus-Based-Aspects

In print in **ACTAS ICP**.

Abstract

The aim of the contribution is identification of BNC as to the English proverbs used here, trying to get at the substance of what is basic here. For this, as a filter, a number of proverb lists have been used. Thus, over 100 most frequent English proverbs with their contexts and variants have been found. The results have been used to describe the lexical stock used here, as well as the most frequent (syntagmatic and paradigmatic) variants. The final list of proverbs offers, for each proverb, its frequency, a variability label, and a tentative evaluation as candidates for Matti Kuusi's international type system of proverbs.

1. Introduction

While it is true that proverbs are widely used, nobody really knows how often and how many are used altogether, let alone how many proverbs there are in various languages. This lack of knowledge might be somehow disconcerting should proverbs be made the subject of a serious and exhaustive study, especially a comparative one, since it is impossible to study something that is rather unknown as a whole: there are too many loose ends and indistinct boundaries. The practical solution, which may not replace one encompassing the whole field, has been to concentrate *only* on some proverbs chosen for introductory insight, as offered by a large corpus. At best, such results offer an interesting picture of some common features, though based on a limited selection of available data.

At the same time, even this rather limited approach of making a list of proverbs is almost always devoid of the context, meaning, and function of proverbs in these. This may be due to a rather haphazard and false view, which is influenced by unfortunate approaches, mostly interested in a sentence or somewhat larger context only, presupposing namely that there is *no* context necessary while studying proverbs. Likewise, it is impossible so far to say to what extent an average individual may know proverbs, the Bible's contention that King Solomon *'spoke three thousand proverbs and his songs numbered a thousand and five'* seems to be poetic licence only.

An entirely different, though no less problematic, problem is the size of the bulk of proverbs for one language. These proverbs and their figures, being assembled for a long time by many in sometimes voluminous books are *linguistically* a problem, always mixing past and present, namely disregarding the time factor, and have to be synchronically viewed as unreliable. Given rough estimates for a number of proverbs recorded by some proverb dictionaries and lists, there are thousands, or perhaps, tens of thousands, of proverbs, at least in some languages.

A way to partly solve this problem and get at the core is to resort to the large corpus mentioned above that is contemporary and represents a selection of many texts, contexts and users in the belief that such a representative sample says rather more (though not everything) and may reflect, somehow, the language in question as a whole.

Following Permjakov, a number of languages appear to have a paremiological minimum, ranging from 100 proverbs to several hundred, though their selection has so far been based on no safe and reliable criteria. For some reason, Wikipedia has settled on the number of 900 representative proverbs for English. But these do not offer any idea of their frequency and it is just assuming a lot if they are passed for the very proverbial core of a language (including the first attempt in Czech, Čermák 2010). Hence the idea of paremiological minima seems to be less appealing, should one follow (a) objective, corpus-based data and (b) include them in a natural frequency order, i.e. including what a representative corpus has to offer.

This paper intends to delve deeper into the realm of the 100 million British National Corpus (of 100 million words), allowing the researcher to follow ways how proverbs are used in context, and how often, dwell on the premise that this number is quite large and representative enough to give a glimpse of the whole of the language as it is really used at the moment. In doing so, unfortunately, certain things had to be taken for granted, such as the terminological distinction of proverb, proverbial expression, adage, etc. that are collapsed under a single umbrella.

The goal of this paper is to delve rather deeply into the realm of 100 million English text corpus (BNC), trying to identify its proverbs, their frequency, variability and usage; eventually, it is projected in their membership into a proverb general thesaurus that has been offered to us by Matti Kuusi.

2. BASIC PROVERBS

On the academic front, the obvious recognition of the proverbs' importance gave rise to their collection and, since there are too many of them, to their selections in various languages, their final listing and count stopping, for practical and attractive purposes, quite early (usually 100 or a little more occurrences, see above).

On the commercial side, the number of booklets and various lists offering the 'most frequent and familiar' proverbs is so vast that no reliable and exhaustive list or bibliography is available and it is not expedient to take and compare these too seriously.

There is also a third approach trying to assemble basic proverbs for school textbooks and dictionaries.

What they all have in common is a complete lack of reliable criteria for their selection either, supported by a lack of data to draw them from. Thus, not even the best dictionaries will tell what kind of proverbs have been covered and explained and on what basis this selection has been made.

Hence, from a synchronic point of view, it is impossible to say with any certainty what basic proverbs in a language might be, i.e. without knowing their frequency based on reliable and vast data.

3. Basic English Proverbs (120, down to frequency 4)

In English and elsewhere, there is very little suggesting what the basic proverb might be, though a number of estimates and guesses is available. To improve this, all major and available lists of proverbs have been inspected, compared and tested, and a relatively exhaustive control list of their use and form (using key elements of proverbs, such as *silver lining*) has been obtained from BNC (one hundred million words).

Thus the starting point of this research was the British National Corpus on the one hand, and a manifold list of resources in various control lists and proverb collections on the other. Speaking quite simply, the latter had been used to inspect (filter) the former. However, proverbs found in this way have a cut-off point of 120 (i.e. down to frequency 4 viewed as offering hopefully at least some basic information about their behaviour). In a sense, this approach offers in fact then most of all reasonable proverb candidates in BNC. Thus, these results represent 120 proverbs. Proverbs are viewed here as sentences of a kind, made of words (wordforms).

In what follows, some basic statistics may be given.

While the **number of sentences** in BNC is 6,052,190, their lexical stock of proverbs is rather small (650 words), seven of these sentences being compound sentences. The number of the proverbs that have been excluded (for this reason mostly) from any further consideration is 73.

Having inspected the bulk of proverbs (120) taken as a special corpus against the number of words used for their construction, it is evident that proverb frequency is not very high, due to the fact that most corpora are largely still written, while proverbs may be used more often in spoken language. The 120 proverbs are based on 650 word forms (these include, however, 7 compound sentences made of two clauses). Using these figures, the average proverb consists of 5.41 word forms per single proverb.

Thus, the **sum of BNC proverbs** (120), if all of their frequencies and repetitions are taken as whole, is 1,318. This, in turn, suggests that out of the 100 million words of

BNC, the total sum of proverbs occupies 0.0217% of all BNC texts. Should we simplify the situation a bit further and presuppose that all proverbs are sentences, then the total **number of proverbs in BNC** (only 120 most frequent) is 0.0217% of the total of BNC sentences (no attempt has been made, however, to modify this figure, discounting proverb repetitions which are quite frequent).

The **Lexical stock** of these proverbs (made up of 650 word forms, with simple frequency) is the following list:

25× *the*, 25 *is*, 18 *a*, 13 *in*, 8 *of*, 8 *than*, 6 *of*, 5× *you*, 5 *and*, 5 *better*, 4 *are*, 4 *do*, 4 *come*, 4 *not*, 4 *be*, 4 *man*, 4 *to*, 4 *an*, 3× *right*, 3 *things*, 3 *time*, 3 *first*, 3 *power*, 3 *fire*, 3 *eye*, 3 *good*, 3 *two*, 2× *news*, 2 *makes*, 2 *well*, 2 *devil*, 2 *end*, 2 *helps*, 2 *on*, 2 *your*, 2 *eat*, 2 *scratch*, 2 *his*, 2 *words*, 2 *who*, 2 *have*, 2 *go*, 2 *tooth*, 2 *they*, 2 *deep*, 2 *friend*, 2 *has*, 2 *bird*, 2 *what*, 2 *while*, 2 *safety*, 2 *before*, 2 *as*, 2 *worth*, 2 *grow*, 2 *spoil*, 2 *bygones*, 2 *home*, 2 *corrupts*, 2 *no*, 1× *valour*, 1 *want*, 1 *rod*, 1 *might*, 1 *spare*, 1 *nine*, 1 *heads*, 1 *beauty*, 1 *saves*, 1 *a*, 1 *one*, 1 *stitch*, 1 *beholder*, 1 *part*, 1 *bitten*, 1 *once*, 1 *twice*, 1 *discretion*, 1 *two*, 1 *shy*, 1 *waste*, 1 *penny*, 1 *pound*, 1 *at*, 1 *in*, 1 *absolute*, 1 *justifies*, 1 *means*, 1 *absolutely*, 1 *the*, 1 *begins*, 1a, 1 *hand*, 1 *practice*, 1 *perfect*, 1 *bush*, 1 *diem*, and 1 *charity*.

Obviously, it is nouns that are the ultimate and foremost bearers of meaning, followed by much rarer verbs and adjectives.

Having a look at the top only (between frequency 25–2), one can see these:

Nouns: *man, things, time, power, fire, eye, news, devil, end, words, tooth, friend, bird, safety,*
Verbs: *be, come, make, help, eat, scratch, have, go, grow, spoil, corrupt,*
Adjectives: *right, good, deep.*

Despite proverb's *abstract meaning*, surprisingly, they use only a limited number of old noun abstracts, these being quite general, such as *time, power, words, valour, beauty, discretion, practice,* and *charity*. Besides, the avoidance of new or recent abstract nouns (such as *relativity, relation, process*) is rather familiar.

It is not surprising that the frequency of grammar words is highest here (although they need a slight correction and recount, since the cases where a word form linked with a figure have been counted separately, see, for instance, a double frequency of the article *a*). While grammar words are surprisingly limited in their choice (articles, mostly personal pronouns, seven prepositions, etc.), it is even more surprising how few types of meaning are brought about by the nouns mentioned. Obviously, this should not be surprising, though it is just impossible to draw any semantic conclusion and relation to the meaning of proverbs from the point of the component words taken as a whole. Despite this, my paper will deal with the proverb *meaning* (in part 7) viewed as sentences or rather, with their thematic membership.

The goal of this contribution is concerned, next to the problem of **form**, namely of its *identification and variability* (in 6, 5). The **functional aspect** will be limited here to a core of word class combinations. Although some, rather rare, possibilities can be found, too, the core of *monosentential proverbs* consists of the following

1 **(A) - S - V - (A-) S**

2 **S - V - ADV**

3 *S - S*
4 *S - V*
5 *V - V*
6 *S - Gr*

where S (= noun), V (= verb), A (= adjective), ADV (= ADV), and Gr (= grammar word).

4. VARIABILITY IN GENERAL

In any living language, **variability** of form, i.e. existence of **variants** is found everywhere, as that is the primary tool of its development and innovation, but also an interesting meeting point between diachrony and synchrony. In these, most of new formations squeeze eventually the old forms out. At first sight, existence of variation seems to be contradictory to the stable and authoritative form of the proverbs, used through times, being handed over to next generations.

All proverbs, should they undergo, in their manifestations, any comparison between themselves must be always related to the same thing, the same proverb. Hence, a major problem of *proverb identity* arises and has to be solved (the criterion being roughly the same function and meaning for the same form). Variants must adhere to the criterion of the identity, too. This has been discussed and became evident also from the analysis of the data of the Czech National Corpus (Čermák 2004).

To keep various types and cases of **variability** at bay, a basic generalized approach drawing for contemporary study has been used on both:
syntagmatic aspects (linear form, combination, length) and
paradigmatic aspects (synonymy, substitution, inflectional forms, etc.); and
a simplified distinction of **content-grammar** words, i.e.
autosemantic and synsemantic aspects (i.e. nouns, Adjectives, Verbs and Adverbs as against various inflectional endings, such as case and tense forms).

This has been applied to the proverb data studied and encoded using abbreviations based on two scales, such as **P, S** (*Paradigmatic and Syntagmatic*) and **a, s** (*autosemantics, synsemantic*) and their combinations (such as **Sa, Ss, Pa, Ps**; such as, **Ss** standing for syntagmatic and synsemantic, etc.). A special case of a syntagmatic change and, hence, variation is considered to be **shortening**.

5. VARIABILITY OF BASIC ENGLISH PROVERBS, BASED ON BNC

An almost prototypical example of multifaceted proverb behaviour in text (in Čermák 2009) is to be seen in *Every cloud has a silver lining* with a total frequency of 52, which happens to be the fourth most frequent proverb in BNC; it is found and used in many different contexts and functions. As a full form (i.e. without any variant) it is found only six times in BNC, while most of its occurrences show some kind of variation or occur in these only. Its major form of existence is *silver lining*, found in all sorts of contexts, but clearly linked to the full form semantically. This is rather unusual, as we are dealing with the end of the proverb and its rather easy way of dissociating itself and living an independent life. On the other hand, the beginning of the proverb, generally much more prone to separate itself, i.e. *every cloud* in this case, does not seem to exist just by itself, independent of the proverb.

The frequency of the isolated *silver lining* or *silverline* (*lines*), is rather high, in fact higher than that of the proverb itself. Its 57 occurrences (some of them in plural form) do signal an almost independent existence of the form, but there is no way to know this for sure (apart from frequency). So it may be viewed as a problem of identity (two or only one form?). The independent way of existence of what used to be only part of a larger form is to be seen in its new collocations such as, *every cloud had*, but also *clouds had a silver lining*. Thus, one is faced here with the break-up of a proverb and the beginnings of a new, smaller, shorter idiom.

6. English Proverbs Formally and By Frequency (in BNC)

6.1 Frequency List of English Proverbs

It appears that 52 of the first 100 proverbs, i.e. 52% of the first English proverbs from BNC are *invariable*, while 48% have some kind of variants (see examples on this in 6.2).

To have an idea what, in the following, will be discussed, the full list, devoid of variation (see more in 5) will be presented here but provided with reducing frequencies of the proverb occurrence below.

62 Easier said than done, 46 Safety first, 40 You get what you pay for, 52 Every cloud has a silver lining, 37 The early bird catches the worm, 33 Still waters run deep, 32 First come, first served, 32 Forgive and forget, 32 It's better to be safe than sorry, 31 First things first, 31 Prevention is better than cure,

30 Small is beautiful, 29 The proof of the pudding is in the eating, 27 You cannot have your cake and eat it (too), 25 Birds of a feather flock together, 25 There is safety in numbers, 22 Jack of all trades, master of none, 22 Time is money, 21 Beggars can't be choosers, 21 Old habits die hard,

20 All good things come to an end, 19 No smoke without fire, 19 The show must go on, 19 Horses for courses, 18 Actions speak louder than words, 18 Every man for himself, 18 Money talks, 18 There is no time like the present, 17 An apple a day keeps the doctor away, 17 There is no such thing as a free lunch, 16 A friend in need is a friend indeed, 16- Better late than never, 1 One/a picture is worth a thousand words, 15 Don't judge a book by its cover, 15 Fight fire with fire, 15 Knowledge is power, 15 The devil you know is better than the devil you don't, 14 All's well that ends well, 14 Let sleeping dogs lie, 14 No news is good news, 14 There is a time and place for everything, 14 Time is a great healer, 14 When in Rome, do as the Romans do, 14 He who pays the piper calls the tune,

13 Absence makes the heart grow fonder, 13 Easy come, easy go, 13 Forewarned is forearmed, 13 Live and let live, 13 Make hay while the sun shines, 13 Bad things come in threes, 12 Boys will be boys, 12 Let bygones be bygones, 12 Look before you leap, 12 Practice makes perfect, 11 A bird in the hand is worth two in the bush, 11 An eye for an eye, a tooth for a tooth, 11 Carpe diem, 11 Charity begins at home, 11 In for a penny, in for a pound, 11 Power corrupts, absolute power corrupts absolutely, 11 The end justifies the means, 11 Two wrongs do not make a right,

10 Beauty is only skin deep, 10 Count your blessings, 10 Don't/do not look a gift horse in the mouth, 10 No man can serve two masters, 10 Strike while the iron is hot, 10 Waste not, want not, 9 Might is right, 9 Once bitten, twice shy, 9 Two heads are better than one, 8 A stitch in time (saves nine), 8 Beauty is in the eye of the beholder, 8 Discretion is the better part of valour, 8 Spare the rod and spoil the child, 8 Too many cooks spoil the broth, 8 Walls have ears, 8 You are what you eat, 7 Blood is thicker than water, 7 Curiosity killed the cat, 7 Fools rush in (where angels fear to tread), 7 God helps those who help themselves, 7 Money doesn't grow on trees, 7 No man is an island, 7 The customer is always right,

6 Every little bit helps, 6 Great minds think alike, 6 History repeats itself, 6 A man's home is his castle, 6 If you scratch my back, I'll scratch yours, 6 It takes two to tango, 6 One good turn deserves another, 6 People in glass houses shouldn't throw stones, 6 Physician, heal thyself, 6 The bigger they are, the harder they fall, 5 A new broom sweeps clean, 5 Appearances are deceptive, 5 Business before pleasure, 5 Every man has his price, 5 Familiarity breeds contempt, 5 Fortune favours the brave, 5 Honesty is the best policy, 5 History repeats itself, 5 The grass is always greener on the other side of the fence, 5 Tomorrow is another day,

4 Absolute power corrupts absolutely, 4 Christmas comes but once a year, 4 Like father, like son, 4 Close but no cigar, 4 Diamonds are a girl's best friend, 4 Don't count your chickens before they're hatched, 4 Don't try to teach grandma how to suck eggs, 4 Early to bed and early to rise, makes a man healthy, wealthy, and wise, 4 If a job is worth doing , it is worth doing well, 4 Ignorance is bliss, 4 Life begins at forty, 4 Lightning never strikes in the same place twice, 4 Man does not live by bread, 4 Never say never, 4 Seek and ye shall find, 4 Silence is golden, 4 There is no accounting for tastes, 4 Think globally, act locally, 4 To err is human, to forgive divine, 4 You make your bed, you have to lie in it.

Table of distribution of Invariants (separately for each 10 proverbs with descending frequency, marked below) is the following :

(1.) 3, (2.) 3, (3.) 8, (4.) 6, (5.) 6, (5.) 6, (7.) 5, (8.) 7, (9.) 4, (10.) 4 (rest = 6) 4.

6.2 Analysis of a Sample Taken from the Proverbs Having Top Frequency

Let us first briefly inspect the status, formal aspects, and and also text behaviour of the proverbs with the highest frequency (**Fr**) displaying the richest scale of cases and types of use. Due to too many examples, systematic attention (in the sense that it includes all BNC corpus findings), will be on the first half of data (with frequencies 62-25). Next to the overall frequency and abbreviated variation (such as **Sa**, **Ss**, including Invariable), a sample of contextual examples will be offered with a commentary. Also labels for *meaning types* (following Matti Kuusi system) will be offered (see more in 7 and a full coverage in Supplement 2) and a simple note on meaning made (in brackets).

Easier said than done. Fr 62, **J1h** *Actions-Deeds*
(*It is easy to propose, but difficult to accomplish*).
This topmost proverb which is mostly **invariable** may be used as it is (as a sentence), such as in *,Easier said than done, I supposed;* its main use is basically evaluative and based on comparison. It often requires a completion of a subject, such as in *Managing to be positive when you are in pain is easier said than done*, or an introductory phrase, such as in *But I knew that was easier said than done*. In many cases, the proverb uses a complement on its right side (or both on the left and right side) which explains the reasons for its use, as in *Like practically everything in business this is easier said than done, as the plethora of books, theories, advice, and consultants testify*.

Safety first. Fr 46, **Coping and Learning**, **M1b** *Dangerous Situations*
(*One should take precautions first, securing safety*).
The second topmost proverb, which is invariable due to its extremely small length, has reached its position due to its general slogan-like function, where it is dominant, eg., so *'**Safety First**' was not a substitute for lack of ideas and policies : it was deliberately...*

You get what you pay for. Fr 40, *Agreement and Norms*, **L2a** *The nature of business and bargaining*
(*The quality of goods depends on the amount paid*).
Also, the third topmost proverb is basically a statement of a general type of behaviour, where it is often difficult to discern between its metaphorical and literal meaning and function. See, the first could be metaphorical:*you get what you pay forwas ably demonstrated by the decision in 1981 to replace aging first-generation DMU fleets on non electrified outer suburban lines,*while the second refers to a common financial transaction: *but you get what you pay for and a cheap bed will wear out faster than a quality style*. There are quite a few of such instances and to clearly mark the border-line may be difficult.

Every cloud has a silver lining. Fr 52, Sa **T3c Trusting in the future, preparing for the future, dreaming, optimism or pessimism** or E1 *Success*
(*It is possible for something good to come out of a bad situation*).
This is a very popular proverb, finally based on an obvious metaphor, having offered itself profusely to variation; accordingly, its full form is found only 6 times. The nominal form **silver cloud** (also as *silver clouds*) is very dominant and found 57 times, i.e. more than the whole frequency which suggests that the form has long started to have a life of its own. This independent life suggests different variants starting with the past tense

s.c. had, but also such as in *clouds had a silver lining*, etc., (for an exhaustive analysis of this proverb, see more about this proverb in Čermák 2009).

The early bird catches the worm. Fr 37, **T1a *Timing***, Sa
(*Who arrives first has the best chance to succeed*).
Similarly, *the early bird catches the worm* is attested only twice, the rest being uses of the **early bird** only (also 11 times in plural *early birds*), e.g. *Your reply – Never be an early worm!, My, my – you are an early bird!* There is a single paradigmatic variant,*The early bird catches the voter.*

Still waters run deep. Fr 33, **M1e *Precaution*, *Watchfulness***, Sa
(*A person with a calm appearance has considerable inner emotion, character, or intellect and acts secretly*).
Most uses belong to the nominal phrase and idiom **still waters**, such as while *Still Waters project began two years ago*, and the nominal and proprietary versions such as *Still Waters Press, STILL HIGHLAND SPRING WATER*; there are only 5 full version of *still waters run deep,*and two using a slightly different paradigmatic version of it *still waters running deep*. Yet there is no singular use of **water*. Obviously, some versions denoting a geographical feature of water are used literally, such as in *The still watersof the lake reflected the surrounding mountains*. An advantageous feature of balancing between a terminological name quality and and idiomatic one is to be found in *still waters of the swimming pool*.

First come, first served. Fr 32, **T1a *Timing***
(*People will be dealt with in the order they came*).
The proverb which is not metaphorical, is almost **invariable** and used as an independent sentence, and rarely as a nominal phrase, such as *in first come first served* basis, the only exception being a complex syntagmatic variant *running out of funds and first in will be first served and maybe even the only one served*.

Forgive and forget. Fr 32, **H7k *Aggression and Peacefulness***
(*To forgive someone by also forgetting that the wrong they committed ever happened*).
Its use is rather simple, where all of the invariable 32 occurrences of the full proverb are always used, though there is a slight paradigmatic variation in tense, such as *A man forgives and forgets, be forgiven and forgotten*. Its variability is limited, most uses are found either in the infinitive or imperative. *He now wants to forgive and forget Mr. Prescott, Forgive and forget if possible.*

It's better to be safe than sorry. Fr 32, **M1a Precaution, *Watchfulness***, Ss
(*It is better to expend the time or effort to be cautious with one's actions than to feel regret about one's carelessness later*).
Also all forms of the 32 uses of *It's better to be safe than sorry* are rather simple, with a very little syntagmatic variation extending and also emphasizing the proverb, such

as *It was better to be safe than sorry. It's far better to be safe than sorry, especially better to be safe than sorry.*

First things first. Fr 31, **L2a** *The nature of business and bargaining*
(*It is better to keep the order of things and concentrate on the most important things*).
A fully stable, invariable proverb is *First things first*, being formally very dense and small (three words). This does not mean that a slight, limited syntagmatic, in fact an emphatic variation is not possible, appearing usually at the beginning of the proverb, such as in *But first things first, so first things first.*

Prevention is better than cure. Fr 31, T1d *A well-timed beginning, finish, support or aid will pay off* or M1 *Precaution and Watchfulness*
(*One should work to stop something from happening rather than try to combat it later*).
Another almost invariable proverb, *Prevention is better than cure*, is never syntagmatically shortened having only undergone a small lexical, i.e. paradigmatic changes Pa (*better → easier*) as in *Prevention is easier than cure*, and an added double syntagmatic modification of words, such as in *Better an ounce of prevention than a pound of cure.*

Small is beautiful. Fr 30, **C4b** **Little : Big**
(*The belief that something small-scale is better than a large-scale equivalent*).
Invariable is another very short proverb *Small is beautiful*, which is typically used, if not integrated in the body of text, as a slogan, proper name, etc, as in *...who wrote a book entitled Small Is Beautiful*, but is sometimes used in citations, cf. *such clichés as 'Small is beautiful' are not helpful.*

The proof of the pudding is in the eating. Fr 29, **D4b** or **C5 Signals and their Interpretation**
(*The ultimate evidence of testing is trying it*).
Unusually, in an almost half (14) instances, there appears a version of the full, unshortened proverb, allowing thus for a number of variants, mostly Sa, Ss, such as *The proof of the pudding has to be in the eating; Now the proof of the pudding should be in the eating.* In some cases an additional text helps to make the proverb's use clear, such as *And the proof of the pudding is 40% revenue growth worldwide year-on-year*, or *Perhaps the proof of the pudding can be seen in public attitudes, for no such projects can come to fruition.* However, a much larger context is necessary (not provided here) to make an occasional and rather bold use of the proverb comprehensible at all, such as in *The proof of the pudding here is sex role reverse species.*

You cannot have your cake and eat it (too). Fr 27, Sa, Ss **M8a Thrift and stinginess**
(*You cannot enjoy two desirable things at the same time*).
The proverb *You cannot have your cake and eat it too* is almostalways (in 25 out of all 27 occurrences) used in its full form, i.e. without any major change, such as in *You can't have your cake and eat it.* A minor variation does occur, however, paradigmatically, due

to a change of morphology, such as in *Now that's a case of having your cake and eating it, isn't it?* A rather frequent case is a larger context where the proverb is used as a result of it, such as in *You face the real world and you can't have your cake and eat it.* Rarely, the proverb is clipped and loses its end, such as in *The problem the Wedding Industry in Scotland are in for a treat: now you can have your cake.*

Birds of a feather flock together. Fr 25, **H1f *Self* : *Others*, *Company***, Sa
(*People of similar* <u>character</u>, *taste tend to* <u>congregate</u> *or* <u>associate</u> *with one another*).
Being quite familiar, the proverb is often substituted in text by its shortened form only *birds of a feather* (mostly in the plural) *Birds of a feather, aren't they really?* Its full version has been used only once which suggests that the short form has acquired its independent existence as a nominal phraseme.

7. English Proverbs and Their Meaning (as Reflected in Matti-Kuusi classification)

Any attempt at a semantic classification of proverbs is not easy (though Permjakov's dichotomy system seems to be inviting an offering, however, only a skeleton of information, if any). Hence a combined ethnographic classification is undertaken here, trying to fit the 120 English proverbs used into the well-known Proverb thesaurus (*International Type System of Proverbs*, 2000) by Matti Kuusi and Outi Lauhakangas. It was found that out of the rich inventory of proverb types related to all languages, only those proverbs in the 120 inspected were found, going by their frequency, to be really prominent here. All of these are related to the ***social aspects of life*** and proverb use, and are split into 7 classes. Accordingly, these and only these are offered below (with frequencies in BNC offering one proverb as an illustration).

It is interesting to note that none of such familiar fields and topics, as religion, god, nature, animals, weather, etc., have scored higher or has the same frequencies. Hence nine classes (C, E, G, H, J, K, L, M, and T, including the relevant subclass) are used with their brief description (see more in Supplement 1).

8. Notes and Summary

An elaborate, systematic and exhaustive treatment of the core proverbs has been offered here, illustrated in English in the effort to find out what the core consists of and is made of. It is evident that the data may serve as inspiration for basic dictionaries, textbooks, etc., so there is the offer of a practical use of these results, too.

Variability must be viewed as a double phenomenon. Of the two types, one is due to high frequency and familiarity of use, the other is due to periphery and insufficient knowledge. It is evident that only the former could have been inspected here. The highest variability, which is a converse to invariability, is rather great in lower frequencies. The top proverbs are, as a rule, invariable, though their very top frequencies are not.

Generally, there is a pronounced preference of the proverbs inspected here:

To formally have short forms, being lexically rather simple.

To semantically occupy only certain areas being predominant is to the exclusion of other.

Obviously, the core proverbs are an approximation of how humans, through their language, deal with reality in a quantified way.

SUPPLEMENTS:

1 Basic Proverbs by Frequency

See the list above in 6.1.

2 Basic Proverbs Alphabetically (105) down to frequency 5 inclusively.

The table shortlisting research figures, offers:

(1) absolute frequency of the proverb in BNC,

(2) representation and coverage of Matti Kuusi's types (*http://lauhakan.home.cern.ch/lauhakan/int/cerpint.html* values in the third column,

(3) variants : **Inv**(ariable), **S**(yntagmatic), **P**(aradigmatic), **a**(utosemantic), **s**(ynsemantic),

including *shortening* as part of **Sa**, thus *Sa, Ss, As, Aa*.

A bird in the hand is worth two in the bush	Freq. in BNC 11	**C3c12**	variation Sa
A friend in need is a friend indeed	Freq. in BNC 16	**H6b24**	variation Sa
A man's home is his castle	Freq. in BNC 6	**H4b18**	variation Pa
A new broom sweeps clean	Freq. in BNC 5	**T2b10**	variation Sa Pa
A stitch in time (saves nine)	Freq. in BNC 8	**T1d15**	Invariant
Absence makes the heart grow fonder	Freq. in BNC 13	**E1l32**	variation Sa
Absolute power corrupts absolutely	Freq. in BNC 11	**K1b11**	variation Sa
Actions speak louder than words	Freq. in BNC 18	**J1h17**	variation Pa?
All good things come to an end	Freq. in BNC 20	**T4e11**	Invariant
All's well that ends well	Freq. in BNC 14	**T4c13**	Invariant
An apple a day keeps the doctor away	Freq. in BNC 17	**G7b11**	variation Pa
An eye for an eye, a tooth for a tooth	Freq. in BNC 11	**H7m20**	Invariant
Appearances are deceptive	Freq. in BNC 5	**C6b15**	variation Pa
Bad things come in threes	Freq. in BNC 13	**B2d14**	variation Pa

Beauty is in the eye of the beholder	Freq. in BNC 8	**D3c21**	variation Sa
Beauty is only skin deep	Freq. in BNC 10	**C6b23**	variation Sa
Beggars can't be choosers	Freq. in BNC 21	**H3i13**	variation Pa
Better late than never	Freq. in BNC 16	**E1d28**	Invariant
Birds of a feather flock together	Freq. in BNC 25	**H1f 24**	variation Sa
Blood is thicker than water	Freq. in BNC 7	**G1a12**	Invariant
Boys will be boys	Freq. in BNC 12	**C1b11**	Invariant
Business before pleasure	Freq. in BNC 5	**M7f11**	Invariant
Carpe diem	Freq. in BNC 11	**T1c10**	Invariant
Charity begins at home	Freq. in BNC 11	**H2c17**	Invariant
Count your blessings	Freq. in BNC 10	**B2b10**	Invariant
Curiosity killed the cat	Freq. in BNC 7	**H3g15**	Invariant
Discretion is the better part of valour	Freq. in BNC 8	**M4d23**	Invariant
Don't judge a book by its cover	Freq. in BNC 15	**C6d15**	variation Sa
Don't/do not look a gift horse in the mouth	Freq. in BNC 10	**H5g13**	variation Sa
Easier said than done	Freq. in BNC 62	**J1h22**	Invariant
Easy come, easy go	Freq. in BNC 13	**T1j20**	variation Sa?
Every cloud has a silver lining	Freq. in BNC 52	**T3c16**	variation Sa
Every little bit helps	Freq. in BNC 6	**C1b27**	Invariant
Every man for himself	Freq. in BNC 18	**H2c15**	Invariant
Every man has his price	Freq. in BNC 5	**L2a22**	Invariant
Familiarity breeds contempt	Freq. in BNC 5	**H4d11**	Invariant
Fight fire with fire	Freq. in BNC 15	**H7k28 opposite**	variation Ps
First come, first served	Freq. in BNC 32	**T1a18**	Invariant
First things first	Freq. in BNC 31	**M1f11**	Invariant
Fools rush in (where angels fear to tread	Freq. in BNC 7	**J1g29**	variation Sa
Forewarned is forearmed	Freq. in BNC 13	**M1a16**	Invariant
Forgive and forget	Freq. in BNC 32	**H7k29**	Invariant
Fortune favours the brave	Freq. in BNC 5	**M4a13**	Invariant
God helps those who help themselves	Freq. in BNC 7	**H2e12**	variation Sa
Grass is always greener on the other side of the fence	Freq. in BNC 5	**H3f14**	Invariant
Great minds think alike	Freq. in BNC 6	**H1f27c**	variation Sa?
He who pays the piper calls the tune	Freq. in BNC 14	**L2b13**	variation Sa
History repeats itself	Freq. in BNC 6	**T2c11**	variation Pa
Honesty is the best policy	Freq. in BNC 5	**F1b43**	Invariant?
Horses for courses	Freq. in BNC 19	**K1j23**	Invariant

If you scratch my back, I'll scratch yours	Freq. in BNC 6	**H5d**	variation Sa
In for a penny, in for a pound	Freq. in BNC 11	**M8a12**	variation Sa
It takes two to tango	Freq. in BNC 6	**C4a**	Invariant
It's better to be safe than sorry	Freq. in BNC 32	**M1a16**	variation Ss
Jack of all trades, master of none	Freq. in BNC 22	**M6d10**	variation Sa
Knowledge is power	Freq. in BNC 15	**M3a14**	Invariant
Let bygones be bygones	Freq. in BNC 12	**C3d15**	Invariant
Let sleeping dogs lie	Freq. in BNC 14	**M1e24**	Invariant
Live and let live	Freq. in BNC 13	**M4d11**	Invariant
Look before you leap	Freq. in BNC 12	**T1f22**	Invariant
Make hay while the sun shines	Freq. in BNC 13	**T1b11**	variation Sa Ps
Might is right	Freq. in BNC 9	**K1l23**	Invariant
Money doesn't grow on trees	Freq. in BNC 7	**C3b29**	variation Sa
Money talks	Freq. in BNC 18	**K2a22**	Invariant
No man can serve two masters	Freq. in BNC 10	**M6d21**	variation Ss
No man is an island	Freq. in BNC 7	**G1a11**	Invariant
No news is good news	Freq. in BNC 14	**J1e19**	variation Sa
No smoke without fire	Freq. in BNC 19	**C5a18**	Invariant
Old habits die hard	Freq. in BNC 21	**C1d21c**	Invariant
Once bitten, twice shy	Freq. in BNC 9	**M9e15**	variation Sa
One good turn deserves another	Freq. in BNC 6	**H5d09b**	Invariant
One/a picture is worth a thousand words	Freq. in BNC 15	**J1q**	Invariant
People in glass houses shouldn't throw stones	Freq. in BNC 6	**H7b27**	variation Sa
Physician, heal thyself	Freq. in BNC 6	**H1b29**	Invariant
Power corrupts, absolute power corrupts absolutely	Freq. in BNC 11	**K1b11**	variation Sa
Practice makes perfect	Freq. in BNC 12	**M9d27**	Invariant
Prevention is better than cure	Freq. in BNC 31	**T1d11b**	Invariant
Safety first	Freq. in BNC 46	**M1b**	Invariant
Small is beautiful	Freq. in BNC 30	**C4b14**	Invariant
Spare the rod and spoil the child	Freq. in BNC 8	**G3c29**	variation Ss
Still waters run deep	Freq. in BNC 33	**M1e21**	variation Sa
Strike while the iron is hot	Freq. in BNC 10	**T1b15**	Invariant
The bigger they are, the harder they fall	Freq. in BNC 6	**C6f15**	variation Sa
The customer is always right	Freq. in BNC 7	**L2b13**	Invariant
The devil you know is better than the devil you don't	Freq. in BNC 15	**M4c34**	variation S/Aa
The early bird catches the worm	Freq. in BNC 37	**T1a11,M1**	variation Sa

The end justifies the means	Freq. in BNC 11	F1d26	Invariant
The grass is always greener on the other side of the fence	Freq. in BNC 5	H3f14	variation Pa
The proof of the pudding is in the eating	Freq. in BNC 29	D4b11,C5	variation Sa
The show must go on	Freq. in BNC 19	M4a10	Invariant
There is a time and place for everything	Freq. in BNC 14	T1b10	variation S/Pa Ps
There is no such thing as a free lunch	Freq. in BNC 17	L2a23	Invariant
There is no time like the present	Freq. in BNC 18	T1c10	Invariant
There is safety in numbers	Freq. in BNC 25	H3b24	variation Sa
Time is a great healer	Freq. in BNC 14	T1h27	variation Pa
Time is money	Freq. in BNC 22	T1a22	Invariant
Tomorrow is another day	Freq. in BNC 5	T1g14	Invariant
Too many cooks spoil the broth	Freq. in BNC 8	H2a20	variation Sa
Two heads are better than one	Freq. in BNC 9	H3b15	Invariant
Two wrongs do not make a right	Freq. in BNC 11	H7m28b	variation Sa
Walls have ears	Freq. in BNC 8	J1n18	Invariant
Waste not, want not	Freq. in BNC 10	M8a29	Invariant
When in Rome, do as the Romans do	Freq. in BNC 14	H1g10	variation Sa
You are what you eat	Freq. in BNC 8	D4a	Invariant
You cannot have your cake and eat it (too)	Freq. in BNC 27	M8a31	variation Ss Sa
You get what you pay for	Freq. in BNC 40	L2a22	Invariant

A note of thanks for the precise references to the Matti Kuusi type system isdue to O. Lauhakangas.

LITERATURE

BNC. British National Corpus https://ske.fi.muni.cz/bonito/run.cgi/corp_info?corpname = preloaded/ bnc2_tt2&struct_attr_stats = 1&subcorpora = 1.

ČERMÁK, František, 2009. "What One Can Do with Proverbs in Text." In *Phraseologie disziplinar und interdisziplinar*, ed. C. Foldes, 307–321. Tübingen: Gunter Narr Verlag.

ČERMÁK, František. 2004. "Jazyková variabilita: případ přísloví." In Čeština – Universalia a specifika 5, edited by Z. Hladká and P. Karlík, 99–109. Praha: NLN. (= Language Variability: the Case of Proverbs).

ČERMÁK, František. 2010. "The Paremiological Minimum of English." In … *for thy speech bewrayeth thee. A Festschrift for Libuše Dušková*, edited by M. Malá and P. Šaldová, 57–71. Praha: Univerzita Karlova v Praze, Filozofická fakulta.

CHAMBERS, J. K., TRUDGILL, Peter, and SCHILLING-ESTES, Natalie, eds. 2003. *The Handbook of Language Variation And Change* Oxford: Blackwell.

CHRISTY, Robert. cca 1888. Proverbs, Maxims and Phrasemes of All Ages: classified subjectively and arranged alphabetically. New York: G. P. Putnam's Sons.

HRISZTOVA-GOTTHARDT, Hrisztalina and ALEKSA VARGA, Melita, ed. 2014. *Introduction to Paremiology: A Comprehensive Guide to Proverb Studies*. Berlin: DeGruyter.

KUUSI, Matti and LAUHAKANGAS, Outi. 2000-. *The MATTI KUUSI International Type System of Proverbs*. http://lauhakan.home.cern.ch/lauhakan/int/cerpint.html.

LAU, K. J., TOKOFSKY, P., WINICK, S. D., and. MIEDER, W. 2004. *What goes around comes around: The circulation of proverbs in contemporary life*. Logan: Utah State University Press.

MIEDER, Wolfgang. 1993. *Proverbs are Never out of Season, Popular Wisdom in Modern Age*. Oxford: Oxford University Press.

MOHAMMAD, Saber Khaghaninejad. 2015. "The Frequency of Expressions and Proverbs in Different Iranian Generations' Speech Styles." *International Letters of Social and Humanistic Sciences* 9(1): 1–19.

SCHMIDT, Jürgen Erich, ed. 2010. *LANGUAGE and SPACE, An International Handbook of Linguistic Variation*. Berlin: de Gruyter.

STABELL BILGRAV, Jens A. 1985. *20.000 proverbs and their equivalents in German, French, Swedish, Danish*. Copenhagen: H. Heide.

THESAURUS PROVERBIORUM MEDII AEVI 1–13. 1995–2013. Lexikon der Sprichwörter des romanisch-germanischen Mittelalters, Begründet von Samuel Singer, Berlin: W. de Gruyter.

11. Paremiological Minimum of English

In ...*for thy speech bewrayeth thee. A Festschrift for Libuše Dušková*, M. Malá, P. Šaldová, (eds.) Univerzita Karlova v Praze Filozofická fakulta, Praha 2010, 57–71, **Čermák Proverbs 2014**, 225–234.

Abstract

An English corpus-based proverb minimum is presented here with an analysis of their constituent parts.

1. Introduction

Proverbs are far from being dead having been used and repeatedly found useful for centuries. All known languages have them. However, their usage does depend on the situation, type of speaker (who tends to be older and more experienced in contrast to the listener), wishing to refer to a general and recognized experience and norm, and other factors. In teaching a language, proverbs tend to be omitted entirely, as there is precious little they offer to a grammarian or a text-book author.

Being pieces of wisdom of past generations, they may seem to be rather heavy in the language of the easy-going young people of today who may then shy away from what proverbs keep telling and reminding them of what has proved to be a good way of conduct in life and what may be wrong with what they may be doing now.

2. Research of Proverbs

Paremiology has been rather popular both in linguistics and ethnography for some time, which has led to numerous book studies and articles, some of which are to be found in the specialized journal *Proverbium* or the Website *Proverbio*. The present editor-in-chief of *Proverbium*, prof. Wolfgang Mieder, a dedicated researcher and author of many studies, has recently published an international bibliography of proverb research which offers an invaluable insight into contributions in many languages and from many (often widely different) points of view (Mieder 2009).

However, restricting ourselves by the data and their frequency, the results of any research would be somewhat different. Should one ask the uncomfortable questions which proverbs belong among the most common, the question seems difficult, if not impossible to answer. Yet, there is a recent trend of establishing just this, a proverb minimum of a language which is supposed to contain a compressed version of the totality of proverbs. Yet there are problems linked to this. In the sense of quantity, a selection of one hundred proverbs (or a few more) out of several thousand evokes the problem of representation of the whole; in the sense of providing researchers or teachers with a kind of basis for their activities it may seem to be an advantage, etc.

Once assembled in a list, proverbs seem to be a source for at least two types of research. One (A), focussing on odd and rare grammatical or lexical features, etc., may be of a marginal interest, however.

However, much more rewarding research may be oriented on ever new (B) variants of proverbs, to be found amply in the corpora of today's language. This way, a new type of study, never really possible in the past, is made possible. Though variation is an important feature of any language in any of its aspects, proverbs seem to offer a very specific and rich source of data. The explanation is to be sought in the psychology of some speakers. By introducing one's own variant of a proverb, one usually signals one's own interpretation of the old and general truth proverbs offer; this interpretation leading to a change in form, always preserves a substantial part of the proverb unchanged, as the speaker's intention is always not to break the links with the old and generally acknowledged standard form of the proverb.

Obviously, no one really knows, should he/she decide to teach proverbs or introduce them in a new textbook, which of thousands of existing proverbs to choose from.

Following a recent trend of establishing proverb minima for some languages, an attempt is made here to propose such a minimum for the English language for the first time. Despite proposals of a proverb list by individual authors in past (some of which have been consulted here), which can hardly be called minima, the list proposed in the following, based on the British National Corpus, may be viewed as representative and, hence, of some use for others. Despite the fact that it may not be so simple in some cases and that there is, definitely, a corroboration needed based on a much larger corpus (which does not exist, however), it is basically safe to view the proverbs in the list as ordered by typicality and general importance due to their high usage. Yet it has to be stressed that the use and frequency of proverbs must be somewhat different in oral communications and corpora since what BNC offers is largely the written language.

3. Some Features of the English Paremiological Minimum

Because too many proverb variants are found in the corpus, no attempt has been made here to follow this line (B). However, there may be some other aspects (A) worth inspecting. The list below, which is ordered by frequency in the BNC only, has been standardized to a single canonical form for each proverb only (the cut-off point being 1).

Even in this standard form, some features stand out and are in contrast with the standard features of an average text. Thus, as far as mood is concerned, the proverbs are used in the declarative present tense form mostly, while only 12 (out of 100) use the imperative form, although, obviously, all declarative forms have, in fact, the same function, that of advice, admonishing, warning, etc. It is also of some interest, that the prominent proverb feature of impersonality or, rather, impartial approach to the listener, uses passive voice scarcely (only 4 occurrences, apart from the form *bitten*) as well as other means used for impersonality (there are four instances of *you*). Lexical features are not followed here, although two lists, alphabetical and frequency, of all words used in the proverb forms are added making analysis of this feature possible, especially with regard to a little-known aspect of how a meaning of a large unit (sentence in this case) is built out of smaller units (words) which is all the more interesting in this case as almost no compositional effect takes place here giving place to metaphors, etc.

4. English Paremiological Minimum

The number of proverbs found in the BNC is rounded off at one hundred. Unfortunately, at least two final groups in the list of one hundred may not be quite representative, as they have been found only once. Yet, given BNC as (practically) the only representative data source of contemporary English, they have to be taken at their face-value.

Easier said than done. 62
Every cloud has a silver lining. 52
Still waters run deep. 33
Chickens come home to roost. 31
First things first. 31
Small is beautiful. 30
Forgive and forget. 27
Birds of a feather flock together. 25
There is safety in numbers. 25
Time is money. 22

Out of sight, out of mind. 21
First come, first served. 20
Every man for himself. 20
No smoke without fire. 19
Money talks. 18
Better late than never. 16
You cannot have your cake and eat it too. 16
Knowledge is power. 15
A picture is worth a thousand words. 15
There is no such thing as a free lunch. 15

Fight fire with fire. 15
When in Rome, do as the Romans do. 14
Let sleeping dogs lie. 14
Beggars can't be choosers. 14
All's well that ends well. 13
Forewarned is forearmed. 13
Live and let live. 13
Let bygones be bygones. 12
Look before you leap. 12
Practice makes perfect. 12

A bird in the hand is worth two in the bush. 11
The end justifies the means. 11
Easy come, easy go. 11
Two wrongs don't make a right. 11
Like father, like son. 11
Actions speak louder than words. 10
Don't look a gift horse in the mouth. 10
An apple a day keeps the doctor away. 10
First come, first served. 10
No man can serve two masters. 10

Once bitten, twice shy. 9
Waste not, want not. 9
Two heads are better than one. 9
Bad news travels fast. 9
A stitch in time saves nine. 8
Beauty is in the eye of the beholder. 8
Too many cooks spoil the broth. 8
No news is good news. 8
Charity begins at home. 8
Absence makes the heart grow fonder. 7

No man is an island. 7
Strike while the iron is hot. 7
Make hay while the sun shines. 7
Curiosity killed the cat. 7
Blood is thicker than water. 7
Out of sight, out of mind. 6
It takes two to tango. 6
The early bird catches the worm. 5
All good things come to an end. 5
Don't count your chickens before they're hatched. 4

Where there's a will, there's a way. 4
Silence is golden. 4
Early to bed and early to rise, makes a man healthy, wealthy, and wise. 4
The grass is always greener on the other side of the fence. 4
All that glitters is not gold. 3
Do unto others as you would have them do unto you. 3
Spare the rod and spoil the child. 3
To err is human, to forgive divine. 4
Lightning never strikes in the same place twice. 4
Beauty is only skin deep. 3

He who hesitates is lost. 3
Love is blind. 3
One swallow doesn't make a summer. 3
Business before pleasure. 2
If at first you don't succeed, try, try again. 2
An ounce of prevention is worth a pound of cure. 2
A rolling stone gathers no moss. 2
You can't teach an old dog new tricks. 2
Don't put all your eggs in one basket. 2
A fool and his money are soon parted. 2

Many hands make light work. 2
Don't change horses in the middle of the stream (mid-stream). 2
Revenge is sweet. 2
Every man has his price. 2
Don't put all your eggs in one basket. 2
A friend in need is a friend indeed. 1
The road to hell is paved with good intentions. 1
Diamond cuts diamond. 1
Haste makes waste. 1
Don't judge a book by its cover. 1

You can lead a horse to water, but you can't make him drink. 1
Never put off till tomorrow what you can do today. 1
When it rains, it pours. 1
As you sow, so shall you reap. 1
Discretion is the better part of valour. 1
Rome was not built in a day. 1
The road to hell is paved with good intentions. 1
Time and tide wait for no man. 1
There is no fool like an old fool. 1
When the cat's away, the mice play. 1

LITERATURE

ČERMÁK, František. 2003. "Paremiological Minimum of Czech: The Corpus Evidence." In *Flut von Texten – Vielvalt der Kulturen. Ascona 2001 zur Methodologie und Kulturspezifik der Phraseologie*, edited by H. Burger, A. Häcki-Buhofer, G. Greciano, 15–31. Hohengehren: Schneider Verlag.

ČERMÁK, František. 2004a. "Text Introducers of Proverbs and Other Idioms." In *Phraseologismen als Gegenstand sprach- und kulturwissenschaftlicher Forschung*, edited by C. Földes and J. Wirrer, 27-46. Hohengren: Schneider Verlag.

ČERMÁK, František. 2004b. "Jazyková variabilita: případ přísloví." In Čeština - Universalia a specifika 5. Praha: NLN.

ČERMÁK, František. 2007a. *What One Can Do with Proverbs in Text*, In Čermák 2007 Frazeologie a idiomatika... (also: Proceedings of Vezsprém Europhras)

ČERMÁK, František. 2007b. *Frazeologie a idiomatika česká a obecná*. Praha: Karolinum. (= Czech and General Phraseology)

KUUSI, Matti. 1972. *Towards an International Type-System of Proverbs*. Helsinki: Academia Scientiarum Fennica.

MIDER, Wolfgang. 2009. *International Bibliography of Paremiology and Phraseology*. Vol 1: A–M, Vol 2: N–Z. Berlin – New York: de Gruyter.

MIEDER, Wolfgang. 2004c. *Proverbs. A Handbook*. London: Greenwood Press Westport.

PERMJAKOV, Grigorij Ľvovič. 1971. *Paremiologičeskij Eksperiment. Materialy dlja paremiologičeskogo minimuma*. Moskva: Nauka.

APPENDICES

ALPHABETICAL LIST OF WORDS MAKING UP THE ENGLISH PAREMIOLOGICAL MINIMUM

Statistics: 100 sentences, 667 tokens (text words), 356 types.

a absence actions again all all's always an and apple are as at away away bad basket be beautiful beauty bed before beggars begins beholder better bird birds bitten blind blood book broth built bush business but by bygones bygones cake can cannot can't cat catches cat's change charity chickens child choosers cloud come come cooks count cover cure curiosity cuts day day deep diamond discretion divine do doctor doesn't dog dogs done don't drink early easier easy eat eggs end ends err every eye fast father feather fence fight fire first flock fonder fool fool for forearmed forewarned forget forgive free friend gathers gift glitters go gold golden good grass greener grow hand hands has haste hatched have hay he heads healthy heart hell hesitates him himself his home horse horses hot human if in indeed intentions intentions iron is island it its judge justifies keeps killed knowledge late lead leap let lie light lightning like lining live look lost louder love lunch make makes man man many masters means mice middle midstream mind mind money moss mouth need never new news news nine no not not not numbers of off old on once one one only other others ounce out part parted paved perfect picture place play pleasure pound pours power practice prevention price put rains reap revenge right rise road rod rolling romans rome rome roost run safety said same saves serve served shall shines shy side sight silence silver skin sleeping small smoke so son soon sow spare speak spoil still stitch stone stream strike strikes succeed such summer sun swallow sweet takes talks tango teach than that the them there there's they're thicker thing things thousand tide till time to today together tomorrow too too travels tricks try try twice two unto valour wait want was waste water water waters way wealthy well what when where while who will wise with without words words work worm worth would wrongs you you your

FREQUENCY LIST OF WORDS MAKING UP THE ENGLISH PAREMIOLOGICAL MINIMUM

29 the 27 is 22 a 13 in 11 of 10 you 10 to 8 no 8 and 8 don't 7 first 6 an 5 two 5 man 5 make 5 do 5 than 4 all 4 out 4 your 4 it 4 as 4 makes 4 good 3 put 3 never 3 money 3 before 3 better 3 come 3 fire 3 time 3 when 3 with 3 one 3 can't 3 let 3 early 3 there 3 worth 3 like 3 can 3 every 2 friend 2 well 2 that 2 live 2 be 2 look 2 spoil 2 at 2 many 2 news 2 beauty 2 while 2 there's 2 unto 2 not 2 are 2 basket 2 eggs 2 bird 2 his 2 fool 2 end 2 twice 2 waste 2 horse 2 easy 2 old 2 served 2 sight 2 for 2 has 2 have 2 forgive 2 things 2 home 2 deep 2 chickens 2 come 2 road 2 diamond 2 hell 2 paved 1 mice 1 strikes 1 place 1 same 1 lightning 1 silence 1 err 1 child 1 was 1 divine 1 human 1 play 1 way 1 love 1 blind 1 valour 1 doesn't 1 swallow 1 he 1 skin 1 only 1 who 1 lost 1 rome 1 hesitates 1 built 1 other 1 on 1 rise 1 side 1 man 1 glitters 1 fence 1 fool 1 wise 1 wealthy 1 grass 1 greener 1 always 1 healthy 1 gold 1 them 1 day 1 bed 1 golden 1 rod 1 spare 1 you 1 intentions 1 tide 1 wait 1 others 1 away 1 cat's 1 would 1 ands 1 parted 1 cover 1 change 1 work 1 light 1 lead 1 drink 1 off 1 till 1 him 1 water 1 soon 1 but 1 its 1 price 1 haste 1 judge 1 cuts 1 indeed 1 need 1 intentions 1 sweet 1 by 1 middle 1 horses 1 book 1 revenge 1 (mid-stream) 1 stream 1 again 1 try 1 try 1 ounce 1 so 1 prevention 1 shall 1 succeed 1 discretion 1 summer 1 part 1 business 1 reap 1 if 1 pleasure 1 ound 1 dog 1 today 1 rains 1 new 1 tomorrow 1 tricks 1 what 1 pours 1 rolling 1 cure 1 sow 1 stone 1 teach 1 moss 1 gathers 1 will 1 thing 1 free 1 words 1 such 1 rome

1 romans 1 lunch 1 fight 1 eat 1 too 1 cannot 1 cake 1 picture 1 thousand 1 knowledge 1 power 1 sleeping 1 leap 1 practice 1 bygones 1 bygones 1 bush 1 justifies 1 perfect 1 hand 1 beggars 1 choosers 1 dogs 1 lie 1 forewarned 1 forearmed 1 all's 1 ends 1 late 1 run 1 still 1 waters 1 beautiful 1 roost 1 small 1 done 1 easier 1 said 1 lining 1 cloud 1 silver 1 forget 1 imself 1 smoke 1 mind 1 talks 1 without 1 feather 1 flock 1 birds 1 numbers 1 together 1 safety 1 onder 1 island 1 heart 1 grow 1 hot 1 hay 1 strike 1 iron 1 cooks 1 broth 1 beholder 1 too 1 begins 1 absence 1 news 1 charity 1 sun 1 catches 1 worm 1 takes 1 tango 1 hatched 1 where 1 count 1 they're 1 killed 1 cat 1 shines 1 curiosity 1 water 1 mind 1 blood 1 thicker 1 eye 1 gift 1 mouth 1 louder 1 words 1 keeps 1 doctor 1 apple 1 day 1 wrongs 1 right 1 means 1 go 1 actions 1 speak 1 father 1 son 1 away 1 bad 1 travels 1 heads 1 one 1 saves 1 nine 1 fast 1 stitch 1 once 1 bitten 1 serve 1 masters 1 want 1 not 1 shy 1 not

12. Paremiological Minimum of Czech: The Corpus Evidence

In *Flut von Texten – Vielvalt der Kulturen*. Ascona 2001 zur Methodologie und Kultur-spezifik der Phraseologie, H. Burger, A. Häcki Bufofer, G. Greciano (eds.), Schneider Verlag, Hohengehren 2003, 15–31, **Čermák Proverbs 2014**, 205–224.

Abstract

A 100 million corpus of contemporary Czech yielded a frequency-based list of the basic Czech proverbs. It is accompanied by an analysis of the constituent parts.

1. Introduction: Data for Proverb Research

The quest for a *paremiological minimum*, initiated by Y. Permjakov, has been rather popular in past decades and quite a few languages have been reported to have one now (see, among others, Permjakov 1989, Grzybek 1984, Mieder 1995). The way it has usually been constructed reflects the possibilities linguists or paremiologists have had at their disposal, these being, basically, of a double nature. They included either a collation of various views reflected in old proverbial dictionaries and collections or results of a *sociological enquete*, usually modest in size, which one could have undertaken under the limited circumstances.

The latter method, used also for Czech by Schindler (Schindler 1993), tries to elicit answers to leading questions, which are based on a list of proverb beginnings and to which selected informants are asked to add the missing part. The obvious problems, to name just two are: (1) where does this list come from and on what basis is it based and selected since, obviously, one cannot go out asking people to answer several thousand questions, i.e. the full list based on a large proverb dictionary. The second problem (2) is more subtle. Due to the linear character of our speech, it is obvious that it is the beginning of one's speech, rather than its end, which should be used in the elicitation method and suggested to informants in such a research.

In most cases, this is really true and it works. However, some questions have to be raised, such as the following. Are the beginnings of such an enquete (questionnaire) questions of the most familiar parts and do they elicit the rest of the proverbs, if known, in a reliable, foolproof way? This problem has not been tested extensively, so far, and it is doubtful whether this assumption should be taken for granted without any shadow of doubt. I would contend it on two random Czech examples where I think the opposite might be true, i.e. in some cases at least: *polní tráva* (i.e. the second half of *Světská sláva polní tráva*, corresponding roughly to the English *Fame is short-lived*) and *holé neštěstí* (i.e. the second half of *Líná huba holé neštěstí*, corresponding roughly to the English *You get nothing if you don't ask*, literally *Lazy mouth sheer disaster*) where the second half of the second example seems, alongside with the first one, to have a life of its own. It just may be possible that, if this is used in eliciting the full proverb, one would succeed as well.

There is, however, a third point (3) which should be raised here, too. The enquete method strives to arrive at what is usually termed as *knowledge* of proverbs. However, it is not quite clear, unless this is explicitly and carefully investigated by the questionnaire what this boils down to. Does this mean an active or a passive knowledge, and in what degree in the latter case and how reliable are the answers obtained?

Thus it appears that this presumption that sufficient information about a knowledge of proverbs can be elicited from native speakers is far from being ideal. This could be made to look even more doubtful should one want (4) to conduct the research on a truly *representative sample* of population. However, this often happens to be difficult, mostly for financial reasons. All of this raises, yet again, the question of reliability and best methods of research to be used and the quality of its results.

In contrast to this, an alternative approach, though not quite its converse, is made possible nowadays by the existence of a very *large corpora*. Such an investigation, some results of which, holding for the Czech language, which I would like to present here now, has a different basis, possibilities and limitations, too. First, it can be based on (1) *multiples of data*, which is now much larger than anything before; in the case of the representative Czech National Corpus (CNC, see also Čermák 1998b and address: http://ucnk.ff.cuni.cz), it is based on a one hundred million words corpus, one of the largest in Europe now. Second, the corpus covers (2) *written language* mostly, which is not, presumably, the mode in which the use of proverbs is preferential, this being a drawback.

Third, it is an (3) *active use* (implying a prior knowledge, of course) of the recorded language coming from, in fact, a few people (authors) that is investigated and not a representative sample of the population (known also as the production versus reception problem). However, the number of these people, whose contributions make up the whole of such a large corpus, is so great that this can hardly be seen as a serious drawback. One should recall that the older sociological approach is not quite clear in this point and one does not quite know, in fact, whether one is investigating the active or passive aspect of use. Fourth, (4) next to the enormous advantage, available for the first time, of being able to study the *proverb use in actual contexts* (see my Europhras 97 contribution, Čermák 1998a), such an approach makes it now possible to see, document, and study a *full variability* of proverbs, too, which has not been possible before.

The present research has been based on a large phraseological data-base, assembled for over 15 years, which tries to record and subsequently compile as the last, i.e. fourth volume, of the *Czech Idiom Dictionary*, what may be viewed as the largest coverage of the contemporary Czech language in this region (Čermák – Hronek – Machač 1983, 1988, 1994, see also Čermák 2003). All of the 243 frequent proverbs included here and in current use have been tested against the 100 million words corpus of CNC. The results obtained modify and complement the results and figures presented in my previous paper (Čermák 1998a), which were based on a small part of the corpus only, still under construction then. The present results differ considerably from both the minimum proposed by Schindler and myself (see 4 and Appendix).

2. Formal Aspects of Czech Proverbs

In the following, only aspects concerning proverb length, its variants, transformations, and some general syntactic features will be studied.

2.1 The Total and the First 100 Proverbs

For the 241 proverbs tested against CNC, 2,776 textual occurrences have been recorded. This suggests that the *average frequency* of use per one proverb is almost 12 (11.52). Some of the other aspects of form were predictable, such as mean proverb length, others have been corroborated.

Thus, it was possible to establish a mean frequency of proverbs for the whole of the written language. Subtracting 12,770 words (4.6 words times 2,776, i.e. the average proverb length times the total number of all proverb occurrences, see below) from the total length of CNC (100,000,000 words), gives 99,987,230, i.e. a 'clean', non-proverb length of CNC. This, in turn (12,770 : 99,987,230), suggests two interesting facts, namely:

(1) that *0.128% of the corpus is made up of proverbs*. In other words, a proverb may be expected to occur in written Czech texts, on that average.

(2) Each time, it follows a span of almost *36,000 text words* (99,987,230: 2,776 = 36,018.5). Due to a high representation of technical and scientific texts in CNC (25%), having, as a rule, next to no proverbs, these average figures would be somewhat higher, should this genre be discounted (more about distribution in this respect in 3.1). Obviously, no attempt has been made here to further distinguish between dictionary and grammar words, etc.

The *mean length* of the Czech proverb has been confirmed establishing previous research as valid (see Čermák 1998a). This is now *4.6 words per proverb* for the total of the results obtained.

To obtain at least some preliminary information about the formal structure of the proverbs studied, the first 100 have been chosen for further analysis. These (1,564 occurrences from the total) represent over a half of all proverb forms attested in their text use (54.6%). For the sake of simplicity, certain conventions have been adopted (where the reflexive *se* is not counted separately from its main verb, while on the other hand, prepositions, conjunctions, etc., are viewed as separate words). The distribution of proverbs by their length gives the following table:

Length No of instances
2 words 4×
3 words 22×
4 words 33×
5 words 14×
6 words 14×
7 words 6×
8 words 5×
9 words 0×
10 words 1×

The 4 shortest Czech proverbs made up of 2 words only consist of *Pravda vítězí* (Truth will prevail), *Sliby chyby* (x Fine words butter no parsnips), *Příklady táhnou* (People learn by examples, cf. lat. Exempla trahunt) and *Peníze nesmrdí* (x Money do not stink, cf. lat. Non olet). The mean length of this sample is 4,4 words, while the longest proverbs are made up of 8 and 10 words, respectively, i.e. *Jak se do lesa volá, tak se z lesa ozývá* (x You get as much as you give) and *Tak dlouho se chodí se džbánem pro vodu, až se ucho utrhne* (x It's the last straw that breaks the camel's back). However, the table clearly shows that the highest concentration of proverbs is in the region of 3 and 4 words. In general, a mere glimpse at the less frequent layers (bands) of proverbs, not included in this analysis, reveals that the above distribution is to be found there, too (with the exception of the two-word proverbs).

A word of caution is due here, however. Most of the counts here seem to be satisfied with a simple word count which could be somewhat misleading, however. This is due to a mechanical inclusion of all types of words, irrespective of their length, function and complexity. In view of the paramount oral, spoken use of proverbs and pressure on their communicative economy, it seems that the mean proverb length count could be equally, if not more, important, if it is calculated in *number of syllables*. This count, however, has not been undertaken here, so far.

The 100 proverb sample analyzed can be split into two unequal halves by the presence of a simple *sentence* and two-clause sentence; there is 62% of simple sentences to be found here, while 38% of proverbs are made up of two clauses. A further slow increase in the representation of two-clause proverbs is to be observed in less frequent bands of the total.

2.2 PROVERB VARIANTS

Analysis of the types and distribution of proverb variants deserves a separate detailed study, which is not possible here, although the wealth of information obtained from the corpus makes it possible now. Hence, only some major points and general tendencies will be raised here in a preliminary way.

Out of the total of 241 proverbs which have been analysed, *over 40% (42.8%) have variants* of one or another type. This is hardly surprising, although their full range has never been recorded before. An obvious and simple presumption is that number of variants should be directly proportional to their frequency. But is it really so? On the whole, it is, but not quite. The following table gives variant distribution related to descending frequency. No attempt is made here to distinguish their types, however.

Frequency Band	No of Proverbs	No of Variants (in %)
89–20×	41	80.5
19–10×	48	60.4
9–5×	59	40.0
4×	12	50
3×	14	35.7
2×	15	0.0
1×	18	16.6

It is somewhat surprising that almost 17% of even those proverbs which have been attested only once in CNC, i.e. the proverb periphery, do have variants. The very high variant representation of over 80% for the highest frequency band of proverbs could be viewed as a surprise as well. The general explanation might be sought both in that the highest frequency of use makes them somewhat 'battered' because of their constant clash with all sorts of contexts and a frequent need to make them more fitted to these various contexts. This is supported and enabled by an absence of any codification or artificial petrification of proverbs which seem to live a life of their own.

An illustration of the *types of variants* is offered below. It is based on an analysis of 7 of the 10 most frequent proverbs and their variants, namely:

(1) *Oko za oko, zub za zub* (An eye for an eye and a tooth for a tooth),
(2) *Účel světí prostředky* (The end justifies the means),
(3) *Mnoho povyku pro nic* (Much ado about nothing),
(4) *Vlk se nažral a koza zůstala celá* (lit. The wolf has eaten and the goat remained whole),
(5) *Naděje umírá poslední* (lit. Hope dies last),
(6) *Za málo peněz málo muziky* (* You get what you pay),
(7) *Boží mlýny melou pomalu, ale jistě* (The mills of God grind slowly, but they grind small).

Basically, three broad variant types are attested, (A) syntagmatic, (B) paradigmatic, and (C) complex and mixed ones.

A *Syntagmatic variants* are made of *reduction* mostly (e.g., No 1 is used by its first half only), or *addition* of either a short commentary, quantifier (such as *vždy* 'always') or modalizer (usually a particle, e.g.,*však*, *přece* 'however')

B *Paradigmatic variants*, usually less frequent, are made of *morphological* or *lexical alternations* (such as a change of tense, number or negation, e.g., Účel vždy světil prostředky, No 2) and some rather special cases (*Vlk se nažral a koza chcípla* 'The wolf has eaten and the goat perished', No 4).

C *Complex and mixed variants* are made up of A and B combinations. Sometimes it is rather difficult to decide on the dividing line between a variant and a new formation, as in *Ráda se skrývá za boží mlýny s jejich příslovečnou pomalostí* ('She likes to hide behind the mills of God with their proverbial slowness', see No 7).

It is obvious that the shortest, i.e. two-word proverbs do not have any variants at all, since a variant would mean a fifty percent change of it and that would imply the threat of losing its identity. On the other hand, it may be surprising that also the longest proverbs may not have any variants at all (8 words: *Jak se do lesa volá, tak se z lesa ozývá* x You get as much as you give) or a single one only (10 words: *Tak dlouho se chodí se džbánem pro vodu*, až se ucho utrhne x It's the last straw that breaks the camel's back). It is evident that most of variant profusion is to be found in middle-sized proverbs.

2.3 SYNTACTIC FORM OF CZECH PROVERBS

While sentence representation has been briefly mentioned above (2.1), the subject and predicate situation needs some explanation here. Due to the proverb's generalized meaning, it is reasonable to look for a formal means of expressing this. Mostly, this is to be sought in the form of *subjects*. Indeed, an analysis of the first 100 proverbs confirms that the general nature of the proverb meaning is mediated through its subject choice and form. There is, however, a distinct dividing line to be observed between HUMAN and NON-HUMAN subjects, while the distinction between PERSONAL and IMPERSONAL is also prominent, as one might expect. In the HUMAN sphere, there are altogether 52% of impersonal forms expressing the personal subject of various types, including verb forms, general personal pronouns such as *kdo* (who), *všechno* (everything, all), *každý* (everybody), *nic* (nothing). These are complemented by only very few generalized nouns, namely člověk (2x, man, person), čert (1x, devil) and, oddly, *mistr* (1x, master).

On the other hand, 66% of subjects, i.e. 2/3, belong to NON-HUMAN subjects, nouns represented by abstracts mostly (such as čas time, *konec* end, *pravda* truth, *rada* advice) or animal names (such as *vlk* wolf, *pes* dog) and a few concrete nouns (such as *ruka* hand, *strom* tree or šaty dress). It is evident that *proverbs manifest a pronounced tendency to avoid personal subjects of any sort*, although their scope of use is almost exclusively related to humans and aspects of their life.

Missing verbal *predicates* (19%) figure here prominently, being based, mostly, on ellipsis of *být* (to be). This contrasts with the prevailing and prominent verbal character of standard Czech sentences. It may be of interest that such an ellipsis is to be found mostly in middle-sized proverbs again, with little or none in either of the extremes (e.g., out of the four shortest two-word proverbs, only one does not contain a verb, namely *Sliby chyby* x Fine words butter no parsnips). On the other hand, no tendency to mediate a generality of meaning through the choice of verb has been recorded, as this seems to be taken care of by subjects, exclusively.

2.4 PROVERB TRANSFORMATIONS

The fact that some proverbs give rise, by a transformation of a kind, to other and subsequently independent idioms, is both familiar and rather frequent. The obvious cases for Czech are *tichá* voda (73), *práce kvapná* (117), *ranní ptáče* (142), *zakázané ovoce* (118), *dočkej času* (120), *cesta do pekla/pekel* (145), *s chutí do toho* (outside the minimum), *vrabec v hrsti* (23), figures referring to the list in the Appendix. Most of these happen now to be standard noun idioms on the collocational level, having developed from proverbs.

There is, however, a problem of criteria for drawing *the line between transformations* that are fixed and stable and those that are not. Even a large corpus does not provide conclusive evidence and one's subjective personal judgement may not be reliable. Hence, on the basis of a rather high frequency, the following transformations might be considered as candidates for new idioms: *oko za oko* (3), *dvakrát měř* (28), *komu není rady* (99), *jeden za osmnáct* (44), *kdo chce kam* (50), *jak se do lesa volá* (75), etc. The transitory character of these is reflected in the CNC in their often, but not always, being followed by an ellipses marking a pause and their unfinished character. This is definitely a matter for further research, fitting well into one of the most sensitive problems of phraseology, namely that of stableness and fixity of its units.

3. FUNCTION AND DISTRIBUTION OF CZECH PROVERBS

While general types of text function of proverbs have been explored in a previous contribution (Čermák 1998a), a more specific research is needed into ways how proverbs are integrated into text. Evidence shows that it is not true that proverbs are not integrated into text, i.e. that they do form an independent unit which has just been inserted into text. There are, in fact, three general types of formal presence of proverbs in the text to be distinguished (which does not say anything about their semiotic status and integration, however).

Generally, proverbs are used as

(A) *independent sentence* (only formally, contrary to older views, see above),
(B) *commented sentence* (usually by modelizers or particles of a kind) (...),
(C) *embedded sentence* (i.e. into a larger one).

Thus, to illustrate this briefly, the following proverbs behave differently:
Kdo seje vítr, sklízí bouři (only type A, see 113)
Boží mlýny melou pomalu, ale jistě (both type A and B, see 10)
Pozdě bycha honit (both type A and C, see 18).
In the following, a different kind of data will be presented, however, characterizing proverb genre distribution and frequency bands.

3.1 Genre Distribution of Czech Proverbs

The distribution of 10 most frequent Czech proverbs have been scrutinized on the evidence of CNC, i.e. in their 585 cumulative occurrences in a hundred million corpus (SYN2000). To give some of the background of this representative corpus, constructed on a number of sociolinguistic researches and reading and lending statistics, it is necessary to mention its gross figures.

SYN2000 (in %)
FIC: fiction 15
PUB: newspapers and journals 60
S-H: social sciences and art (incl. law, etc.) cca 14
S-N: non-social sciences (incl. technology, cca 11
administration, natural sciences, economics, medicine, manual hobbies, etc.)

The distribution of proverbs in the corpus is given in the following table, where the summary average figures are most revealing.

PROVERB:	FIC	PUB	S-H	S-N (%)
1	16.3	73.3	6.9	3.5
2	5.9	81	10	3
3	23.3	53.4	21	2.3
4	23.6	74	2.2	-
5	30	50	18	-
6	8.3	75	16.6	-
7	36	39.5	24.4	0.8
8	19.2	67.3	11.5	1.9
9	2.6	76.3	13.2	7.9
10	15.8	71	13.2	-
Average	19.8%	64.4% 1	3.7%	2%

As expected, the highest prominent contribution to the proverb use is due to *fiction* (where 15% of its representation in CNC offers 20% of the proverbs). The figures for *newspapers* are more or less conformant (60% representation offers 64%) and, similarly and, perhaps, somewhat surprisingly, also the *social sciences and art* (14% : 13.7%). Presumably, *non-social and technical sciences* should not contribute to the proverb use at all. The 2 percent in the statistics are not a counterexample, however. Rather, these are to be explained by a too broad classification of some texts which, in this particular case, include also journals on hunting and manual hobbies, where some proverbs are to be found, too, due to commentaries used and a loose type of style.

3.2 FREQUENCY DISTRIBUTION OF CZECH PROVERBS

To come back to what has been briefly mentioned above (2.2), a detailed survey of the distribution bands of all 241 proverbs investigated will be offered. The conclusion to be drawn from this data confirms, broadly, our intuition. Thus the decreasing frequency gives rise to the growing number of proverbs. Or, to put it differently, proverb frequency is inversely proportional to their number in the rank (band). However, this correlation does not represent a gradual and smooth curve, as there seems to be a prominent break around the frequency band of 12. Due to the limited number of evidence, which is still not satisfactory even in such a large corpus, only a belief might be voiced at this stage of research. Namely, that the *first Zipf's law* might also apply for the distribution of proverbs. Quite a few calculations seem to point to a constant of +/–80 in this case (obtained by the number of proverbs of a band multiplied by the frequency of that band).

FREQ	NO of Proverbs	FREQ	No of Proverbs
89	1	19	2
88	1	18	1
71	1	17	4
50	1	16	3
48	1	15	7
44	1	14	7
40	2	13	4
39	3	12	10
37	1	11	10
35	1	10	7
34	1	9	8
33	2	8	8
32	1	7	16
31	1	6	11
30	1	5	16

29	1
27	2
26	1
25	3
24	2
23	1
22	2
21	2
20	3

(= 2332 occurrences = 84% of all proverbs)

4. Czech Paremiological Minimum: A Concolusion

The differences in the form and content of the paremiological minima are due to two sets of factors. The first is *cultural* which is no business of a linguist to go into; here, other disciplines must take over explaining these. From a *linguist's point of view*, however, it seems that these are basically to be explained both by a different methodology and, primarily, by sufficient or, rather more often, an insufficient amount of data.

The latter might explain why Schindler's minimum is so different. His 4 proverbs topping the list with a 100% familiarity with respondents, whose number was rather limited, do not figure so prominently in the CNC data (ranking there as Nos 23, 7, 14, and 12; namely, *Bez práce nejsou koláče, Jak si usteleš, tak si lehneš, Pro dobrotu na žebrotu, Co Čech to muzikant*) and are overshadowed by other proverbs. An additional factor, mentioned above, which is difficult to measure, however, is the spoken-written language difference, although some doubt remains as to the traditional method of elicitation, too.

Both types of factors should probably be considered, should we want to explain why there is no overlap at all between the Czech corpus-based results and some older *traditional approaches for other languages*. Thus, the 15 most frequent American English proverbs suggested by Higbee and Millard (quoted from Mieder 1995) have no counterparts in the Czech list at all, while Whiting's (Whiting 1989) 33 most common proverbs overlap with the Czech proverb list in only 13% (4 proverbs), the rest being different. This both shows that, on the basis of previous sociological research as conceived by Permyakov, (1) no comparison seems to be really worthwhile across languages in this way and that, to be able to do that in the way suggested in this paper, (2) much more data is needed.

No really convincing criteria has been offered for the size of **a paremiological minimum**. Hence, its selection, somewhere on the decreasing frequency scale, is rather an *arbitrary* one. Thus, in the Appendix, only those proverbs are listed whose frequency is 10 or higher. By way of illustration, the first 50 proverbs are provided with an English equivalent (where *lit.* = literal equivalent, *cf.* = non-cognate proverb, = = cognate proverb, * = free translation).

APPENDIX: Paremiological Minimum of Czech FREQ in CNC

1 Účel světí prostředky. 89
  (= The end justifies the means.)
2 Nic není zadarmo. 88
  (*lit.* Nothing is for free.)
3 Oko za oko, zub za zub. 76
  (= An eye for an eye and a tooth for a tooth.)
4 Mnoho povyku pro nic. 71
  (= Much ado about nothing.)
5 Pravda vítězí. 50
  (= Truth will prevail.)
6 Vlk se nažral a koza zůstala celá. 48
  (*lit.* The wolf has eaten and the goat remained whole.)
7 Naděje umírá poslední. 44
  (*lit.* Hope dies last.)
8 Všechno zlé je k něčemu dobré. 40
  (*cf.* Every cloud has a silver lining.)
9 Za málo peněz málo muziky. 40
  (* You get what you pay.)
10 Boží mlýny melou pomalu, ale jistě. 39
  (= The mills of God grind slowly, but they grind small.)
11 Stará láska nerezaví. 39
  (* Old love is never forgotten.)
12 Sliby chyby. 37
  (*cf.* Fine words butter no parsnips.)
13 Čas jsou peníze. 35
  (= Time is money.)
14 Kdo umí, umí. 34
  (* He is certainly good at it.)
15 Když dělají dva totéž, není to totéž. 33
  (= No two people do anything quite alike.)
16 S jídlem roste chuť. 33
  (* The more one has the more one wants.)
17 Kdo hledá, najde. 33
  (= Search and you shall find.)
18 Pozdě bycha honit. 32
  (*cf.* It is late to shut the stable door after the mare is gone.)
19 Šaty dělají člověka. 32
  (*cf.* Fine feathers make fine birds.)
20 Všude dobře, doma nejlíp. 32
  (= There is no place like home.)

21 Tonoucí se stébla chytá. 31
  (= Drowning man clutches at a straw.)
22 Nic netrvá věčně. 30
  (*cf.* All good things come to an end.)
23 Lepší vrabec v hrsti než holub na střeše. 29
  (= A bird in hand is worth two in the bush.)
24 Konec dobrý všechno dobré. 27
  (= All's well that ends well.)
25 Výjimka potvrzuje pravidlo. 27
  (= The exception proves the rule.)
26 Není všechno zlato, co se třpytí. 26
  (= All that glitters is not gold.)
27 Do třetice všeho dobrého. 25
  (*cf.* Third time lucky.)
28 Dvakrát měř, jednou řež. 25
  (*cf.* Look twice before you leap.)
29 Pod svícnem bývá tma. 25
  (*cf.* There are often low goings-on in high places.)
30 Každý svého štěstí strůjcem. 24
  (*cf.* Life is what you make it.)
31 Peníze nejsou všechno. 24
  (* Money is not everything.)
32 Přání je otcem myšlenky. 24
  (*cf.* This is wishful thinking.)
33 Bez práce nejsou koláče. 23
  (*cf.* No cross no crown.)
34 Bližší košile než kabát. 22
  (= Nearest my coat, but nearer my skin (shirt).)
35 Kdo nic nedělá, nic nezkazí. 22
  (lit. He who does nothing, spoils nothing.)
36 Zvyk je železná košile. 22
  (*cf.* Habit is second nature.)
37 Nula od nuly pojde. 21
  (*cf.* Twice nought is nought.)
38 Příležitost dělá zloděje. 21
  (= Opportunity makes the thief.)
39 Člověk míní a bůh mění. 20
  (= Man proposes, God disposes.)
40 Jablko nepadne/nepadá daleko od stromu. 20
  (*cf.* Like father, like son. He is a chip of the old lock.)
41 Každý začátek je těžký. 20
  (= The first step is always the hardest.)

42 Na hrubý pytel hrubá záplata. 19
(*cf.* Meet rudeness with rudeness.)

43 Příklady táhnou. 19
(*cf.* People learn by examples, Examples work miracles.)

44 Jeden za osmnáct, druhý bez dvou za dvacet .18
(*cf.* They are tarred with the same brush.)

45 Čí chleba jíš, toho píseň zpívej. 17
(cf. Don't quarrel with your bread.)

46 Chybovat/mýlit se je lidské. 17
(= To err is human.)

47 Lež má krátké nohy. 17
(*cf.* Lies have short wings.)

48 Sejde s očí, sejde s mysli. 17
(= Out of sight, out of mind.)

49 Darovanému koni na zuby nekoukej. 16
(= Don't look a gift horse in the mouth.)

50 Kdo chce kam, pomozme mu tam. 16
(*lit.* Let us help him who wants [to get] somewhere.)

51 Řemeslo má zlaté dno. 16

52 Ve zdravém těle zdravý duch. 16

53 Dobrá rada nad zlato. 15

54 Kde není žalobce, není ani soudce. 15

55 Kdo dřív přijde, ten dřív mele. 15

56 Padla kosa na kámen. 15

57 Peníze nesmrdí. 15

58 Trpělivost přináší růže. 15

59 Vrána k vráně sedá. 15

60 Čas všechny rány hojí/zhojí. 14

61 Kdo jinému jámu kopá, sám do ní padá. 14

62 Mluviti stříbro, mlčeti zlato. 14

63 Pro dobrotu na žebrotu. 14

64 Ruka ruku myje. 14

65 S poctivostí nejdál dojdeš. 14

66 Strach má velké oči. 14

67 Všechno má svůj konec. 14

68 Zítra je taky den. 14

69 Člověka po řeči, ptáka po zpěvu poznáš. 13

70 Kdo lže, ten krade. 13

71 Sytý hladovému nevěří. 13

72 Tichá voda břehy mele. 13

73 Co Čech, to muzikant .12

74 Jak se do lesa volá, tak se z lesa ozývá. 12

75 Kdo chce psa bít, hůl si najde. 12

76 Kdo s čím zachází, tím také schází. 12

77 Kdo šetří, má za tři. 12

78 Láska hory přenáší. 12

79 Není šprochu, aby na něm nebylo pravdy trochu. 12

80 Pýcha předchází pád. 12

81 Ráno moudřejší večera. 12

82 Tak dlouho se chodí s džbánem pro vodu, až se ucho utrhne. 12

83 Co na srdci, to na jazyku. 11

84 Čert nikdy nespí. 11

85 Komu se nelení, tomu se zelení. 11

86 Kuj železo, dokud je žhavé. 11

87 Ne samým chlebem živ je člověk. 11

88 Neštěstí nechodí po horách, ale po lidech. 11

89 Pes, který štěká, nekouše. 11

90 Podej někomu prst a chce celou ruku. 11

91 Žádný strom neroste do nebe. 11

92 Žádný učený z nebe nespadl. 11

93 Co můžeš učinit dnes, neodkládej na zítřek. 10

94 I mistr tesař se utne. 10

95 Kdo rychle dává, dvakrát dává. 10

96 Kdo se směje naposled, ten se směje nejlíp. 10

97 Když se dva perou, třetí se směje. 10

98 Komu není rady, tomu není pomoci. 10

99 Lépe pozdě než nikdy. 10

100 Neštěstí nechodí/nechodívá (nikdy) samo. 10

LITERATURE

ČERMÁK, František, HRONEK, Jiří, MACHAČ, Jaroslav, eds. 1983. *Slovník české frazeologie a idiomatiky. Přirovnání*. Praha: Academia (= Dictionary of Czech Phraseology and Idiomatics. Similes).

ČERMÁK, František, HRONEK, Jiří, MACHAČ, Jaroslav, eds. 1988. *Slovník české frazeologie a idiomatiky. Výrazy neslovesné*. Praha: Academia (= (Dictionary of Czech Phraseology and Idiomatics. Non-Verbal Expressions)

ČERMÁK, František, HRONEK, Jiří, MACHAČ, Jaroslav, eds. 1994. *Slovník české frazeologie a idiomatiky. Výrazy slovesné. A-P, R-Ž*. Praha: Academia. (Dictionary of Czech Phraseology and Idiomatics. Verb Expressions)

ČERMÁK, František. 1998a. "Usage of Proverbs: What the Czech National Corpus Shows." In *Europhras '97*, edited by P. Ďurčo, 37–59. Bratislava: Akadémia PZ.

ČERMÁK, František. 1998b. "Czech National Corpus: Its Character, Goal and Background." In *Text, Speech, Dialogue, Proceedings of the First Workshop on Text, Speech, Dialogue – TSD'98, Brno, Czech Republic, September, 1998*, edited by P. Sojka, V. Matoušek, K. Pala, and I. Kopeček, 9–14. Brno: Masaryk University.

ČERMÁK, František. 2001. "Substance of Idioms: Perennial Problems, Lack of Data or Theory?" *International Journal of Lexicography* 14 (1): 1–20.

ČERMÁK, František. 2004. "Propositional Idioms". In *Europhras 2000*, edited by Ch. Palm-Meister, 15–31. Tübingen: Stauffenberg Verlag.

GRZYBEK, Peter. 1984. "How to Do Things with Some Proverbs: Zur Frage eines parömi(ologi)schen Minimums." In *Semiotische Studien zum Sprichwort, Simple Forms Reconsidered I*, edited by P. Grzybek and W. Eismann, 351–358. Tübingen: Günter Narr.

GRZYBEK, Peter. 1995. "Foundations of Semiotic Proverb Study." *De Proverbio, An Electronic Journal of International Proverb Studies* 1(1).

MIEDER, Wolfgang. 1995. "Paremiological Minimum and Cultural Literacy." *De Proverbio, An Electronic Journal of International Proverb Studies* 1(1). (http://info.utas.edu.au/docs/flonta/).

PERMJAKOV, Grigorij Ľvovič. 1989. "On the Question of a Russian Paremiological Minimum." *Proverbium* 6: 91–102.

SCHINDLER, Franz. 1993. *Das Sprichwort im heutigen Tschechischen. Emprirische Untersuchung und semantische Beschreibung*. München: O. Sagner.

WHITING, Bartlett Jere. 1989. *Modern Proverbs and Proverbial Sayings*. Cambridge, Mass.: Harvard University Press.

D
SEMANTIC AND FUNCTIONAL TYPES AND CLASSES OF PROVERBS

In their reflection of human doings, feelings and attitudes (here, in Part D) proverbs tend, by their frequency, to reflect also what types of these are common or less common. Some of the common fields, such as friendship, reason, wisdom, laugh, and numbers are looked into and compared. In contradistinction to data gleaned mostly from the corpora, data in this last section comes from an international dictionary, The ROUTLEDGE DICTIONARY of WORLD'S PROVERBS based on very many diverse languages offering a rich insight into these.

13. WISDOM IN PROVERBS? (DO PROVERBS SUGGEST WISDOM?)

In **Čermák Proverbs 2014**, 197–204.

ABSTRACT

Wisdom is associated with older and more experienced people mostly, although what is considered wisdom in various cultures may vary. This is usually a kind of essence of the proverbs in general.

1. INTRODUCTION AND QUESTIONS

Obviously, trying to pin down what may be considered a wise saying among proverbs is a futile effort as all proverbs are traditionally considered to be drops of essence containing wisdom, though some do seem to sound wiser, such as *The apple does not fall far from the tree*, some less so. Yet it is in fact relevant to ask if all the proverbs really express some kind of wisdom. Leaving the problem open, it may be enough to say that it is, at least, definitely not true that only those proverbs containing the words *wisdom* and *wise* must tell us something about wisdom. Hence, a limitation of the scope is necessary: to make it really simple, let us concentrate on wisdom proverbs only, i.e. those having this loaded word in their form. Before doing so, however, some other general questions, seemingly futile for some, about **people using proverbs** might and should be asked.

2. QUESTIONS ABOUT *WISDOM*

Since frequent attributes attached to proverbs include *wisdom*, one may naturally ask a couple of questions based on this premise. Therefore:

1 *Is a man/woman often using proverbs wise, i.e. one displaying some kind of wisdom?*
2 *Is a paremiologist studying proverbs professionally and extensively a particularly wise person, then?*

A simple answer is that it is not the knowledge of proverbs but one's respect to and realisation of proverbs in life that is of importance.

3 *Is it then so, that, on a closer look, a person may be wise and not use proverbs much?*

A general attitude might be that he/she may be wise, though more background knowledge would be called for.

4 *Since an appropriate use of a proverb may be heard from an adolescent or child, too, would the boy or girl then be rightly called wise and full of wisdom, too?*

The question would probably get a negative answer, while it might be pointed to such aspects as maturity, experience, that are missing, etc.

5 *Is, then, wisdom a privilege of only old, mature, and experienced persons meaning that the proverb user is acquainted with typical contexts and is able, among other things, to perceive human follies in these?*

To be on the safe side, the answer may not be very definite either way. There are old fools around, too.

Yet, it does not seem that the scope of wisdom and people using wisdom proverbs is sufficiently explained in this way, as other aspects are still missing, such as the type of the listener and his ability to realize that hearing a proverb, a golden nugget of experience, is being passed on to him/her. Hence, itemizing generalized features of wisdom and proverbs may seem to be rather futile.

Let us, then, abandon this line of thinking and merely observe what wisdom proverbs tell us and, perhaps, importantly, how they are phrased. The following observations are taken from international proverbs grouped under the heading of *wisdom* (Routledge Book of World Proverbs, 2006).

3. Wisdom Proverbs

3.1 Wisdom and *Type of Person* to have it

Standard, usually acknowledged qualities related to one's age and experience, listed explicitly in conjunction with wisdom, include such attributes as **maturity**, **age**, **hard--thinking**, **born ability**, or **education and study**, cf.

Mature man: (Ripeness is in wisdom, not in years. (Unknown)),
Thinking Man: (Thinking is the essence of wisdom. (Persian)),
Able Man: (Wisdom is not attained with years, but by ability. (Roman))
Studious Man: (Wisdom grows by study. (Roman),

where the idea of wisdom acquired naturally in most cases is, oddly enough, contrasted with an **inborn capacity** (Wisdom is not attained with years, but by ability (Roman)).

Yet also some non-standard possibilities or types of speakers are considered, such as **early-rising, child** or **poor man**, cf.

Early-Riser: (He who rises early will gather wisdom. (Danish))
Poor man-uninfluential: (A poor man's wisdom goes for little. (Dutch))
Child-inexperienced: (A child's wisdom is also wisdom. (Yiddish)).

3.2 Ways how Wisdom May be Attained

Perhaps the most straightforward way how knowledge and mastery of wisdom is achieved mentioned in proverbs is related to basic **moral discrimination**, cf.

Ability to discriminate: The first step toward wisdom is to distinguish what is false. (Roman)
Knowing false-true: ('Tis wisdom sometimes to seem a fool. (Roman))

All other ways seem to stress the necessity or usefulness of **learning, either positive or negative**, cf.

Positive learning, also from mistakes of others, even enemies: Wisdom is learned through the wisdom of others. (Yoruban)
It is best to learn wisdom from the follies of others. (Roman)
Even from a foe a man may learn wisdom. (Greek)

Negative learning: By committing foolish acts, one learns wisdom. (Singhalese)

Wisdom may be achieved in a negative way, too, by not doing the expected, cf.

Wisdom in Silence: Not to speak is the flower of wisdom. (Japanese)
Talking comes by nature, silence by wisdom. (Yiddish)

This is not far from using one's wisdom while resorting to a trick
Wisdom used through trick: To feign stupidity is, in certain situations, the highest wisdom. (Roman)

3.3 WISDOM DEFINED NEGATIVELY

Conversely, certain ways of behaviour are not considered to be wise and one is dissuaded from adopting such paths. These may relate to one's **superficial appearances and possessions**, cf.

Dressing and apparel: Wisdom does not consist in dress. (Roman)
Beauty-Attractiveness: Rarely are beauty and wisdom found together. (Roman)
Property: Wisdom is better than gold and silver. (Jamaican)

Or they may point to the **real essence of wisdom** instead of what is usually taken as a sign of it, cf.

Brain-not Face: Wisdom is in the head and not in the beard. (Swedish)

Or, some **ways of expression are challenged**, such as, cf.

Eloquence is not wisdom: Enough of eloquence, but little of wisdom. (Roman)
Speech capacity is not wisdom: Speech is given to all, wisdom to few. (Roman)

3.4 WISDOM AND PRACTICE

Finally, wisdom may be contrasted with **ways how it is used and how many times when it is used**.

Wisdom and foolishness are incompatible: 'Tis altogether vain to learn wisdom, and yet live foolishly. (Dutch)

Wisdom is inversely proportional to physical strength: Once I had strength but no wisdom; now I have wisdom but no strength. (Persian)

Wisdom must be accompanied by virtue: Wisdom and virtue are like the two wheels of a cart. (Japanese)

A seldom stressed aspect of a special kind relates wisdom to negative **practice combined with fear**, cf.

Wisdom is due to fear of one's superior: To fear the master is the beginning of wisdom. (Roman)

4. Conclusion

Going from such a limited proverb basis may not be enough, but even this handful of proverbs explicitly offered by the dictionary gives rise to some doubts and other questions that this contribution has started with. Inspecting the types of persons (3.1) attributed to wisdom and respective proverbs, one may wonder, why, for example, influential people such as politicians, priests, teachers, and, perhaps, philosophers, are rarely mentioned as those related to wisdom proverbs. Is it, perhaps, due to them being professional demagogues busy with their own propaganda than really wise men using (proverb) wisdom?

Postscript

Nevertheless, despite all of this and of his being a paremiologist, for a number of other, personal, reasons based on my knowledge of him, I think Wolfgang Mieder is a wise man who happens to know many wisdom proverbs.

Literature

ČERMÁK, František. 2015. "Wisdom in Proverbs", In *Bis dat, qui cito dat. Gegengabe in Paremiology, Folklore, Language, and Literature. Honoring Wolfgang Mieder on His Seventieth Birthday*. Eds. Ch. Grandl and K. J. McKenna, 95–98. Frankurt am M.: Peter Lang.

JAMES, Alexander. 2007. *The World's Funniest Proverbs*. Bath: Crombie Jardine.

PEARSALL, Judy and HANKS, Patrick, eds. 2001. *The New Oxford Dictionary of English*. Oxford – New York: Oxford University Press.

STONE, Jon R., ed. 2006. *The routledge book of world's proverbs*. London – New York: Routledge.

14. Proverbs on Friends and Friendship

In **Actas ICP 11, 2018**, 15–27.

Abstract

Friend is a familiar notion, probably in any language and culture. Yet it is far from clear what it means exactly, especially in human life. On the basis of the Routledge international dictionary of proverbs based on many languages, some of its 200 hundred items in various languages are inspected as to the identity and quality of the notion of friend and friendship. In doing so, such familiar contrast as friend-enemy will discussed. Friendship will be seen here as both as state and domain of actions between friends and it will be shown that not all proverbs fit in or support the familiar notion of someone close to oneself, ready to help, stressing, on the other hand such observations as:

There is no life without friendship,

a proverb coming from Roman times.

This is a first attempt at a systematic survey of major aspects of friend-friendship relationship, open to discussion.

1. Introduction

It is obvious that to get at the essence of the **friend-friendship phenomenon** in proverbs linguistically one must have sufficient data to be able to arrive at any conclusions. Secondly, it will be inspiring to inspect the verbal image of proverbs in more than one language. Both requirements seem to be satisfied by the Routledge international dictionary of proverbs (J. R. Stone, 2006) drawing on 130 languages and, in the author's selection, offering some 17,000 proverbs. Of course, the selection must be subjective but, unfortunately, no firm objective data on the use and frequency of proverbs are available anywhere; thus, the choice of proverbs and languages is entirely his. This holds for the topic of friend/s in proverbs, too, which covers all of the proverbs the author has included. The total number of proverbs found here is, surprisingly, high (about 200). Finally, it must added that the topic of friends-friendship being universal apparently, includes proverbs that repeat themselves in many languages and are overlapping.

Friend is a familiar notion in, probably, any language and culture. Yet it is far from clear what it exactly means, especially in human life. The word itself is one of the most frequent in any language (freq. 266 in Frequency Dictionary of American English, 2010, standing in close neighbourhood of *father*), though proverbs related to it are far from common in use, even though friends and friendship are highly valued and considered to be pillars of the culture and everyday life.

A representative Oxford English Dictionary of Proverbs (Simpson 2015) records only six proverbs having the word *friend*. One would expect that among these such noble, edifying, elevating, and spirit-enhancing truths and pieces of wisdom that proverbs patently remind us, i.e. of indications of companionship, support, loyalty, and faithfulness would appear, since such is somebody one knows, likes, and trusts as a friend. However, even in the very few proverbs on friends in the dictionary there is one in a quite different strain, namely *Save us from our friends*, which does not fulfill these expectations, going contrary to our shared ideal of the word. The Oxford English Dictionary is based on the largest stock of excerpts and there seems to be a good basis for the inclusion of such 'strange' proverbs as the one mentioned. It may be that the divide between words and notions is somewhat different in this case and one may, in fact, use the notion of friend, perhaps, more often than the word or proverbs related to it. Such an ambivalent picture suggests friend and friendship to be complex and, up to an extent, complicated; the respective proverbs might seem to have slightly different shades of meaning in various languages with a background history of its own.

Quite a few people give the topic of friendship more than a passing thought. Yet, a classic, not to be omitted, is found in Cicero already.

Cicero, Marcus Tullius, *Laelius de Amicitia*

Cicero, Marcus Tullius, a Roman philosopher, politician, and orator some 2000 years ago, paid thoughtful attention to friendship in one of his speeches in some detail. Let us follow his thoughts on this for a while and notice some of his observations which might seem surprisingly modern.

The question, whether the longing for friendship is felt on account of weakness and want, so that by the giving and receiving of favours one may get from another and in turn repay what he is unable to procure of himself; or, although this mutual interchange is really inseparable from friendship, whether there is not another cause, older, more beautiful, and emanating more directly from Nature herself.

When the characters of friends are blameless, then there should be between them complete harmony of opinions and inclinations in everything without any exception; and, even if by some chance the wishes of a friend are not altogether honourable and require to be forwarded in matters which involve his life or reputation, we should turn aside from the straight path, provided, however, utter disgrace does not follow, for there are limits to the indulgence which can be allowed to friendship.

Let this law be established in friendship: neither ask dishonourable things, nor do them, if asked.

Ask of friends only what is honourable; do for friends only what is honourable and without even waiting to be asked; let zeal be ever present, but hesitation absent; dare to give true advice with all frankness; in friendship let the influence of friends who are wise counsellors be paramount...

Two rules in friendship: first, let there be no feigning or hypocrisy; for it is more befitting a candid man to hate openly than to mask his real thoughts with a lying face; secondly, let him not only reject charges preferred by another, but also let him avoid even being suspicious and ever believing that his friend has done something wrong.

Some of his observations include the following:

Friendship is nothing else than an accord in all things, human and divine, conjoined with mutual goodwill and affection.

What is sweeter than to have someone with whom you may dare discuss anything as if you were communing with yourself?

Friendship cannot exist except among good men.

Friendship was given to us by nature as the handmaid of virtue, not as a comrade of vice.

For friendship excels relationship in this, that goodwill may be eliminated from relationship while from friendship it cannot.

Friendship adds a brighter radiance to prosperity and lessens the burden of adversity by dividing and sharing it.

For it is love (amor), from which the word 'friendship' (amicitia) is derived, that leads to the establishing of goodwill.

You should love your friend after you have appraised him; you should not appraise him after you have begun to love him.

Complaisance gets us friends, plain speaking, hate.

To begin our quest, however, and return to our time and to **open our search** into the essence of this friend-friendship topic in proverbs let us start with some that seem to be traditionally and prototypically acknowledged to be accepted generally. The gist of the topic seems to include ideas expressed by the following proverbs.

There is no life without friendship. (Roman)
A friend in need is a friend indeed. (English)
All are not friends who smile on you. (Dutch)
A man's oldest friend is his best. (Roman)
The image of friendship is truth. (Egyptian)

All are old. Two proverbs come to us from Roman times, one from the ancient Egypt pointing down, under the notion, at its substance. The English proverb conveys perhaps the most acknowledged feature of proverbs related to a friendly help in need, but the Dutch one brings in a trace of doubt warning the user that not everything is as it looks and one should look under the surface of friendship.

2. FRIENDS AND FRIENDSHIP

2.1 FRIEND: IDENTITY AND QUALITIES

It is not so easy to identify a friend quickly, since the notion of friend is highly personal for everyone, based on experience but it is necessary to distinguish it from other common notions. It is evident that there is a lot of difference between friend and lover or friend and politician, even though some people may disagree. There is the feature of permanence and solidness which separates them. However, there is also a way to distinguish friend from neighbour and brother, if we stick to proverbs.

Friend and/or Brother

The way brother is related to friend is to be seen in the following proverbs **preferring friend to brother** in some cases:

A brother may not be a friend, but a friend will always be a brother. (Poor Richard)
A friend by thee is better than a brother far off. (Irish)

while the real difference may not be so great, cf.

At the narrow passage there is no brother and no friend. (Arabian)

However, this brother-friend scale goes on:

A good neighbour is a good friend. (Mexican)
A good neighbour is better than a brother far off. (Danish)
A friend to my table and wine, is no good neighbour. (French)

A possible relation between lover and friend may be expressed as in:

The same man cannot be both friend and flatterer. (Poor Richard)
Absence, and a friendly neighbor, washeth away love. (English)

Note: **Poor Richard** is a pseudonym of the famous American diplomat, politician and inventor Benjamin Franklin.

2.2 FRIEND AND FRIENDS

Need of Friends

Every man or woman, next to one's family, must have some friends, since friendship is necessary *in life:*

Friends are flowers in the garden of life. (Portuguese)
There is no need like the lack of a friend. (Irish)

Support and Help

A complex proverb suggests **main types of support** in difficult or painful situation, advising us:
Go to friends for advice; to women for pity; to strangers for charity; to relatives for nothing. (Spanish)

Perhaps the commonest idea of friend is expressed by someone **ready to help one** in any way, cf.

A friend is known in time of need. (French)
A friend is proven in time of necessity. (Roman)
Friends are known in time of need. (Dutch)
Friends are proved by adversity. (Roman)
Friends are known in times of danger. (Irish)
A friend is not known till he is lost. (Italian)

To stress this feature of help and assistance, often a stronger name is used, namely **good friend**:

A good neighbor is a good friend. (Mexican)
A good friend is better than silver and gold. (Dutch)
A friend's frown is better than a fool's smile. (Danish)

Availability, Consolation and Advice

In this sense, friend is a safeguard in crisis being **invaluable**, **ready to help**, **available**, when needed, and also as a **source of consolation** and **advice**:

A friend at one's back is a safe bridge. (Dutch)
A friend is better than money in the purse. (Dutch)
A friend is the solace of life. (Roman)

On the road between the homes of friends, grass does not grow. (Norwegian)
A mile walk with a friend has only one hundred steps. (Russian)
The road to a friend's house is never long. (Danish)
Only your real friends will tell you when your face is dirty. (Burmese)
A friend by thee is better than a brother far off. (Irish)
To lose a friend is the greatest of all losses. (Roman)

Most friends one relies on are **old friends** since there is a joint experience and time enjoyed together, cf.

A man's oldest friend is his best. (Roman)
Old age comes with friends. (Albanian)
Old friends and old wine are best. (German)

True Friend and Companion

A very special case in one's life **is true friend,** since no-one has too many of these. They are those one trusts. True friends are **permanent companions in one's life**:

A true friend is a rare bird. (Roman)
A true friend is a second self. (Roman)
A true friend is certain when certainty is uncertain. (Roman)
A true friend laughs at your stories even when they're not so good, and sympathizes with your troubles even when they're not so bad. (Irish)
True friends are tested in adversity. (Roman)
The name of friend is common, but a faithful friend is rare. (Roman)

Friend and Myself/Oneself

Friends help one to understand himself or herself better offering kind and **helpful criticism** and suggesting a picture of oneself:

A friend is one soul in two bodies. (Roman)
A friend's eye is a good mirror. (Irish)
If you have a good friend, you don't need a mirror. (German)
Tell me who's your friend and I'll tell you who you are. (Russian)
When the character of a man is not clear to you, look at his friends. (Japanese)

Friends Are not Ideal

No-one is perfect, therefore one should not idealize one's friends, be aware of his/her qualities and only then safely rely on them, such as in:

A friend is to be taken with his faults. (Portuguese)
A friend's faults may be noticed, but not blamed. (Danish)
Unless you bear with the faults of a friend, you betray your own. (Roman)
Looking too closely at the affairs of a friend spoils the friendship. (Yoruban)
Silence is wisdom and gets a man friends. (Roman)
Old friends and old ways ought not to be disdained. (Danish)
Once a friend, always a friend. (Kurdish)
One can care little for man, but we need a friend. (Chinese)

However, friends may be demanding and even dangerous and hence, worse than an enemy, as in:

Save us from our friends. (Italian)

The idea is an old one, found, eg., in OVID *Ars Amatoria* I. 751, AD 2, *Non est hostis metuendus amanti. Quos credis fidos effuge: tutus eris,an enemy is not to be feared by the lover. Shun those whom you believe friends; then you will be safe.*

Yet, to switch to a lighter side of this solemn and grave aspect, a quite different and, in fact, a **humorous proverb** may be added, cf.

One may live without one's friends, but not without one's pipe. (Irish)

Making Friends

Ways to meet and make friends are many, some highly personal, professional or social. Thus, many different types of friends are made and one's behaviour is adapted or restricted to this. In many cases, it is property and riches that influence the status of friends. Cf.
Make a friend when you don't need one. (Jamaican)
Have but few friends though many acquaintances. (Danish)
Over the bottle many a friend is found. (Yiddish)
A friend that you buy with presents, will be bought from you. (Roman)
Make new friends, but don't forget the old ones. (Yiddish)
It is as bad to have too many friends as no friends at all. (Roman)
He who makes friends of all keeps none. (German)
People of the same stock and trade are friendly. (Irish)
Spend a new penny on an old friend and share an old pleasure with a new friend. (Chinese)
You can hardly make a friend in a year, but you can easily offend one in an hour. (Chinese)

Friendship, however, may be **opportunistic and selfish**:

Prosperity is never friendless. (Greek)
Success has many friends. (Greek)
In prosperity you may count on many friends; if the sky becomes overcast you will be alone. (Roman)
In happy times we reckon many friends; but if fortune fails, we will have no friends. (Roman)

Spending Time and Life with Friends

Living with friends may be both pleasurable and sincere, but also demanding time and energy. However, the extent of this relation should not be overtaxed, cf.

Friends and wine: the older the better. (Spanish)
Friends are like fiddle strings: they must not be screwed too tight. (Italian)
Friends are sometimes troublesome. (Roman)
Friends are thieves of time. (English)
Many friends will sit at the same table. (German)
One must be wary while meeting friends, especially those who take different views, cf.
A thousand cups of wine do not suffice when true friends meet, but half a sentence is too much when there is no meeting of minds. (Chinese)

Relations between Friends

True friends expect you to do the same for them what they would do for you. Real friends are tested over time and actions. Yet, some caution, even sacrifice and a lot of consideration is necessary when a friend is concerned, cf.

Mind neither storms nor snows for the sake of a friend. (Georgian)
He is my friend that grinds at my mill. (Danish)
He is my friend that succors me, not he that pities me. (Danish)
Keep your mouth, and keep your friend. (Danish)
Speak well of your friend; of your enemy, neither well nor ill. (Italian)
Keep your friends close, your enemies closer. (American)
Tell your friend a lie; if he keeps it secret, tell him the truth. (Spanish)
Friends are to be regarded from deeds, not words. (Roman)
A small house will hold a hundred friends. (German)
A stone from the hand of a friend is an apple. (Moroccan)

When interests of two friends clash, it is better to be prudent in such a dangerous situation, cf.

He who judges between two friends loses one of them. (French)

If a minor clash is imminent, it should be quickly removed, amicably.
Win a bet of your friend, and drink it on the spot. (Portuguese)

Mutual Dealings

A possible pitfall in one's relation with friends is property and money, cf.

If you lend money to a friend, you lose both money and a friend. (Korean)
He that lends loses a friend. (German)
Your friend lends and your enemy asks payment. (Dutch)
Trade knows neither friends nor kindred. (French)
The Devil is a great friend of the wealthy. (Spanish)
Promises may make friends, but performance keeps them. (German)

Just a note to lending-money proverb: it is not clear why the author chose to attribute it to Korea. The proverb is very common elsewhere, made immortal by Shakespeare in 1601 in Hamlet (I, iii), cf.
Neither a borrower nor a lender be; For loan oft loses both itself and friend.

Losing a Friend

Although friends are a life-long achievement, they may, by natural causes, be parted, cf.
He that ends a friendship was never a good friend. (German)
Poverty parts friends. (Portuguese)
Long absence changes friends. (French)
The best of friends must part. (English)
When death takes your friends, it is a warning to yourself. (Yoruban)

2.3 FRIENDSHIP: THE STATE, PROCESS AND ACTIONS

Some aspects of friendship suggest friendship's substance, quality and how to maintain it.
Substance of Friendship

Friendships know no age. (Spanish)
Friendships should be immortal, enmities should be mortal. (Roman)
True friendship is seen through the heart, not through the eyes. (American)
Friendship always benefits; love sometimes injures. (Roman)
Shared friendship is a double friendship. (German)
Gold is proved in the fire, friendship in need. (Danish)
To give counsel, as well as take it, is a feature of true friendship. (Roman)

There is no better friend in winter than a warm cloak. (Spanish)
Of clothing, the newer the better; of friendships, the older the better. (Chinese)

Quality of Friendship

He who sows courtesy reaps friendship, and he who plants kindness gathers love. (Spanish)
Suspicion is the poison of friendship. (French)
Hatred watches while friendship sleeps. (French)
The friendship of a great man is like the shadow of a bush, soon gone. (French)
The friendship of officials is as thin as paper. (Chinese)
The friendship of the great is fraternity with lions. (Italian)

Maintaining Friendship

In forming new friendships, forget not old friends. (Roman)
Little presents maintain friendship. (French)
Short visits make long friendships. (English)
To preserve friendship one must build walls. (Italian)
The one who sows charity reaps friendship and he who plants kindness gathers love. (Spanish)
While you seek new friendships, take care to cultivate the old ones. (Roman)

2.4 INAPPROPRIATE FRIENDS

Not all friends are friends in the positive, prototypical way mentioned above, cf.
A friend to all is a friend to none. (German)
A friend to everybody is a friend to nobody. (Spanish)
The constant friend is never welcome. (Yiddish)
The false friend is like the shadow of a sundial. (French)
A false friend and a shadow attend only while the sun shines. (Poor Richard)
The tongue of a bad friend cuts more than a knife. (Spanish)
Our own kin are the worst friends, said the fox, when he saw the dogs after him. (Danish)
The courts of kings are full of men, empty of friends. (Roman)
A lazy shepherd is a wolf's friend. (Welsh)
A thief and darkness are friends. (African)

3. FRIENDS AND ENEMIES

The usual opposite of friend, the **enemy**, may not be general, sometimes it is not mentioned at all, yet it exists. One can draw a lesson or two from some enemies, too, cf.

One enemy can harm you more than a hundred friends can do you good. (German)
One enemy is too many, a hundred friends is too few. (Indian)
Speak well of your friend; of your enemy, neither well nor ill. (Italian)
A friend is got for nothing, an enemy has to be paid for. (Yiddish)
If you would keep your secret from an enemy, tell it not to a friend. (Poor Richard)
In the house of your enemy, make the wife your friend. (Spanish)

The **role of enemy** may become blurred and get various interpretations, cf.

My friend's enemy is often my best friend. (German)
Wine is first a friend, then an enemy. (Unknown)
Your friend lends and your enemy asks payment. (Dutch)
A reconciled friend is a double enemy. (Spanish)
He cannot be a friend to any one who is his own enemy. (French)
The enmity of the wise is better than the friendship of fools. (Egyptian)
A courageous foe is better than a cowardly friend. (Chinese)

Sometimes, human **folly and enmity** may meet in a single proverb, cf.

A foolish man may be known by six things: anger without cause, speech without profit, change without progress, inquiry without object, putting trust in a stranger, and mistaking foes for friends. (Arabian)

4. Other and Nonhuman Friends

Obviously, *friend/s* are sometimes extended to mean **non-humans** as well. A few of those include dog, book, and other, not necessarily living objects, cf.

A book is a friend. (American)
A dog is a man's best friend. (American)
A dog with a bone knows no friend. (Dutch)
He who goes to bed with dogs, will wake up with fleas. (German)
The cat is friendly, but scratches. (Spanish)
The cock cannot profit by friendship with the fox. (Georgian)
Night has no friend. (French)

5. Inscrutables and Unknowns

Although the **origin and etymology** of proverbs is usually old, quite misty and unreliable, being patently a feature usually avoided by most paremiologists. Hence many proverbs are just not clear as to their origin and may never be. A small attempt at proverbs that might seem to be less comprehensible has been made in some cases producing mixed results and leaving question marks pending, such as:

A friend's meat is soon ready. Being allegedly French but it is nowhere properly explained, suggesting thus more than one interpretation.

Many friends will sit at the same table. It is difficult to pin down where it comes from (Germany?) as well as its meaning (it could mean friends only or negotiating enemies, etc.)

Friendship is but a name; fidelity but an empty name. This rather sad proverb is attributed to Ovid, *Nomen amicitia est, nomen inane fides* suggesting that, after an end of friendship, one's love may have been a real friendship but also a symbiotic attachment or a kind of egotism only.

Friends may meet, but mountains never greet. This may be Italian, but is found also in German or Czech (*setkávají se lidi s lidmi, ale ne hory s horama*), but the allusion to it is found in Shakespeare already (As you like it).

A friend at court is worth a penny in one's purse. It is supposed to be Irish meaning that a friend, coming to court for you, is very valuable (more than a penny (= cent) in your purse (= wallet)), but there is a lot of historical sediment burying this.

6. A CONCLUSION AND A MORAL

Obviously, sex seems to avoid friendship (in proverbs, not in life, perhaps), and the same holds for politics and friendship. In fact, Thomas Jefferson said to William Hamilton in 1880 this:

'*I never considered a difference of opinion in politics, in religion, in philosophy, as cause for withdrawing from a friend.*' Of course, this relationship is open to interpretation again and we shall never know whom Jefferson had taken for friend.

So, is there a moral to all of this? Yes and no: all proverbs do offer their own specific morals, so to speak.

Yet, two proverbs may deserve to be singled out in conclusion, one reaffirming the unshakeable status of proverbs in life, the other pointing to a hidden logical and philosophical link between proverb and truth:

A friend is the solace of life. (Roman)
Truth is better than friendship. (Indian)

LITERATURE

BRAY, Alan. 2003. *The Friend*. Chicago: University of Chicago Press.
CICERO, *Cicero on Friendship*, Lacus Curcio, *Laelius de amicitia*.
CICERO, Marcus Tullius. 1971. *Laelius de Amicitia, Selected Works*. New York: Penguin Books Ltd.
DAVIES, Mark. 2010. *Frequency Dictionary of American English: 5000 Words*. London – New York: Routledge.

LEPP, Ignace. 1966. *The Ways of Friendship*. New York: The Macmillan Company.

SPEAKE, Jennifer, ed. 2015. *The Oxford Dictionary of Proverbs*, Oxford Quick Reference. Oxford – New York: Oxford University.

STONE, Jon R. 2006. *The Routledge Book of World's Proverbs*.London – New York: Routledge.

15. Reason and Thought: Pillars of Intelligent Behaviour Found in Proverbs

In **Actas ICP 10, 2016**, 149–160.

1. Introduction

Motto:

Many complain of their looks, but none of their brains. (Yiddish)
A brain is worth little without a tongue. (French)
Against reason no sword will prevail. (Japanese)

Any deliberate action, physical or intellectual, starts as a vague idea somewhere in the brain, being based

(**A**) on a **reason** in one's **mind**.

Being triggered off by another person's action, inspiration or impetus, supported by memory, experience or belief, it is finally:
(**B**) shaped and elaborated by **thought**. This thought, if conscious, is viewed as a *judgement*. Before it reaches its final form, it is often scrutinized and checked against the background of:

(**C**) one's **wisdom** including judgments on the *folly* of the others (or oneself), if apparent.

All of these phases (A-B-C, i.e. mind, thought and wisdom) might, then, be viewed as steps or stages preceding any intelligent behaviour. As all of these are frequent mental phenomena and processes, repeated over and over again, they have not escaped their being recorded in language as valuable observations of human life, taking on a linguistic form. In the following, then, all of these stages will be taken up and viewed in the light of relevant proverbs, while their various shades and ramifications will be noted.

Thus, about 300 proverbs of, mainly, the three semantic areas mentioned have been selected, mostly from the data offered by the Routledge dictionary, but also other resources.

However, the proverbs brought together here from many languages of the world have been originally selected by the author (which is why many proverbs did not make it to the list used here). The basic proverb data of his is assembled in *The Routledge Book of World Proverbs*, that has been compiled and edited by Jon R. Stone (2006). He inspected proverb collections (mostly written in English) from over 100 languages and after filtering them, offers here a selection of over 17,000 proverbs. This selective character of the data has been made even more prominent by the author of this contribution (responsible for a further filtering out of many). In this way, obviously, a rather subjective basis relating to the narrow topic of this contribution has been achieved almost preventing one from formulating any general conclusion. Yet, hopefully, the gist and the tenor of the three fields is captured here in a more or less responsible coverage.

Since the terms *wisdom* and *wise* (see also Čermák, 2015) comes up quite often here, it should be clearly stated, that, in a sense, most proverbs in a language, indeed, are based on the popular and traditional wisdom of people. To avoid possible confusion between this general sense and the narrower approach chosen here, it has been decided, that only such proverbs will be considered and included in the treatment here that are based on, or rather, that contain basic key-words. These keywords include:

fool, judgement, mind, think, thought, reason, wise and *wisdom*.

2. Relevant Meaning of the Terms Used

All of these words obviously seem to be related to various phases and aspects of one's thought, at least in a basic way. Some are rather broad in their meaning or polysemous, but proverbs containing them do point rather directly to their basic or original meaning. To make this relation of the key-words used in their reflection in the proverbs selected (motivation), each of the three phases **A** (Mind and Reason, in 3.), **B** (Thought and Judgement, in 4.), and **C** (Wisdom and Folly, in 5.) are briefly introduced by a dictionary note and definition indicating the relevant (and basic) meaning reflected by the proverbs that follow. This information is based on the *New Oxford Dictionary of English* (2001).

3. Mind and Reason (A)

DICTIONARY: *Mind*: the faculty of consciousness and thought.

Reason: power of the mind to think, logically processing what is right, practical, or possible; common sense.

For an **Opening**, let us consider two powerful and general proverbs that may be brought forward setting up the scene of mind and reason:

Be master of mind rather than mastered by mind. (Japanese)
May we have a sound mind in a sound body. (Roman)

Obviously, both seem to represent an ideal situation for thought. Following these, however, main specific aspects are given, belonging to A group outlined where proverbs grouping similar features of thought are brought together. The country or ethnicity of these and all of the following proverbs are simply taken from the source dictionary and are thus open to discussion, obviously. It is to be stressed that many similar ideas are found in more than one language.

3.1 MIND OPEN TO EXPERIENCE AND THOUGHT

A prerequisite for a sound thought is being conditioned by one's milieu using the experience gained from it. In doing so, a few basic caveats and conditions should be observed relating to a ready communication linked with compassion, outside inspiration, as well as disturbing influences and fluctuation, including discipline and concentration, etc. Thus,

See with your mind, hear with your heart. (Kurdish)
A closed mind is like a closed book: just a block of wood. (Chinese)
A mind enlightened is like the halls of Heaven; a mind in darkness is like the realm of Hell. (Chinese)
Put your mind under lock and key. (Japanese)
Rage and anger hurry the mind. (Roman)
Much bending breaks the bow; much unbending the mind. (Roman)
Man's mind changes morning through evening. (Korean)
Man's mind cannot be foretold. (Japanese)

3.2 NATURE OF THE MIND

Human mind, if sound and in a reasonable state, has always been highly appreciated as a basic characteristic of man. Hence the following proverbs stating this:
A sound and vigorous mind is the highest possession. (Roman)
Reason is absent when impulse rules. (Roman)
Reason can generally effect more than blind force. (Roman)

However, next to its decisive role in life in general, the human mind is specific for every individual, and is often improved only if compared to and attuned to minds of other people, their experience being thus enriched.

Reason is the guide and light of life. (Roman)
Many heads, many minds. (Greek)
Men's minds are as different as their faces. (Japanese)
Against reason no sword will prevail. (Japanese)
Reason does not come before years. (German)

3.3 MIND: INFLUENCES ON AND INSPIRATION FOR

Inspiration for one's mind and its orientation is often due to outside factors, being both significant and insignificant. However, there seems to be a correlation between the type of mind and its external inspiration. Yet, the mind must be active and effective at all times.

It is the mark of a great mind to despise injuries. (Roman)
Little minds are caught by little things. (Roman)
Little things please little minds. (Dutch)
Man's mind is a watch that needs winding daily. (Welsh)

3.4 REASONING WITH PEOPLE

Relations with other people may be based on the contact and proper experience gained from clever and reasonable people, who often share the same type of thought. It is reasonable not to get into disputes with such people.

Reason not with the great, 'tis a perilous gate. (French)
Great minds think alike. (German)

3.5 TWO AREAS OF APPLICATION: REASON AND LOGIC

While deliberating on a reaction to something, one should be aware of the fact that things do not happen without reason. This has to be recognized and taken into account. On a general level, it is reason and common experience that has become basis for legislature and law, making it predominant in one's thought and reactions.

Every why has a wherefore, every rhyme a reason. (English)
Reason is the spirit and soul of the law. (Roman)

4. THOUGHT AND JUDGEMENT (B)

DICTIONARY: *think*: have a particular opinion, belief,

thought: an idea or opinion produced by thinking or occurring suddenly in the mind, thinking
judgement: the ability to make considered decisions, an opinion or conclusion

As a default set of wise proverbs, serving as an **Opening** of this part, there might be those chosen expressing some very basic and general desiderata and, in fact, advices for everyday life:

Think well of all men. (English)
Thoughts are toll-free, but not hell-free. (German)
Think much, speak little, write less. (Spanish)
Think of three things: whence you came, where you are going, and to whom you must give account. (Poor Richard)

Moving over from reason and mind to thought and thinking processes, we deal with a kind of logical continuation of these. This area might, again, be best viewed as reflecting three more or less separate aspects. Most proverbs here are declarative in their nature, but quite a few assume the form of advice and recommendation. The three areas are related to the independence of thought, ways of thinking and, finally, to shared advices and common sense attitudes.

4.1 INDEPENDENCE OF THOUGHT

The first group is traditionally concerned with *freedom of thought* where all outside interference is generally considered to be unacceptable. This is expressed in many languages in slightly different ways pointing, basically, to the same core.

Thought is free. (English)
Our thoughts are free. (Roman)
No one deserves punishment for a thought. (Roman)

4.2 HOW WE THINK AND SHOULD THINK

The second area presents proverbs related to our *ways of thinking* where one should be aware of the difference of reality and wishful thinking: one does not always think the way he/she should.

Natural logic makes one think and make analogical judgement on two things mostly: the basis of one's past experience and inference from a part to the whole.

We judge of the present from the past. (Roman)
From one you may judge of the whole. (Roman)

On a more concrete level, however, one goes in life by superficial, surface signs that signal, supposedly, some internal state of affairs or quality, such as in:

Abroad we judge the dress; at home we judge the man. (Chinese)
Do not judge of the ship from the land. (Italian)
Do not judge the dog by its hairs. (Danish)
Never judge a book by its cover. (Italian)

The general experience and its urgency derived from the past may be so strong that quite a few proverbs insist on a *shared knowledge*, on what one should do, by expressly refuting or refusing, in fact, the wrong idea and procedure.

This approach may be introduced by a negative imperative **Do not**, such as in:

Do not judge by appearances: a rich heart may be under a poor coat. (Irish)
Don't judge hastily of a ragged boy or a shaggy colt. (Irish)
Don't judge of men's wealth or piety, by their Sunday appearances. (Poor Richard)
Do not judge your friend until you stand in his place. (Danish)
Don't judge a man by the words of his mother, listen to the comments of his neighbors. (Yiddish)

A change of the original thought, due to an important new experience, may point to obvious *change of opinion or thought.*

When you meet a man, you judge him by his clothes; when you leave, you judge him by his heart. (Russian)
Judge of the daughter by the mother. (Roman)
It's easy to be wise after the event. (English)

A plea for impartiality is voiced by the first of the following proverb. That is accompanied by a positive and unexpected experience derived from a turn of affairs.

No one is a good judge in his own cause. (Portuguese)
A pleasant thought never comes too soon. (Danish)

An etymological note: Usually, it is impossible to track down the origin of a proverb to its beginning linked to a nation or even a person/author, and many proverbs do come up repeatedly under various disguises. One of a few exceptions is linked with Poor Richard which is a pseudonym of a natural scientist and diplomat Benjamin Franklin who used it for his popular *Almanac* that he published in many volumes (1732 to 1758). Of course, this does not mean that Franklin had coined lots of proverbs, he just collected them.

Let us add a few more, rather rare, thoughts and proverbs at the same time:

Who judges best of a man, his enemies or himself? (Poor Richard)
Darkness and night are mothers of thought. (Dutch)
Many complain of their memory, few of their judgment. (Poor Richard)
Bodily fatigue affects the mind less than intense thought. (Roman)

4.3 ADVICE AND WARNINGS

Finally, many proverbs take the form of an advice, warning or admonition, such as:

Thinking is not knowing. (Portuguese)
Be slow in thought but quick in action. (Spanish)
Think with the wise, but talk with the vulgar. (Greek)

Also here, a direct *imperative voice* is used to enhance the importance of the proverb.

Judge a tree by its fruit, not by its leaves. (Roman)
Judge not of a ship as she lies on the stocks. (Arabian)
Judge not the horse by its saddle. (Chinese)
Judge a man by the reputation of his enemies. (Arabian)
Judge of the daughter by the mother. (Roman)

The problematic role of a person who finds himself in the position of a (real) judge from whom an objective pronouncement is expected, is commented on by such provebs as:

He is no judge who listens to one side only. (Korean)
The good judge condemns the crime, but does not hate the criminal. (Roman)
Let not the shoemaker judge beyond his last. (Roman)
Who judges others, condemns himself. (Italian)
He who judges between two friends loses one of them. (French)
Second thoughts are wiser thoughts. (Greek)
Take your thoughts to bed with you, for the morning is wiser than the evening. (Russian)
Older is not always wiser. (Unknown)

5. Wisdom and Folly (C)

DICTIONARY: *wisdom*: good judgement, quality of being wise.
folly: lack of good sense; foolishness, a foolish act.

Being aware that wisdom is the internal state everyone would like to achieve while no one likes to be taken for a fool, let us choose, as suitable:

Opening the following three proverbs introducing the last part of the thought process:

No one is at all times wise. (Roman)
No one alone is sufficiently wise. (Roman)
No one is born wise. (German)

Knowing that fools are all around us at all times making our life difficult, some attention should be paid to them, too. There are many types of fools (or, to put it more strongly, idiots, etc.), many of them standing in opposition to wise people. In fact, most of the proverbs on fools are like that, being defined against the background of wisdom. What may appear surprising, given the profusion of fools in real life as against a relative scarcity of wise people, is that there are, in fact, far fewer proverbs about fools than about wisdom and the wise.

5.1 The Fool and the Wise Man

Such aspects of both, as their behaviour, ways of talking, kind and degree of action and decision making, are stressed here, in the following proverbs.

A fool gives full vent to his anger, but a wise man keeps himself under control. (Italian)
A fool may meet with good fortune, but only the wise profits by it. (Dutch)
A fool says what he knows, and a wise man knows what he says. (Yiddish)
The fool speaks, the wise man listens. (African)
A fool takes two steps where a wise man takes none. (Yiddish)
A fool throws a stone into a well, and it requires a hundred wise men to get it out again. (Italian)
A fool will ask more questions than the wisest man can answer. (Unknown)
A fool finds pleasure in evil conduct, but a man of understanding delights in wisdom. (Italian)

Wisdom may be inspired from very different sources, such as:

The fool inherits, the wise acquires. (German)
The fool wanders, the wise man travels. (Unknown)
The wise follow their own decisions; the foolish follow public opinion. (Chinese)
The wise understand by themselves; fools follow the reports of others. (Tibetan)

Unfortunately, a fool may be considered to be wise, if he/she knows when to stop speaking.

The fool who is silent passes for wise. (French)
A fool who can keep silent is counted among the wise. (Yiddish)

5.2 WISDOM AND ITS NATURE

Wisdom, that is firmly anchored to virtue, ability to act and the negation of folly, is both a never-ending state and process, as well as one that is easy to avail, once it is achieved.

Wisdom and virtue are like the two wheels of a cart. (Japanese)
A wise man, a strong man. (German)
Wisdom rides upon the ruins of folly. (Danish)
The doors of wisdom are never shut. (Poor Richard)
Wisdom is the least burdensome traveling pack. (Danish)

However, a popular link of wisdom to human age, is a problematic conclusion, cf.

Wisdom is learned through the wisdom of others. (Yoruban)
Wisdom is not attained with years, but by ability. (Roman)
Up to seventy we learn wisdom – and die fools. (Yiddish)

In real life, wisdom, or rather, realization of the best solution, may come a bit late, inspired by external events, such as in:

Everybody is wise after the fact. (American)
Everyone is wise until he speaks. (Irish)
The wise are ever learning. (German)

5.3 WISDOM: OUTWARD FEATURES AND APPEARANCES

Continual cheerfulness is a sign of wisdom. (Irish)
Not to speak is the flower of wisdom. (Japanese)
Rarely are beauty and wisdom found together. (Roman)
Wisdom does not consist in dress. (Roman)
Speech is given to all, wisdom to few. (Roman)
A wise man hides his wisdom, a fool reveals his folly. (Yiddish)
Those who have white hair are old enough to be wise. (Roman)

Sometimes, it may be useful to remind himself or other people of the intrinsic link to foolishness, such as in:

He is not a wise man who cannot play the fool on occasions. (Italian)
'Tis wisdom sometimes to seem a fool. (Roman)

5.4 Ways to Wisdom

Although wisdom is not learned at school, there are certain ways to approach it, but it is never fast, cheap, and easy. Some of the ways leading to wisdom are captured in proverbs like:

It is best to learn wisdom from the follies of others. (Roman)
The first step toward wisdom is to distinguish what is false. (Roman)
Ripeness is in wisdom, not in years. (Unknown)
Thinking is the essence of wisdom. (Persian)
The morning is wiser than the evening. (Czech)
Wisdom grows by study. (Roman)
A wise man may learn from a fool. (French)
To fear the master is the beginning of wisdom. (Roman)
The beginning of wisdom is to call things by their right names. (Chinese)
Adversity and loss make a man wise. (Welsh)
Wisdom is a good purchase, though we pay dear for it. (Dutch)
A fall into a ditch makes you wiser. (Chinese)

The fact that it may be enough just to partly indicate, hint at or imply precious wisdom and avoid use of the full formulation, is known from many cultures and languages, cf. for example:

Half a word to the wise is enough. (Dutch)
which is found elsewhere, too, as in English *A word to the wise...*or in Czech, etc.

Explicit recommendations and observations may wind up this wisdom list, including additional features of wisdom:

By committing foolish acts, one learns wisdom. (Singhalese)
Better to lose with a wise man than win with a fool. (Yiddish)
A wise man will make tools of what comes to hand. (Roman)
What the fool does at last the wise man does at first. (Spanish)
Wise men learn by other men's mistakes, fools by their own. (Italian)

5.5 THE WISE MAN

Quite a few proverbs on wisdom have already been mentioned above. So, who is a wise man? Whoever might be considered to be a wise man is summed up by the following proverbs and the features they convey:

A wise man is known by what he does not say. (Spanish)
He is wise who watches. (Roman)
The wise man has long ears and a short tongue. (German)
Wise man, even when he holds his tongue, says more than the fool when he speaks. (Yiddish)
Wise men learn from their foes. (German)
A wise man turns chance into good fortune. (Roman)
However, a wise man's profile stands out best, if he/she is compared to or contrasted with a fool:

Fools build houses and wise men live in them. (German)
Fools look to tomorrow, wise men use today. (Scottish)
A wise man does nothing against his will, nothing from sorrow, nothing under coercion. (Roman)
He is the wisest man who does not think himself so. (French)
If everyone were wise, a fool would be the prize. (German)

5.6 SUBSTANCE AND VALUE OF WISDOM

Finally, getting to the very semantic core here, some of general features of wisdom and its value in life might be found reflected in these proverbs:

Wisdom is better than gold and silver. (Jamaican)
Wisdom is the least burdensome traveling pack. (Danish)
He is not a wise man who cannot play the fool on occasions. (Italian)

A child's wisdom is also wisdom. (Yiddish)
All wise men think the same; every fool has his own opinion. (Indian)

Yet, folly being all around us, one may be depressed by this and heave a sigh, such as in:

What use is wisdom when folly reigns? (Yiddish)
With how little wisdom the world is governed! (Roman)

Finally, a rather philosophical conclusion, summing it all up, might be perhaps seen in these three proverbs:

It is not always good to be wise. (German)

Wise lads and old fools were never good for anything. (Italian)
There are no wise men without fools. (English)

6. Conclusions?

Since most of the proverbs here, and definitely all of what has been mentioned and indicated above, is focused on wisdom, it is just impossible to top it by a major 'wisest' proverb beating the rest. Fortunately, such a proverb does not exist.

On a lower level, however, a very polite way, in fact an understatement, taking all of what has been said so far is rendered by a summary, joking conclusion and understatement:

Some are wise and some are otherwise. (English)

Should this sound too pessimistic vis-a-vis the paramount folly all around us, it might be a minor consolation at least, to remember Seneca and his pronouncement:

No man was ever wise by chance.

Literature

ČERMÁK, František. 2015. "Wisdom in Proverbs", In *Bis dat, qui cito dat. Gegengabe in Paremiology, Folklore, Language, and Literature. Honoring Wolfgang Mieder on His Seventieth Birthday*. Eds. Ch. Grandl and K. J. McKenna, 95–98. Frankurt am M.: Peter Lang.

JAMES Alexander. 2007. *The World's Funniest Proverbs*. Bath: Crombie Jardine.

PEARSALL, Judy and HANKS, Patrick, eds. 2001. *The New Oxford Dictionary of English*. Oxford – New York: Oxford University Press.

STONE, Jon R., ed. 2006. *The routledge book of world's proverbs*. London – New York: Routledge.

16. LAUGH PROVERBS: DO THESE REALLY CAPTURE LAUGHING?

In **Actas ICP 9, 2016**, 291–298.

ABSTRACT

Some 160 international proverbs coming from many countries (based on Routledge dictionary) have been analyzed in an attempt to find more general features and aspects of laughter as it is mentioned by proverbs. The analysis, based on the lexical stock of the proverbs only, may be seem as problematic, as the only context of laugh/ter is that of the proverb. Yet, the bulk of proverbs seems to suggest some features at least, along the lines of oppositions, if any, its main actors (arguments), namely the laughing subject, person or object being laughed at and, of qualities and circumstances why and when the laughter occurs.

1. INTRODUCTION

It may not be far from truth that the universal character of proverbs covers all important and recurrent situations in human life. Generally, this is a comfortable knowledge as most common situations based on tradition and experience will almost always be linked to a proverb or two. Due to the ambiguous character of many situations, there is, however, an obvious question to be asked: do proverbs capture all of the main aspects that they seem to be related to? In the following, an attempt will be made to delve into the sphere labeled by or linked with laugh, laughter, and laughing. Yet, it is obvious that people around the world may not always find the same things funny or ridiculous in the same way.

A preliminary answer to the question implied in the title of the contribution may be sought in five selected proverbs that follow, though a more definitive answer one may gather from the totality of this contribution. Hence compare the role of laugh in:

Laughter is the best of medicines. (English)

Laughter makes good blood. (Italian)
That day is lost on which one has not laughed. (French)
Time spent laughing is time spent with the gods. (Japanese)
Laughter is the hiccup of a fool. (Japanese)

To pinpoint to the notional scope where laughter occurs, let us have a look at corpus collocations of *laugh* (BNC), including *loud, softly, gave, loudly, makes, joking, heartily, nervously, harshly, bitter, cry,* and, perhaps, *merry.* Obviously, most of these do not imply joy and mirth.

2. DATA

Since the decision from where to use the data for this topic has been made by choosing those offered in the *Routledge Dictionary of Proverbs* (2006), which collects proverbs from many languages, it may seem that there is a danger of a biased choice that the original author of the dictionary has made. To settle this, an inspection of two alternative sources helped: the *Concise Oxford Dictionary of Proverbs* (2008) having over 1,000 proverbs altogether, and *Wiki English Proverbs* (Wikipedia) listing almost 800 proverbs.

However, proverbs listed in both of them offer much less as far as laugh(ter) is concerned: namely, 5 items in the Oxford Dictionary, and 4 in Wiki (with variants) only, which is patently less than the international Routledge dictionary's offer. Its full inventory contains 159 entries which, having been reduced, by removing many variants, to 82, seems definitely the best source to be used available. True, the Routledge international dictionary is a translation of proverbs from many languages standing against two English-only resources. Comparing these, one finds there is little ground for this as all of the proverbs from the English-only sources are included in the Routledge dictionary, too. Moreover, due to the international character of many proverbs, which often defy any quest as to where they originated, some of these, though labeled as coming from an unfamiliar country or people, may seem familiar nevertheless. In the following, I will refer to the bulk of such proverbs as the *Laugh-corpus.*

3. AN ANALYSIS

Laughter, being both a physical and psychological reaction, as captured by proverbs, suggests that any analysis of its has to include description of some of its aspects, at least. These include (1) oppositions, if any, its main actors (arguments), namely the (2) laughing subject, person or (3) object being laughed at and, perhaps, (4) qualities and circumstances why and when the laughter occurs.

3.1 OPPOSITIONS

While Matti Kuusi's system (Lauhakangas 2001) offers basically only **laughter** versus **crying** or *laughter* versus *sorrow* and *tears* oppositions, these are modified in our Laugh-corpus as often also having *weep/weeping*, with some rare possibilities such as *lament* or *jaundice*, cf.

All things are cause for either laughter or weeping. (Roman)
A woman laughs when she can, and weeps when she pleases. (French)
Beware of laughing hosts and weeping priests. (German)
He who laughs much weeps much. (Turkish)
The weeping bride makes a laughing wife. (German)
Everyone is born crying, not even one laughing. (Spanish)
Sometimes the mouth laughs when the heart cries. (German)
Better to die of laughter than of jaundice. (Spanish)

In general, it is surprising that this opposition (the two versions being very similar) is rather simple and constant being used in only variants of the same situation. In other uses, laugh or laughter are not mentioned as clear opposites of something else.

3.2 WHO LAUGHS?

Oddly enough, however, the largest single group of those who laugh are **fools** (or a fool), simply because of their lack of understanding, education, or knowledge, cf.

A fool is known by his laugh. (German)
A fool laughs when others laugh. (Danish)
By much laughter you detect the fool. (Roman) or
Fools laugh at the Latin language. (Roman)
Laughter abounds in the mouth of fools. (Roman)
There is nothing more foolish than a foolish laugh. (Roman)
The more fools, the more laughter. (French)

Prominent are those fools who laugh at the Latin language or those who laugh because the others laugh, too. Naturally, due to a rather blurred meaning of fool, it is quite possible to encounter fools in many 'laughable' situations.

Women, too, laugh in many situations, but a **women's laugh** is different, the respective proverbs signalling that they are whimsical, changeable in their mood, etc., cf.

The laughter, the tears, and the song of a woman are equally deceptive. (Roman)
A maid who laughs is half taken. (English)
The weeping bride makes a laughing wife. (German)

The thief's wife does not always laugh. (Italian)
A woman laughs when she can, and weeps when she pleases. (French)

A rather rare case associates laughing with **friend**, suggesting a friendly support and sympathy as in:

*A true friend **laugh**s at your stories even when they're not so good, and sympathizes with your troubles even when they're not so bad.* (Irish)

Other than human subjects appear here, too, though these are also linked to humans, i.e. by personification, or anthropocentric principle.

A glad heart seldom sighs, but a sorrowful mouth often laughs. (Danish)
Sometimes the mouth laughs when the heart cries. (German)
A mind conscious of innocence laughs at the lies of rumor. (Roman)
The laughter of the cottage is more hearty and sincere than that of the court. (Roman)

The laughter that is mentioned here is of quite a different type, one concealing sorrow or weeping (which points to an opposition above), expressing pride and disdain of innocence or the sincerity of an informal situation as opposed to the formality of another.

Note that in one case a Roman god Jupiter becomes the subject here, too.
Jupiter laughs at lovers' deceits. (Roman)

Unreasonable and inexperienced people may produce a laugh, too. But that, too, is rather foolish.

*He **laugh**s at scars who never felt a wound.* (German)
*He that **laugh**s at his own joke, spoils the fun of it.* (Danish)

Here also the following British proverb may be interesting to mention, namely:

Love laughs at locksmiths,

which may not seem quite clear nowadays, but which happens to be a modernized version of Shakespeare's proverb referring to Venus and Adonis and the way how obstacles ('locks') are being overcome.

Semantically, it is noticeable that in the data inspected so far, there are hardly any neutral proverbs in the sense of pure, sincere joy and laughter.

It is rather typical to note that **formally** most of the proverbs in this second group (2) use pronouns and other general means, though no specific nouns for subjects: namely *he* (13×), *you* (2×), *one* (1×), *no one* (1×), *man* (2) and, exceptionally, *fool(s)* (7×).

3.3 WHAT DOES ONE LAUGH AT?

Objects or targets of laughing may be numerous and highly subjective. Only frequent situations are captured by proverbs, some of them being quite general and almost philosophical, or related, obviously, to **human nature** in general, such as in:

*One half of the world **laugh**s at the other half.* (French)
*A man shows his character by what he **laugh**s at.* (German)

People laugh at other peoples' misfortune, or failure, too, adding **mockery or even ridicule** by which laughter turns sour or becomes unreasonable. See examples in:

*The **laugh** is always on the loser.* (German)
*The world **laugh**s at those who fall.* (German)
*Who **laugh**s at others' ills, has his own behind the door.* (Italian)

On the other hand, it is a sign of self-composure and control to be able to laugh (ironically) at oneself, if there is a reason for that, this attitude being almost **philosophical**, as in:

*It is a great art to **laugh** at your own misfortune.* (Danish)
*It is better for a man to **laugh** at life than to lament over it.* (Roman)

*When the mouse **laugh**s at the cat, there is a hole nearby.* (Nigerian)
*Fools **laugh** at the Latin language.* (Roman)
*They will be hushed by a good deed who **laugh** at a wise speech.* (French)

*Jupiter **laugh**s at lovers' deceits.* (Roman)
*A mind conscious of innocence **laugh**s at the lies of rumor.* (Roman)

Despite the unpleasant kind of laughing mentioned above, popular wisdom also offers reasonable advice or a warning as a basis of good behaviour, stating what one should not laugh at, such as in:

*Do not **laugh** at a deformed person today; you may be him tomorrow.* (Yoruban)
***Laugh** not at a man because he is old, for age will also come to you.* (Chinese)

There is also self-induced laughter due to physical reasons which can be initiated at will, such as in:

He who tickles himself, can **laugh** *when he likes.* (German)
Those who tickle themselves may **laugh** *whenever they please.* (German)

3.4 LAUGHTER QUALITIES AND CIRCUMSTANCES

Laughing occurs when the situation is appropriate and certain conditions, qualities and circumstances are present. Apart from a general reference to laughing related to a good state of one's health as in:

A good **laugh** *and a long sleep are the best cures in the doctor's book.* (Irish)

The most common and frequent relation of laughing is found and repeatedly pointed out by its link with either it occurring as the *last* reaction to what has gone on before or, at least, to its *duration* if triumphant, such as in

He **laugh**s *best who* **laugh**s *longest.* (Swedish)
He **laugh**s *best who* **laugh**s *last.* (Dutch)
He who **laugh**s *last* **laugh**s *longest.* (English)
He who **laugh**s *last* **laugh**s *best.* (German)

On the other hand, laughter may be a reaction to many things, either nice and humorous or unpleasant, but it may be a sign of the speaker being rather silly or imprudent, or just a sign of the situation being so humorous that one does not realize that it (i.e. the unpleasant thing) may happen also to him/her next day. Compare, for example,

He that **laugh**s *on Friday may cry on Sunday.* (French)
If you **laugh** *today, you will cry tomorrow.* (Portuguese)
Much **laugh**ter, *little wit.* (Portuguese)

An acknowledgement of justified laughter is also possible, though quite rare:

Let them that win **laugh**. (Roman)

However, laughter may serve to conceal other things, such as sorrow, pain or even triumph, as in:

He who **laugh**s *overmuch may have an aching heart.* (Italian)
He who **laugh**s *much weeps much.* (Turkish)
The tears of an heir are **laugh**ter *in disguise.* (Roman)

Laughter may be rather improper sometimes as in the first example, or amused in memory as in the second:

*He who made fun of the old man, **laugh**ed at first and cried afterwards.* (Spanish)
*He who **laugh**s alone is recalling his little sins.* (Spanish)

Finally, laughter may be odd, as a sign of someone ill-mannered or even dangerous and life-threatening, as in:

*Meaningless **laugh**ter is a sign of ill-breeding.* (Arabian)
*He **laugh**s ill that **laugh**s himself to death.* (German)

4. Final Proverbs and Conclusion(s)

Oddly, laughing stands out sometimes as a feature of quite general, almost philosophical situations, both because of the opposites implied or its relative nature. Therefore, it might be proper to wind up this little 'laughing' survey by pointing to just this feature. The relative nature of laughter may be either general as in:

*One half of the world **laugh**s at the other half.* (French)
*If you want to make God **laugh**, tell him your plans.* (Spanish)

Or highly personal as in,

*When a father helps his son, both **laugh**; when a son helps his father, both cry.* (Spanish)
*When man partakes of the earth, there is **laugh**ter; when the earth eats man, there is great wailing.* (Chinese)

Though they are effective in both cases. Yet, finally, it may be advisable not to laugh sometimes as in:

*Ill-timed **laugh**ter is a dangerous evil.* (Greek)

There is little here that could be pointed at as a clear feature of laughter by way of a summary, most cases seem to be obvious. Nevertheless, let us just remind ourselves that people often laugh in proverbs when laugh is close to weeping, or laughing people are just fools sometimes, not quite discriminating between 'good' and 'bad' laugh, so to speak.

*Among those who stand, do not sit; among those who sit, do not stand; among those who **laugh**, do not weep; among those who weep, do not **laugh**.* (Yiddish)

When a father gives to his son, both **laugh***; when a son gives to his father, both cry*. (Yiddish)
No one becomes a laughing stock who eagerly **laugh***s at himself*. (Roman)

Seldom comes a loan **laugh***ing home*. (English)
The nose-drop **laugh***s at the tear-drop*. (English)

LITERATURE

CONCISE OXFORD DICTIONARY of PROVERBS (Oxford Quick Reference), 2008, J. Simpson. Oxford U.P.

ČERMÁK, František, 2014. *Proverbs: Their Lexical and Semantic Features*. The University of Vermont, Burlington, Vermont: Proverbium in cooperation with the Institute of the Czech National Corpus, Supplement Series, Vol. 37, ed. W. Mieder.

ČERMÁK, František, 2013. *Základní slovník českých přísloví*. Praha: NLN (= Basic Dictionary of Czech Proverbs).

LAUHAKANGAS, Outi, 2001. *The Matti Kuusi international type system of proverbs*. Helsinki: Suomalainen Tiedeakatemia.

LAUHAKANGAS, Outi, 2014, *Proverbs as Precision Guided Humor*. In *Actas ICP14 Proceedings, of the 8 Colóquio Interdisciplinar sobre Provérbios. The 8th Interdisciplinary Colloquium on Proverbs*, IAP-AIP (International Association of Paremiology), eds. Rui Soares. Outi Lauhakangas: Tavira.

The ROUTLEDGE DICTIONARY of WORLD'S PROVERBS, ed. Jon R. Stone. 2006. London New York: Routledge.

WIKI ENGLISH PROVERBS (Wikipedia) https://en.wiktionary.org/wiki/Category:English_proverbs (2014).

17. NUMBERS IN PROVERBS

In **Actas ICP 8, 2015**, 298–305.

ABSTRACT

Numbers and proverbs may seem an incongruent combination. Since most current types of human experience are covered by proverbs and some of it may be numbered, this may become a research question, however odd and rare it sounds. On the basis of a proverb corpus (Routledge dictionary), proverbs containing cardinal numbers have been collected and inspected, accompanied by their frequency of use. Except for some very basic first numbers and round numbers such as thirty or hundred, hardly any other have been found in use here. However, despite this result, which could be expected, some minor, yet interesting ways of this type of use could have been pointed at here. In the following, such aspects are inspected as symbolic use, motivation and its absence in their use (Four eyes see more than two vs One bird in the hand is worth four in the air) and rare metaphorical transfers. A detailed inspection of proverbs containing one, first, two, hundred, thousand, and, in more detail, usage of three and seven is offered. A typical feature of some cases is a loose use of numbers, defying, obviously, their otherwise exact character. However, the general answer to the main research question, is, that most of the use of numbers is not projected in the respective proverbs where they occur.

1. INTRODUCTION: DO NUMBERS HAVE A ROLE TO PLAY IN PROVERBS?

Despite a seemingly marginal use of numbers (or rather figures) in proverbs one may ask what role, if any, numbers play in their constitution and build up. More specifically, do numbers/figures stand for what we use them for in mathematics, and, even, in everyday calculations, i.e. operations where *exact* quantities are measured and handled?

Certainly, such proverbs as:

(1) *A stitch in time saves nine*

can hardly be viewed as expressing anything exact making one circumspect as it is impossible to perceive any mathematical justification in the use of *nine*. Why *nine* and not *ten*, for example? Having noticed the rhyme appearing here (*time : nine*) the suspicion increases as one may realize both that *nine* is not motivated in any way while it is used, surprisingly, for another purpose, not quite consistent with mathematics, or rather, arithmetics, namely rhyme-buildup. Some people might even be tempted to think that wisdom as a basic message proverbs offer cannot be calculated and marriage of the two, numbers and wisdom, to put it very simply, cannot be reconciled.

Looking into their statistics in the corpus used (that of *Routledge Dictionary of World Proverbs*, Jon R. Stone, 2006), i.e. in its 14,149,618 words, one observes that the sum total of all occurrences here is very low, indeed, namely a mere 0.03% of all its words. There are over 17,000 proverbs selected here from over 100 languages.

All of this may seem point to the futility of adopting a similar point of view. But let us look first, before giving the idea up, at one more example:

(2) *A man at five may be a fool at fifteen.*

Though not in so many words, the proverb, based on experience, almost certainly refers to two human (A) age periods, (B) experience and (C) reason that may (D) not be directly proportional to the age groups. Hence, in this case, numbers do refer clearly to something rather familiar, and their use is *motivated* here, somehow. The problem as to how and to what extent remains open, however. Thus, at least some cases of numbers appearing in proverbs may have reason for this in a way that is not quite clear yet, though some may not. This, then, suggests a justification of this contribution, to investigate, on a very modest scale, the problem suggested by the title and, specifically, by the two examples above. More broadly, this quest started here tries to follow the lexical features, if any, of numerals within a general quest for lexical motivation of proverbs (see also Čermák 2014).

2. Numbers Represented in Proverbs

In the following, only simple and basic cardinal numbers (with some notable exceptions) occurring in proverbs will be briefly inspected. Proverbs using ordinal numbers have not been found in sufficient quantity. It is not surprising that the appearance of these instances is both unbalanced and, in some cases, even missing. A simple survey offers the numbers inspected and their frequencies in proverbs available.

• 1/one (1285×), first (829×), once (122×), 2/two (238×), second (27), twice (74), 3/ three (85×), third (20×), 4/four (25×), 5/five (9×), fifth (2×), 6/ six (8×), sixth (1×), 7/seven (35×), 8/eight (5×), 9/ nine (23×), 10/ ten (6×)

•11/eleven (1×), 12/ twelve (3×), 13/thirteen (1×), 14/ fourteen (0), 15/ fifteen (2×), 16/ sixteen (1×), 17/ seventeen (0), 18/eighteen (1×), 19/nineteen (0)

• 20/twenty (21×), 30/thirty (9), 40/forty (7), 50/fifty (4), 60/ sixty (2), 70/ seventy (4), 80/ eighty (3), 90/ninety (0), 99/ninety-nine (1)

• 100/hundred (1073×), 1000/thousand (70×), 1 000 000/million (1×)

This inventory does not reveal much, apart from the obvious predominance of *one*. Their use and some features will be shown later, in 4.

3. Number Symbolism and Proverbs

To allay fears that one might, by adopting this kind of approach, arrive at mystical, religious or numerological conclusions, it must be categorically stated that no such irrational aspect has been looked for, found, and inspected here, despite the profusion of books on the subject. Proverbs are very rational and there is hardly anything mystical in them in general, let alone in those supported by numbers if they happen to appear here. Thus, no connection or collocation could be found between numbers and such words as *sacred*, *holy* or *divine*; the same holds for *god*, while a loose and single use of *one* in the sole *One God, one wife, but many friends* can hardly serve as a counterargument.

4. The Use of Numbers in Proverbs: What is Counted and Numbered

In what follows, numbers in proverbs will be inspected as to where they appear, and the possible reasons for their use, at least in some cases, will be looked for. Specifically, their motivated and unmotivated use will be distinguished, next to their metaphorical use, if any.

Likewise, despite a number of instances where numbers are used because of their symbolic value, which lies outside the scope of proverbs however, no mention or reference will be made to these.

4.1 RARELY USED NUMBERS IN PROVERBS

Next to numbers *not appearing* in proverbs at all, such as 24, 17, 19 or almost any higher uneven ones, such as 77, 239, etc, there are some numbers that do appear, but rather rarely. These include 11, 13 or 18, cf.

Rain before seven, fine before eleven.
Between age ten and thirteen, bend the twig while it be green.
Even the Devil was handsome at eighteen.

It seems that even with scarcely represented numbers in proverbs, a basic division can follow cases where (**A**) use of a numeral is *motivated* or (**B**) it is *not motivated*. Let us have a look at some examples:

(**A**) *There's more to a marriage than **four** bare legs in a bed.*
Four eyes see more than two.
Between age ten and thirteen, bend the twig while it be green.

(**B**) *Where there are six cooks, there is nothing to eat.,*
The lazy servant takes eight steps to avoid one.

By extension, some types of use may be viewed, however, as *partially motivated*, such as:

(**C**) *A fifth wheel to a cart is but a hindrance.*
One word beforehand is better than ten afterwards.

On the other hand, a multiple graded use of numerals may have a mixed character. Rather, they may be used for a kind of emphasis, often linked with some funny aspect stressed.

One Russian is a drunk; two Russians a chess game; three Russians a revolution; four Russians a string quartet.
Twelve highlanders and a bagpipe make a rebellion.

As a part of this, a ***random motivation within a known limit*** may be discerned here, such as:

A man at sixteen will prove a child at sixty.
He that is not brave at twenty, strong at thirty, rich at forty, or experienced at fifty, will never be brave, strong, rich or prudent.

It may be that the power of round numbers (such as 20, 30 or 50) is part of the choice behind this type of motivation.

Often, it is difficult to discern **any direct motivation** at all while there may, though **indirectly**, be some *associations* employed, such as in:

At twenty years of age the will reigns; at thirty the wit; at forty the judgment.
As you are at seven so are you at seventy.
Up to seventy we learn wisdom and die fools.
A man as he manages himself may die old at thirty, or young at eighty.
A habit at three years is a habit at eighty.

4.1.1 THE CASE OF *THREE* AND *SEVEN* IN PROVERBS AND PROBLEMS OF THEIR INTERPRETATION: A DETAILED LOOK

A slightly higher, though still rather rare are number 3 (85x) and 7 (with frequency of 35) these being, outside proverbs, often used for their symbolic meaning and the fact that they are prime numbers in cases such as:

*All good things are **three**.*

Let us have a brief look at these first.
Obviously, there are problems with the kind and quality of motivation, reflecting a generalized experience here.

A kind of (**A**) **motivation** of the situation captured by the proverbs related (**1**) to the *outside world*, which is shared by many, presumably, should be distinguished from that formed by relations and situation (**2**) *inside the group* outlined by numbers, shared by those who have this kind of experience. Consider tentatively e.g.,

A1 *Fish and guests stink after three days.*
It takes three generations to make a gentleman.
Three removals are as bad as a fire.

A2 *Children: one is one, two is fun, three is a houseful.*
Where there's three, there's always one fool.
Two's company but three's a crowd.

A loose, (**B**) not quite convincing **ad hoc motivation** that can be viewed by some as both *subjective and relative,* may be found in:

(**4**) cases supported by **loosely generalized experience** (overlapping with A1), e.g.,
Spring has come when you can put your foot on three daisies.
He who has three enemies must agree with two.
Justice is three votes of five.

Finally, the majority type groups together (**C**) ***totally unmotivated cases*** that are either rather (5) *simple, based on a random choice* (of conspicuous items usually) or on (6) *humorous, playful items*, e.g.,

(**5**) *Three things without rule: a woman, a pig, and a mule.*
Three things in the world worth having: courage, good sense, caution.
Three things grow overnight: profits, rents, and girls.

(**6**) *Three women, three geese, and three frogs make a fair.*
The cat has nine lives: three for playing, three for straying, three for staying.

The case of the numeral **seven** is basically similar to that of **three** where the same types of non/motivation can be found. Using the same typology, some typical examples show this.

(**A**, *no motivation*)
Many look with one eye at what they give, but with seven at what they receive.
A false story has seven endings.
Seven will not wait for one.

(**B**, *motivation*)
Rain before seven, fine before eleven.
Six hours' sleep for a man, seven for a woman, eight for a fool.
Seven is company, nine is a brawl.

(**C**, **partial**, *ad hoc motivation*)
A cat has nine lives, as the onion seven skins.
As one is at seven, so one is at seventy.
Seven trades but no luck.

However, due to the special symbolic character of *seven*, some instances tend to use *seven* as a

(**D**) *sufficient number*, ***even plenty***, such as in:

Keep a thing for seven years and you'll find a use for it.
A handful of good life is better than seven barrels of learning.
One fool may ask more questions than seven wise men can answer.
Turn your tongue seven times before speaking.

4.2 More Frequent Numbers Used in Proverbs

Due to their highest occurrence, it is difficult to distinguish for the numeral **one**, **two** and, at the other end, *hundred and thousand*, any clear features of use.

One (1285×) has a standard role to play even here: next to its pronominal use as a general subject or object (*One cannot drink and whistle at the same time*) and substitute, some of its instances do point at the basic counting, naturally, eg., *One swallow doesn't make a summer*.

However, **two** (238×) assumes its numeral function fully, though, apart from mere counting, *two* uses seem to be rather special. These include:

(A) existence of **competition**, **quarrel** or **fight** between two people, etc, e.g.,
Two captains will sink the ship.
Two bulls cannot live in one stable.
Two dogs seldom agree over one bone.

(B) Great **difference** or **opposition**,
To love and be wise are two different things.
He who judges between two friends loses one of them.

(C) A third tendency to be found points to an **emphasis**, or **strengthening**, fortifying of the number, such as in:
Two heads are better than one.
Two men may meet, but never two mountains.

Oddly enough, **hundred** (1073×) and much less used **thousand** (70×) seem to be almost identical in their use showing, however, no special tendencies or subtypes, both of them meaning just 'very many, plenty', cf.

Victory has a hundred fathers but defeat is an orphan.
One fool makes a hundred.
In a hundred years our teeth will no longer hurt.
Success has a thousand fathers.
Though footless, a word can travel a thousand miles.
There are a thousand ways of dying, only one of being born.

In contrast to *hundred*, used only in singular, there are a few cases of **thousands**, i.e. the plural form, signifying an **indefinitely large quantity**. In this feature, it is close to many uses of one and other numerals where the original numerical meaning is completely lost, cf.

Thousands drink themselves to death before one dies of thirst.
There are as many thousands of different pastimes as there are individuals.
He who could foresee affairs three days in advance would be rich for thousands of years.

5. CONCLUSIONS

To sum up briefly, one can say that there are a good many cases where the numerical meaning is either lost or made to mean something indefinite with reference to a larger amount or quantity.

Semiotically and lexically, many numerals, in fact their majority (except *one*) are used, next to a standard motivated use, as unmotivated, or partially unmotivated. It is peculiar that this partial un/motivation can assume more than one way, suggesting, in some cases, that there are subtypes of the same usage of partial motivation.

The general conclusion is that numerals used in proverbs are usually not what they should be in standard language and should not be confused with real counting procedures.

LITERATURE

ČERMÁK, František. 2014. *Proverbs: Their Lexical and Semantic Features*. Proverbium in Cooperation with the Institute of the Czech National Corpus. Burlington, Vermont: University of Vermont.
STONE, Jon R., ed. 2006. *The routledge book of world's proverbs*. London – New York: Routledge.

18. Dog and Cat Proverbs: Comparison of English, Czech, Finnish and Other Languages

In **Čermák Proverbs 2014**, 183–196.

Abstract

Although the coexistence of dogs and cats with humans is universal and taken for granted, reflection of this fact in language, notably in proverbs, may not be so obvious. The paper tries to inspect this question in 6 languages, namely in Czech, English, German, French, Finnish, and Russian using as a starting point, those cat- and dog- proverbs that are to be found in a large recent Czech dictionary of idioms. Hence, ten proverbs are inspected in these languages, their equivalents as well as possibilities to describe them in a unified metalanguage.

1. General and Introductory Remarks

Historically, all idioms and phrasemes have been coined to reflect a recurrent and generally shared experience, drawing on those words and things that were in the centre of such experience and observation. Though specific within the larger framework of phraseology, this holds for proverbs, too. Things, or rather, animals, in our case dogs and cats, have always been around and people have observed and coined proverbs expressing many different types of experience related to these two animals. Both dog, having some 15,000 years of cohabitation with man, and cat with a slightly shorter period of domestication have become indispensable in many respects as human companions, helpers and, increasingly, pets.

Next to horse or cop or even elevator laws, there exist ingenious and funny Murphy's dog/canine laws reflecting an intimate and varied experience of dogs, but, oddly enough there seem to be none about cats. It is impossible to list thousands of sayings and observations about dog and cat, being widely different in different languages (not all of them being proverbs, of course), having been coined anonymously or by some famous people letting us know their preference for, usually, one of the two animals.

Trying to pinpoint what they have in common is a problem, but there might be at least one saying summing up many features of both animals and their role in the human life in a rather clever and witty way: *Dogs have owners, cats have staff.*

General and probably universal coexistence of these two animals with man makes one wonder, if there is a common feature or features that proverbs in different languages jointly reflect.

A first look may not confirm this suggestion, as there are many dog and cat proverbs that are **difficult to find in more than one language**. Let us have a look, briefly, at English first. Proverbs such as:

Give a dog a bad name and hang him,
Why keep a dog and bark yourself? or *Let sleeping dogs lie,*
do belong, it seems, to this kind. Likewise French,
Chien en vie vaut mieux que lion mort (The living dog is better than a dead lion),
Bon chien chasse de race (From their parents children inherit both good and bad qualities),
Qui veut noyer son chien l'accuse de la rage (Give a dog a bad name and hang him),
or German:
Den Letzten beißen die Hunde (It is the dog that bites since it is the last),
Kommt man über den Hund, kommt man auch über den Schwanz (Once you deal with the most difficult part, the rest will have to be dealt with, too).
Also, Finnish offers some specific proverbs, such as:
Ei ole koiraa karvoihin katsominen (Do not judge the dog by its hair),
Se koira älähtää, johon kalikka kalahtaa.(The dog will howl, which is hit by the stick).

A Czech classic (Čelakovský, from 1852) having collected the largest list of proverbs offers no less than 117 proverbs where *dog* alone may be found (leaving *cat* aside for the moment). He, too, offers some specific proverbs, such as:

Koně chromého, psa líného, sluhy opilého stejné jsou služby (The services of a lame horse, lazy dog, and drunken servant are the same),
Zadarmo ani pes neštěká (Not even a dog barks for free),
Dobrý pes lepší než zlý člověk (A good dog is better than an evil man), etc.

In contrast to this, the number of cat proverbs seems to be somewhat smaller in general.

Contrary to this, Guyla Paczolay (1997) registering 106 proverbs in 55 European languages records **3 common proverbs** found relevant in this impressive number, he scrutinized:

A barking dog does not bite,
When the cat is away, the mice will play,
All cats/cows are alike in the dark.

Given the diversity of resources of this important and unique collection investigated here it is obvious that his results represent a cross-section of what was available though what criteria have been used here in the selection of items for this is not clear. Obviously it is difficult if not impossible to draw a line between commonality or familiarity and frequency.

Going by **corpora** resources, it is only the BNC and CNC here that might help, though the results are both meagre and mutually different. The British National Corpus has only:

Barking dogs seldom bite 12
Let sleeping dogs lie 12
Dog eat dog 8,

while The Czech National Corpus offers as the most frequent:
Život je pes 12 (It's a dog's life)
Pes je nejlepší přítel člověka 11 (A man's best friend is his dog).

This makes one wonder what the criteria for selection of such a study could be, if any.

Leaving aside the Internet where some proverbs may be found too, though no safe information about the whole framework they fit in, the only other, rather traditional resource left are **dictionaries**. Next to large monolingual dictionaries, there are collections of proverbs of varying size and quality to be found in various languages, basically showing that there is no reliable comparison of these possible. Thus, for example, the New Oxford Dictionary of English chose to include 9 dog proverbs, while Duden has only 5, as well as a Czech dictionary (SSJČ, Slovník spisovného jazyka českého) offering another 5, too, etc., their problem being, among other things, a poor discrimination between dog proverbs and other dog idioms.

This is why the problem of **selection** of proverbs for comparison seems to be open, as well as the idea that there might be a small group of proverbs shared by more languages. However, in the following, attention will be paid to ten dog and cat proverbs selected and described in the *Czech Dictionary of Phraseology and Idiomatics IV* (Sentence Expressions, 2009), which, as it has turned out, happens to have a fair representation of this type of living proverbs being both sharply discriminated from other types of dog and cat idioms, and containing more than one foreign language equivalent to the Czech core. These happen to have a rather high frequency, too. Hence, data from 6 languages, namely Czech, English, German, French, Russian, and Finnish will be examined, drawn mostly from this dictionary. The ten proverbs taken from this dictionary and given below in the English version first, will be examined in some detail in (3) and (4).

However, the two last proverbs (Nos 9 and 10) do not seem to be used in English.

1 You can't teach an old dog new tricks (*Starého psa novým kouskům nenaučíš*)
2 A barking dog never bites (*Pes, který štěká, nekouše*)
3 It's easy to find a stick to beat a dog (*Kdo chce psa bít, hůl si najde*)

4 A dog is a man's best friend (*Pes je nejlepší přítel člověka*)

5 Dogs bark, but the caravan goes/rolls on (*Psi štěkají, ale karavana jde dál.*)

6 It is unlucky have a black cat cross your path (*Černá kočka přes cestu znamená neštěstí /smůlu*)

7 When/while the cat's away, the mice will play (*Když kocour není doma, myši mají pré*)

8 All cats in the dark are grey (*Potmě je každá kočka černá*)

9 Too many dogs is the hare's death (*Mnoho psů, zajícova smrt*)

10 It's a dog's life (*Život je pes*)

For the following, three general theses, based on a preliminary observation, may be formulated:

Thesis 1: There is no linguistically discernible motivation of proverbs by the dog/cat component.

Thesis 2: Despite the unfathomable preferences for dogs or cats in real life, there are more proverbs related to dog than cat.

Thesis 3: Modern (urban) life has changed to such an extent that many proverbs have gone out of use.

2. Dog and Cat in the Rest of Phraseology and Idioms

Before going on with dog and cat proverbs, a brief picture of the whole dog and cat scene in phraseology might be of interest. Also here, the same Czech resource has been chosen, though limited to similes only, the number of other types of idioms and phrasemes being much larger, going, in fact, into the hundreds. Sixty-three Czech dog and cat similes used as a starting point have been examined semantically and functionally and compared with their equivalents in English, German, and French, e.g.:

scratch Cz *mít drápy jako kocour*, **E** have claws like a *cat*, **G** Krallen wie eine *Katze* haben, **F** !avoir des griffes de *chat*;

beat so cruelly Cz *zbít/seřezat někoho jako psa* n. *zabít/zastřelit někoho jako psa*, **E** !knock the living daylights out of so. !beat. so. to a pulp/jelly, **G** j-n abknallen/ erschiessen wie einen (tollen) *Hund*, **F** abattre/ tirer qn comme un *chien*;

be furious Cz (*být*) *vzteklý jako pes*, **E** be like a rabid *dog*, be as cross as two sticks, **G** wie ein toller *Hund* sein, **F** être comme un *chien* enragé.

It is perhaps surprising that every single idiom had to be semantically classified separately (a shortened version of the metalanguage, not to be mixed with definition, is given above in bold). This means that there are no synonyms found here, each idiom having a specific meaning. On the other hand, it may be interesting to note that despite the many differences between the four languages compared, the highest correspond-ence between these languages is to be found between Czech and English. Obviously, starting with the Czech data, all of them having the structure and function of simile does not mean that equivalents in the other three languages have to have the same structure and function, as the examples show.

To give just an illustration of the field of similes covered elsewhere (Čermák 1994) it might be revealing to say that the most common similes based on *dog* (*pes*) are those expressing
loyalty (26%),
tiredness (24%),
though the combination *like a cat and dog* is also prominent.

The percentages belong to the overall frequency of all dog and cat similes and these semantic fields mentioned are just three out of 63 covering this whole semantic sub-field.

Anyway, both dog and cat similes and proverbs represent only a minor part of all idi-oms of this type.

3. Dog and Cat Proverbs: A Comparison and Notes

Out of the ten proverbs examined in six languages, six are recorded by Hans Walther (1963, etc) as being Latin and coming from the Middle Ages at least. However, this does not mean that they could not be older, cf. Latin *Qui iugulare canem vult, invenit cito causam* (He who wants to strangle the dog finds a reason soon). Generally, there is hardly any better international resource since Latin has influenced most European languages enormously.

Some proverbs refer to a rather complicated and changing history behind them. Thus, contrary to a prevailing view that meeting a black cat brings ill luck, in Great Brit-ain black cats are a symbol of good luck. The Scottish people still believe that a strange black cat's arrival to one's home signifies prosperity. It is also believed that a lady who owns a black cat will have many suitors. In French, however, most of the black cat symbolism has been overshadowed by the Paris amusement and entertainment centre *le chat noir* that has become popular also elsewhere. A strange turn had been taken in German where it has become a tradition to wall up a cat in the foundation of a house, dam, etc., averting thus ill luck to the place.

Despite a general decline in the proverbs use, there are contrary examples found. Such is No 5 below on the relation of caravans and dogs whose first occurrence is attest-ed in R. Kipling's *Beast and Man in India* (1891) which is generally considered to be com-ing from the East, namely Arabic countries. Most dictionaries do not record it yet as it is relatively new and spreading under the influence of English probably, but itseems to be rather familiar, which is the case of Finnish, where it is used, too.

Equivalents related to Czech where all of the ten expressions have the character of proverbs may be different elsewhere, however, note the parentheses ( ) standing for loose equivalents or ! preceding it that points to a non-proverb phraseme having a different function. There are, however, many variants and smaller points that will not be gone into here.

The comparative list includes:

CZECH	English German	French Russian	Finnish
1 *Starýho/starého psa novejm/novým kouskům nenaučíš.*	You can't teach an old dog new tricks. Du kannst einem alten Maestro keine neuen Stücke beibringen.	On n'apprend pas un vieux singe faire la grimace. (Gorbatogo mogila ispravit.)	Ei vanhaa koiraa opeteta., Ei vanha koira opi uusia tapoja.
2 *Pes, který štěká, nekouše.*	A barking dog never bites; His bark is worse than his bite. Hunde, die bellen, beissen nicht.	Chien qui aboie ne mord pas. (Lajušaja sobaka ne kusaetsja.)	Haukkuva koira ei pure.
3 *Kdo chce psa bít, hůl si najde.*	It's easy to find a stick to beat a dog. (Ein billiger Vorwand findet sich immer.)	Qui veut noyer son chien, l'accuse de la rage. Byla by sobaka, a palka budet.	Joka haluaa koiraa lyödä, kyllä keppi löytyy.
4 *Pes je nejlepší přítel člověka.*	A dog is a man's best friend; A man's best friend is his dog. Der beste Freund des Menschen ist der Hund.	(Le chien est le meilleur ami de l'homme.) Sobaka (lučšij) drug čeloveka.	Koira ihmisen paras ystävä.
5 *Psi štěkají, ale karavana jde dál.*	Dogs bark, but the caravan goes/rolls on. Die Hunde bellen, aber die Karawane zieht weiter.	Les chiens aboient, la caravane passe. Sobaka laet, veter nosit., Sobaka laet, a karavan prochodit mimo.	Koirat haukkuu, karavaani kulkee.
6 *Černá kočka přes cestu znamená neštěstí / smůlu.*	Black cat crossing your path is unlucky. Schwarze Katze über den Weg bringt Unglück.	Chat noir traversant votre route porte malheur. Черная кошка приносит несчастье, если пересекает путь	Musta kissa tietää vaaraa/ Kun musta kissa menee tien yli, se tietää huonoa onnea.

CZECH	English German	French Russian	Finnish
7 *Když kocour není doma, myši mají pré.*	When/while the cat's away, the mice will play. Wenn die Katze aus dem Haus ist, tanzen die Mäuse (auf dem Tisch).	Quand le chat n'est pas là, les souris dansent. Póp v gostjach, čerty na pogoste, bez kotá myšám máslenica.	Kun kissa ei ole kotona, hiiret hyppii pöydällä.
8 *Potmě je každá kočka/ kráva černá.*	All cats in the dark are grey. Bei Nacht sind alle Katzen grau.	La nuit, tous les chats sont gris; C'est blanc bonnet, et bonnet blanc. V temnote vse koški sery.	Pimeässä kaikki kissat ovat mustia.
9 *Mnoho psů, zajícova smrt.*	He didn't have a cat/snowball in hell's chance; !be hopelessly outnumbered. Viele Hunde sind des Hasen Tod.	(Beaucoup de chiens, c'est la mort du lièvre.), (Il est difficile de se battre contre vents et marées.)	Monta koiraa, jäniksen kuolema.
10 *Život je pes.*	It's a dog's life. ! Ein Hundeleben (führen)	C'est une chien de vie. Žizn' bezžálostna, Éto sobač'ja žizn'.	Koiran elämää.

There are only few cases where the starting Czech proverb does not have a good equivalent in the other languages (such as English No 9, German No 3 or Russian No 1).

4. Meaning of Proverbs and a Summary

Semantically, the ten proverbs inspected here fall into three types, basically, though all of them bear on man (human being) one way or another. The largest (1-3, 5-6, 9) relates directly to man and situations he finds himself in, including ability to learn, proclivity to threat contrasted to real action, his belief, reaction to minor threats, etc., in which man is also used in the metalaguage; three (Nos 7, 8 and 10) are recalling and naming situations, mostly difficult and unpleasant, while there is only one (No 4) where dog figures in the metalanguage directly as an epitome of loyalty. It is only this proverb where thesis No 1 above seems to be suspended. Below, the ten semantic classes are illustrated by English and Czech examples only.

1 · man old learns with difficulty
- *Starýho/starého psa novejm/novým kouskům nenaučíš. (You can't teach an old dog new tricks.)*

2 · man threatening is not dangereous
- *Pes, kterej/který štěká, nekouše. (A barking dog never bites.)*

3 · man punishes under a pretext easily
- *Kdo chce psa bít, hůl si najde. (It's easy to find a stick to beat a dog.)*

4 · dog is loyal
- *Pes je (nejlepší) přítel člověka. (A dog is a man's best friend.)*

5 · man disregards the unimportant
- *Psi štěkají a karavana jde/de dál. (Dogs bark, but the caravan goes/rolls on.)*

6 · man believes in superstition
- *Černá kočka přes cestu znamená neštěstí /smůlu. (It is unlucky have a black cat cross your path.)*

7 · supervising tempts wilfulness
- *Když kocour není doma, myši mají pré/hody/posvícení. (When/while the cat's away, the mice will play.)*

8 · it is difficult to discriminate, they all merge
- *Potmě je každá kočka/kráva černá. (All cats in the dark are grey.)*

9 · man yields to superiority
- *Mnoho psů, zajícova smrt.* ('*Too many dogs is the hare's death*', He didn't have a cat's/snowball's chance in hell.)

10 · life is hard
- *Život je pes. (It's a dog's life.)*

The metalanguage developed in the Czech dictionary is the one an onomasiological dictionary and taxonomy used in this dictionary is based on; it was explained in a previous contribution (Čermák, 2010, Proceedings of Tavira) and it is not to be mistaken for definition of these proverbs. As it is, it gives a skeletal meaning only, which, due to its relative brevity, was found useful for the classification of proverbs and other sentential idioms.

One can only speculate as to why so many qualities attributed to dog and cat are forgotten or marginal now, which corpus data and frequencies confirm while only few are retained and in use. The motivation for using just these dog and cat proverbs is also to be found in the corpora though much more data is called for.

Literature

ČELAKOVSKÝ, František Ladislav. 1852. *Mudrosloví národa slovanského ve příslovích*. Praha: České museum.

ČERMÁK, František. 1998. "Animal Phraseology: The Case of Dog and Cat", In *Proceedings of Europhras 2010 Granada*.

ČERMÁK, František, HRONEK, Jiří, and MACHAČ, Jaroslav. 2009. *Slovník české frazeologie a idiomatiky. Výrazy větné*. Praha: Leda (= Dictionary of Czech Phraseology and Idiomatics. Sentence Expressions).

ČERMÁK, František. 2003. "Paremiological Minimum of Czech: The Corpus Evidence." In *Flut von Texten - Vielvalt der Kulturen. Ascona 2001 zur Methodologie und Kulturspezifik der Phraseologie*, edited by H. Burger, A. Häcki Bufofer, and G. Greciano, 15–31. Hohengehren: Schneider Verlag.

ČERMÁK, František. 2007. *Frazeologie a idiomatika česká a obecná. Czech and General Phraseology.* Praha: Karolinum.

ČERMÁK, František. 2010. "Frequent Proverbs and Their Meaning: A Proposal of a Linguistic Description (The Core and Paremiological Minima Described)." In *3rd Interdisciplinary Colloquium on Proverbs. Actas ICP Proceedings, International Association of Paremiology,* edited by R. Soares and O. Lauhakangas, 40–65.

ČERMÁK, František. 2010. "The Paremiological Minimum of English." In *...for thy speech bewrayeth thee. A Festschrift for Libuše Dušková,* edited by M. Malá and P. Šaldová, 57–71. Praha: Univerzita Karlova v Praze, Filozofická fakulta.

http://www.fact-archive.com/quotes/Finnish_proverbs

MIEDER, Wolfgang. 2004. *Proverbs. A Handbook.* Westport London: Greenwood Press.

MUIKKU-WERNER, Pirkko, JANTUNEN, Jarmo Harri, and Ossi KOKKO. 2008. *Suurella sydämellä ihan sikana. Suomen kielen kuvailevva fraasisanakirja.* Helsinki: Gumerus.

PACZOLAY, Guyla. 1997. *European proverbs in 55 languages with equivalents in Arabic, Persian, Sanskrit, Chinese and Japanese.* Veszprém: Veszprémi Nyomda Rt.

TITELMAN, Gregory. 1996. *Popular Proverbs and Sayings.* New York: Random House.

VAANANEN-JENSEN, Inkeri. 1990. *Finnish Proverbs.* Iowa City: Pennfield Press.

WALTHER, Hans. 1963-1969. *Proverbia sententiaque latinitatis medii aevi I-VI. Lateinische Sprichwörter und Sentenzen des Mittelalters in alphabetischer Anordnung.* Götingen: Vandenhoeck & Ruprecht

Ten Commandments for Paremiologist or A Paremiological Decalogue

1 *Observe proverbs in languages and compare them, they are not the same, though some may be similar.*
Proverbs are universal and found everywhere, in all natural languages.

2 *View proverbs in the light of the field, area and country.*
Proverbs are interdisciplinary and straddle ethnography, history, linguistics, literature, etc., capturing relevant aspects of traditional human life as they are viewed in these fields.

3 *Do not look for proverbs that are too contemporary, they arise only after being time-tested, their wisdom is intergenerational.*
Proverbs capture traditional, conventional values, and derived social experience, knowledge offered by natural sciences and connections to culture. As such, they are perceived as wisdom inherited from previous generations.

4 *You do not have to adhere to the proverb's truth. However, if you do not, you may risk social sanctioning.*
Proverbs coming from the social sphere express relationships among people, their behaviour, attitudes and actions. Due to tradition, they have the nature of norm, rule, even law. There is a close connection with moral, justice, trade rules, even religious norms.

5 *If a proverb is mentioned by an older speaker, listen to him, since he speaks from general experience, even though you may not like it.*
Proverbs are tradionally used as evaluative expressions of guidance, instruction for another man, but also as reminders and exhortations. The basis for morals is often derived from proverbs.

6 *Realize when a proverb is an emotional evaluation and when it reflects and assesses a matter-of-fact situation and relationship among people.*
Proverbs often express emotions, feelings or state, and comment on a factual relationship between people. Despite their composite nature and condensed content, they tend to be relatively brief.

7 *Should a proverb touch you, consider if it does not happen to offer some generalized and widely accepted knowledge, though that may not be pleasant at the moment.*
Values expressed by proverbs traditionally and pragmatically stress positive values to be recommended to others against opposite, negative values.

8 *Analyze the behaviour of the other person and try to view the proverb he used in an action--relationship.*

Many proverbs express attitudes and subsequent reactions on the acts and behaviour of other people.

9 *Having come across a short proverb, try to figure out what it means and fill it in so that it makes more sense.*

Proverbs tend to be binary, even though in a latent way only (cf. *The truth prevails* and possible implicit second part, eg., *over lies*, etc.).

10 *Think about the reason why and how a proverb relates to the opposite it mentions.*

The two traditional parts of binary proverbs appear in the form of a familiar opposition.

LEXICAL AND SEMANTIC ASPECTS OF PROVERBS

František Čermák

Published by Charles University
Karolinum Press, Ovocný trh 560/5, 116 36 Praha 1
Prague 2019
Typeset by DTP Karolinum Press
Printed by Karolinum Press
First edition

ISBN 978-80-246-4358-8
ISBN 978-80-246-4369-4 (pdf)